This
First Edition
Is In
Tribute
To
Jack Oakie

An enlargement of this portrait of Jack Oakie hung in the Universal Studios Commissary.

GRITS AND GRAVY

I come from the South where I learned to love grits and gravy.

When I came to Hollywood to make movies, the silver screen was serving my favorite dish.

There was lots of corn, and the gravy was dripping all over the place.

This little collection of anecdotes starts in the twenties and uncovers some remembrances of the motion picture industry from the silents through the talkies.

For this Hollywood actor, they are pure "grits and gravy."

— Jack Oakie

The magic of JACK OAKIE
is best described by this
line in *The Sound of Music:*

"How do you hold a moonbeam in your hand?"

JACK OAKIE'S DOUBLE TAKES

JACK OAKIE

Strawberry Hill Press

Strawberry Hill Press
2594 15th Avenue
San Francisco, California 94127

Distributed by
Stackpole Books
Cameron & Kelker Sts.
Harrisburg, Pa. 17105

Manufactured in the United States of America

Edited by Diane Sipes

Book design by Carlton C. Herrick

Special thanks to the University of Southern California Cinema Department and especially Mr. Nuri Erturk for their graciousness in providing photographic reproductions from the Jack Oakie collection for this book.

Library of Congress Cataloging in Publication

Oakie, Jack, 1903-1978
    Jack Oakie's double takes.

    Includes index.
    1. Oakie, Jack, 1903-1978. 2. Comedians — United States — Biography. 3. Moving-picture actors and actresses — United States — Biography. I. Title.
PN2287.017A34 791.43'028'0924 [B] 79-12432 ISBN 0-89407-019-3 pbk.

Jack and Vickie at ceremony dedicating plaque placed by citizen fans in Jack's hometown, Sedalia, Missouri.

My husband enjoyed remembering things. And he remembered everything. He could remember everything he came in touch with, physically and mentally. He never forgot anything whether it were an experience of his own or one that was told him. Every person he met, each experience he had, was cherished. My husband had respect for people and knowledge. And he was in constant search of both. He had a gentle curiosity with which he approached everything.

He almost seemed like a baby looking through newly opened eyes. He always anticipated adventure. And he always found it even in the simplest facts. Because his memory was infallible, I learned many years ago that I needed remember only one thing; that is, that my husband was always right.

It is true that almost everybody has a good memory. What was remarkable about my husband was the way in which he used his accurately retained information. His talent lay in application and his expressions were sifted through a loving, inherent sense of humor. Though you may not have agreed with him, you found that you must have had affection for him. Many people loved him, some just for the way in which he remembered them. He always remembered people, their names, their experiences, even their birthdays. This of course was not always popular with women.

People came up to my husband and said, "You don't remember me . . .," but that was as far as they got, for he did remember them. So very many people loved him, I find that I am but one of millions. To describe his personality, one can say only, "It was a radiance from within."

This 'radiance' was honored by over 20,000 people on October 18, 1960. And many endeared experiences were added to my husband's wealth of remembrances. On October 18, 1960, Sedalia, Missouri, the town where he was born, designated that day to be my husband's day. A monument was erected at 522 West 7th Street, Sedalia, Missouri, and the bronze plaque set in marble reads:

Jack Oakie
Internationally beloved actor
was born here
November 12, 1903

Victoria Oakie
(Mrs. Jack Oakie)

Dear Reader

Long ago in a Golden Era,
When hectically, youth plied
To life's both ends the roaring flame,

With dreams, with work,
With longing heart, he tried
His wanderings to guide.

Follow then this Player's story,
For with gentle hand,
He'll lead you where all dreams are turned
In memory's mystic band.

Pursue those dreams with him,
And see his wondrous land,
Remembering as you do,
That all of this is true.

Victoria Horne Oakie

Jack Oakie, Helen Hayes, Leslie Howard and Mary Pickford.

Contents

Page
ii   Editor's Note
iii   Foreword
1   My Mother Had a Feeling
9   A Double Portion
12   Yellow Silk
17   The Right Place at the Right Time
23   Bows
25   Titular Bishops
29   Sin Town
31   Giants the Jack Killers
37   When We Learned To Talk
41   Fast Company
45   Call of the Wild
51   Unsuitable
55   Sweat Shirt
61   It's a Fascinating Business
71   Chaplin
81   The Redhead
89   Sweetie
91   Let's Go Native
94   Open Door
99   The Turkey Was a Hit
103   Granite
107   Garbophile
109   Jackie-O
113   Tale of Two Cracks
118   Pundits
121   Asta
123   Too Much Dihedral
131   The Spook
141   Iceland
145   Grisha
150   Sheets
152   Car Barns
155   An Unsettling Experience
159   Working for a Quitting Clause
161   Some Sound Thoughts
165   Shoes
170   Benchley
173   Counting
179   Fame at Last
186   Jack Oakie's Films
195   Jack Oakie's Music
198   The Oakie College (Radio)
204   Jack Oakie's Press Stories
206   Jack Oakie's Television
210   Jack Oakie's Vaudeville
215   Acknowledgements to Other Publishers
215   Index of Proper Names

EDITOR'S NOTE

LEWIS DELANEY OFFIELD was born in Sedalia, Missouri, on November 12, 1903. His formal education was in Muskogee, Oklahoma; in Kansas City, Missouri; and in New York City. He worked on Wall Street and held "chorus boy" and "and Company" roles on the New York stage and in vaudeville.

He arrived in Hollywood on June 13, 1927. Wesley Ruggles started his movie career in *Finders Keepers,* starring Laura La Plante, at Universal Pictures, and then signed him to a personal contract.

Mr. Oakie starred in a long list of motion pictures, many of which are today considered "classics." He was known for his love of people, and many of Hollywood's greatest stars learned portions of their trade from him.

He was married to the actress, Victoria Horne, for more than thirty-four years — they were known as one of the happiest couples in Hollywood.

Mr. Oakie brought smiles to the hearts of tens of millions of us. He also left for serious motion picture students a wealth of research material which he and his mother — and later Victoria Oakie — carefully collected over fifty years of active life in Hollywood and the film industry. He has shared with us some small part of that historical material in this book.

He died on January 23, 1978 — but he remains in the hearts of millions of us because of his warm smile, his deep love for humanity, and his true and deep talents as an actor, a singer, a dancer, and a writer.

While working in Wall Street, young Lewis Delaney Offield became very popular for doing his amusing Joe Frisco imitations.

Recognizing the boy's natural talent, Paul Adler, his boss, asked him to help out in a charity show for the Cardiac Society. The show was *Babes In Toyland* and was directed by May Leslie. Sigmund Romberg directed the music and all during the rehearsals he called Lewis "Jack" because he was playing the part of the Jack of Hearts. New Yorkers called him either Oklahoma, Okly, or Okie, because he had just come up from Muskogee. For the *Babes In Toyland* program, Lewis combined Sigmund Romberg's "Jack" with New York's "Okie," to which he added an "a." That was the first time that Lewis Delaney Offield's name read "Jack Oakie."

Paul Adler got him to play in two more charity shows: the Minstrel Show for his men's club, The City Club, and the "Junior League Follies." In both of these he was again directed by May Leslie, who urged him to leave Wall Street and go into show business.

Jack Oakie played in the following Broadway musicals, vaudeville, and motion pictures made in New York, before coming to Hollywood.

BROADWAY MUSICALS

1923 . . . *Little Nelly Kelly* — a George M. Cohan Production at the Liberty Theatre, 234 West 42nd Street

1923 . . . *Sharlee* — a John Cort Production at Daly's 63rd Street Theatre

1924 . . . *Innocent Eyes* — a Messrs. Lee and J.J. Shubert Production at the Winter Garden Theatre

1925 . . . *Artists And Models* — a Messrs. Shubert Production at the Winter Garden Theatre

1927 . . . *Peggy-Ann* — a Lew Fields and Lyle D. Andrews Production at the Vanderbilt Theatre, 38th Street

Vaudeville

1925 . . . "At Home" — Starring LuLu McConnell with Grant Simpson

1926 . . . "At Home"

1927 . . . "At Home" — The sketch played the Keith, Orpheum, and Interstate Circuits

Silent Motion Pictures

Chronicles Of America — made for Yale University by Frank Tuttle and Osgood Perkins

His Children's Children — starring George Fawcett; directed by Sam Wood

Big Brother — starring Thomas Meighan, and little Mickey Bennett (the boy who later starred in *The Dummy*)

Black Is White — starring Tom Wilson

Sour Apples — starring Dorothy MacKaill and Richard Barthelmess

Carmen — starring Martinelli

Foreword

I became interested in writing these remembrances for just two reasons. First, there's a chance that after I'm gone, someone I've never known MAY write a book about me. Second, there's a chance that after I'm gone, someone I've never known MAY NOT write a book about me.

Although the anecdotes are autobiographical and together make a kind of autobiography, that was not my original intention. What I had in mind when I put these down was to try to get some laughs. I guess laughter is still my lifestyle.

For the readers who are not old enough to remember me or the days when I was in the movies, I've started the book with a story about my mother. This introduces my beginnings, and also serves to introduce Ev. She was quite a gal. She had my love and respect, and the history of Hollywood in the 1920's and 1930's also attests to the esteem in which she was held throughout the motion picture industry.

One of the first things I learned in my early days in vaudeville with Lulu McConnell was always to try to avoid that old Chinese act called "Ontoolong." For years my sentimental wife, Vickie, loved to show old Jack Oakie movies at our house; and for years our guests were tormented with full-length pictures.

Then for my sixty-eighth birthday, I was given a most wonderful surprise gift by Jack Haley, Jr. Junior prepared a reel of clips for me — scenes taken from about a dozen of my pictures. The *Oakie Reel* was the forerunner to his *That's Entertainment*, which was also very successful.

Because *The Reel* runs less than an hour (about fifty minutes), it became the perfect entertainment for Oakie guests. It was not "ontoolong." "Let's show them *The Reel*," became our household adage in answer to any request to see an Oakie film. I hope these Hollywood remembrances will be received like *The Reel* — just entertainment, and not on too long.

Well, here we go and, to use the phrase I've written above my name for over fifty-five years, remember: "It's All In Fun!"

Jack Oakie

Jack and "Ev".

MY MOTHER HAD A FEELING

The headlined article in the *Los Angeles Times*, Tuesday, December 2, 1930, read:

"Oakie Entertains Irish Team Friday." Jack Oakie, film star, will serve as master of comedy at the reception banquet held by the Notre Dame Club of California for Knute Rockne's "Fighting Irish" the evening of the squad's arrival in Los Angeles to meet the Southern California Trojans. The affair will be staged Friday night at the Ambassador Hotel, and Oakie has been chosen as the only non-member on the welcoming committee at the dinner.

That Friday night, December 5, 1930, the rally was held as advertised, and I had the best time of anyone there. I was also given one of those very hard-to-get tickets to see the game, and was invited to be Notre Dame's mascot the next afternoon at the Coliseum. I accepted the ticket and the honor although, when I finally got to the game, I spent the whole afternoon cheering for my home team, USC. It didn't help. Notre Dame won — 27 to 0!

That Saturday morning, the day of the game, December 6th, 1930, my mother, Mary Evelyn Offield, whom I always called Ev, was pouring our second cup of coffee at breakfast, when she said, "Lewis." (Although my mother was very proud of Jack Oakie, she never called me by my stage name. I was always Lewis Delaney Offield at home.) "Lewis," Ev said, "I would like you to take me to the bank this morning, so that we can close out the account."

My mother was considered a very bright, very distinguished woman. Ev was a teacher, and had been an educator all her life. She was the founder of her own schools, in both Sedalia, Missouri, and Muskogee, Oklahoma. In New York City, she was a professor of psychology at Columbia University. She also taught at the Scudder's School for Girls. She influenced some of the most accomplished people of our time. Clare Boothe Luce, who was a pupil of Ev's, has often publicly referred to the influence of Mrs. Offield in her life. Dr. Walter Dandy, the great brain surgeon, who, as we say down south, "went to school to my mother," also spoke of Ev with reverence. (At that time Walter Dandy was considered the only surgeon with the stature needed to be sent for to come to Hollywood to operate on George Gershwin.)

When it looked like Paramount Studios meant to keep me on, Ev stopped teaching and came to California to join me. For the first time since Muskogee, Oklahoma, we had a house again — 1759 Taft Avenue, in the heart of Hollywood — and we loved it. Ev's natural wit and warm philosophy charmed the town, and everybody in the cinema capital of the world loved her.

"I would like you to withdraw all the money from the bank this morning," she said. I couldn't believe my ears! I looked at that brilliant lady as if she had lost all her good sense. She was talking about taking out thirty thousand dollars in cash! Our life's savings! All the money we had in the world!

"Ev," I said, as if talking to a child, "you're talking about thirty thousand dollars! You can't take thirty thousand dollars out of the bank and just hold it in your hand!"

in Notre Dame uniform

LEWIS COLLEGE,

GLASGOW, MISSOURI.

THE TRUSTEES AND FACULTY OF LEWIS COLLEGE

Do hereby Certify, That _Mary Evelyn Jump_ has honorably completed the _Classical and Normal_ course in this Institution.

In Testimony Whereof, This Diploma is awarded, and authenticated by the signatures of the President of the Board of Trustees and the President of the Faculty

Done this _Fifth day_ of _June_ in the year of our Lord, 188_8_

Martin L. Curl President of Faculty.

Jas. M. Lewis President Board of Trustees.

NEVER BE   DISCOURAGED

"WE STUDY THE WORD AND THE WORKS OF GOD."   "LET US KEEP OUR HEAVENLY FATHER IN THE MIDST"

CHAUTAUQUA

Literary AND Scientific

CIRCLE

Mary Evelyn Jump

has completed the Four Years' Course of Reading

REQUIRED BY THE

C. L. S. C.

and is enrolled as a Member of the Society of

"THE HALL   IN THE GROVE,"

Lewis Miller
PRESIDENT.

J. H. Vincent
CHANCELLOR.

J. L. Hurlbut
GENERAL SUPERINTENDENT.

Chautauqua, N.Y.
August 18th 1892

HOLY BIBLE

COUNSELORS

Lyman Abbott   _Wilbur C. Atkinson_
J. M. Gibson   _Edward E. Hale_
Henry W. Warren   _James H. Carlisle_

THE OFFIELD SCHOOL FOR GIRLS

MARY EVELYN OFFIELD. A. M.
PRINCIPAL

———

"It is only the ignorant that despise education."
"Capacity without education is deplorable."
"Right training is better than riches."
"Knowledge is power."
"Love is king."

———

SITUATED IN BEAUTIFUL KENDALL PLACE
MUSKOGEE, OKLAHOMA
1912—1914

HOME OF JACK OAKIE

The beautiful home Jack Oakie bought from Bill (Hopalong Cassidy) Boyd for his mother in Beverly Hills.

"We'll put it in a safe-deposit box," she explained simply, as if that was the sort of thing everybody did with money on a Saturday morning.

"No! It's impossible! And besides," I explained, "I don't have time to go to the bank. I've got to be at the football game!"

"I know," she said, "but Lewis, please, you will have plenty of time if we go right over there now and get it done before the bank closes at twelve o'clock."

"Why?" I asked in bad temper. "Why?"

"Because I have a feeling!" she said, and clasped her hands to her heart. "Lewis, please, let's go over there right now."

"No, Ev!" I was adamant. "We'll be the laughingstock of the town."

"Lewis," and now she was adamant, "you call Morris Small and ask him to meet us at the bank."

Morris Small was my agent and business manager. He agreed to meet us at the bank and try to talk my mother out of her foolish hysteria. It was about ten thirty when we three met at the Bank of Hollywood, in the Equitable Building, on the northeast corner of Hollywood Boulevard and Vine Street. Originally, the bank had opened on Vine Street in the location which is now the Hollywood Brown Derby, but it grew too prosperous for that little one-story building and moved into the new Equitable Building, which was built by Bill Davey, also famous for having been married to Gloria Swanson. Morris Small approached mother immediately.

"Good morning, Mrs. Offield. Now tell me what this is all about."

"Morris," I spoke up, "mother wants to close out the savings account because she says she has a feeling! Will you please explain why we can't do a

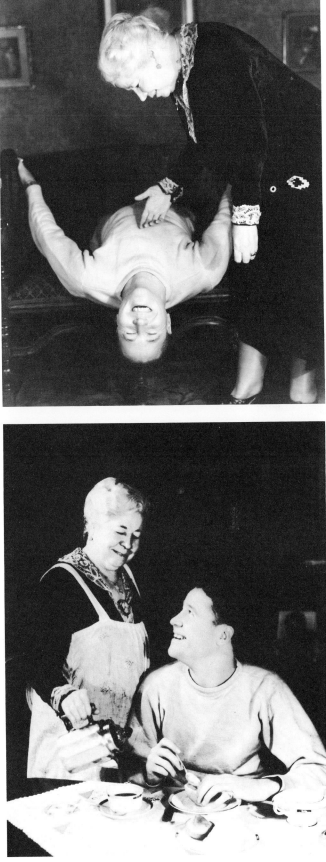

At home.

thing like that! And will you hurry, I've got to get to the football game!" And I turned it over to him.

"Mrs. Offield, that's a large amount of money to take out of the bank. What do you want to do with it?" he asked.

"I want to put it in a safe-deposit box, where it will be safe. Now Mr. Small, please make out the check and have Lewis sign it before the banking hours close at noon, because I'm not leaving here until we take that money out of the bank." Ev was even firmer with Morris Small than she was with me.

"Jack," Morris turned to me, "as long as your mother is so upset, go along with her. On Monday, when there's more time, we can all meet at the office and discuss it more thoroughly."

Morris made out the check, I signed it, and we went over to the desk of Sam Kress, the president of the Bank of Hollywood. We opened the little gate that fenced him off from the rest of the room, and I gave him the check.

"Mr. Kress, will you please cash this," I said, "and please hurry, I've got to get to the Coliseum."

Sam Kress had been a druggist but, because he was one of the greatest greeters Hollywood ever had, he was very popular. When Sam Kress extended that hail-fellow-well-met handshake, he

sure made the receiver feel extremely welcome. It was his personality that got him the job of president of the bank. (Not too long after that Saturday morning episode, he got a job in the wardrobe department of MGM Studios.)

Sam Kress looked at the check and, in his most jovial, good-natured, fun-loving way, said, "Oh, my, you want all this in cash? You know, we don't have that much money in this bank."

That's when Morris Small's ears pricked up. "Mr. Kress," he said, "you have a proper check, drawn up by Mr. Oakie. We expect you to honor it; and we are going to sit right here at your desk until you do."

Morris Small was a businessman, so I guess he recognized the significance of Sam Kress's unusual bit of information. All I knew was that I wanted to get to a football game and everybody was doing everything they could to make me late! Sam Kress took my check to some inner sanctum way off in the back end of the room. We waited. When he returned he was more jovial than ever.

"Mrs. Offield," he said, "your money will be here in just a few minutes." He sat back down in his big leather chair behind his desk, and leaned forward toward Ev. "Mrs. Offield, I want you to know that this bank is as solid as the Rock of Gibraltar!" And he pounded the desk with his fist to demonstrate.

"Mr. Kress," my mother informed him politely, "I have never seen the Rock of Gibraltar, will you please just let us have the money."

The four of us just sat and waited. At noon the guard locked the bank doors. I was becoming more and more worried. Everything always takes so darn long when you're in a hurry. I was sure going to be late for the game!

Finally, Sam Kress got a nod from somebody in the distance. "Well, here it is," he said, announcing the arrival of the money. A couple of men brought in armfuls of money, wrapped in packets with paper bands denoting the amount in each, like 100 $5, or 100 $20, and many, many 100 $1. Thirty thousand dollars made a lot of bundles.

Morris Small spread Sam Kress's morning *Los Angeles Times* and bundled the money into three clumsy newspaper-wrapped packages. Mother, Morris, and I cradled our bundles in our arms as if we were carrying babies. The guard unlocked the door, held it open for us, then closed it and locked it behind us.

We walked down Hollywood Boulevard with our bundles to the Guaranty 6% Savings and Loan. Morris rented one of the largest safe-deposit boxes they had, and we stuffed the money into it, pushing it all down as if it were a lot of old rags.

EDWARD SMALL PRODUCTIONS, INC.

November 12, 1973

Dear Jack:

It's been a long time — 1928, to be exact — since I caught the silent film, "Finders Keepers," on Hollywood Boulevard and saw you for the first time on the screen. This set off a chain of events that over the years enlarged my memory bank with a host of pleasant reminiscences.

I perceived in your "Finders Keepers" performance a talent that could assure you of having a successful career as a comedian. You projected a comedy style different from anything I had seen. It was that mysterious, God-given quality stars possess which no one can define, but we call it Personality. And so I set about to do some checking into your already rather substantial background in the entertainment industry — appearances at the Winter Garden in New York, in vaudeville with Lulu McConnell for three years, stage work, and other silent films I had not seen.

"Finders Keepers" had been directed by Wesley Ruggles, and I learned that he had you under contract — for the rather meager weekly sum of something like $100.00. This was no barrier, as I felt if you could be put under new management (mine), you soon would be doing a lot better than this. But first I had to plot a successful way to get your release from Wesley. It was going to take — and did — maneuvering and salesmanship and springing you was no small task. He was tenacious in his confidence about your future and also viewed your personality as a valuable commodity. But finally the Edward Small Company agency was successful in signing you under its personal management. I should add that Wesley forgave me in time and we became good friends.

Right after this, I believe your first picture was "Fleet's In," followed by "Someone To Love," and then came sound. This advent was no obstacle to you — as it was to some who couldn't weather the transition. And so it was one picture after another, with Paramount being the foremost bidder for your services at that time. Later, I put you in a couple of pictures I made for RKO — "Super Sleuth" and "Toast of New York," in which you co-starred with Cary Grant.

I remember your mother, Evelyn Offield, very well. Evelyn — as everyone called her — was endowed with a musical philosophy: "Music soothes the soul"; "Music calms the nerves"; "Music puts the brakes on." Music was in her soul, and to her it was a panacea for the ills of mankind. She loved show-biz too and might well have had a successful career of her own. Your talent obviously had natural roots. One time we cast Evelyn in a Paramount picture — "Too Much Harmony," directed by Eddie Sutherland — in the realistic role of playing your mother. She was acclaimed as a natural, but I always felt that in her spirited way, this was more of a lark than any real effort toward a career of her own.

You had been doing well and had accumulated a considerable amount of cash — especially for those years — but the big crash of '29 was almost upon us.

As your manager, my office was responsible for both your professional career and your financial matters. My brother, Morris Small, had deposited all your funds in the Bank of Hollywood, which was a private, independent bank.

None of us ever could forget a real life drama we experienced together about this time. It was on a Saturday — and banks were open Saturday mornings in those days. Evelyn got a distinct feeling that you should withdraw your money from the Bank of Hollywood. With some difficulty, she prevailed upon you to do something about her apprehension. You were getting ready to go to a football game and regarded the whole idea as a nuisance. But reluctantly you called the office and my brother Morris agreed to converge on the bank. The place was filled with customers, many of them children who were making their little deposits to their Christmas Club accounts. There was no panic and it appeared that only the usual transactions were taking place. The atmosphere, however, was one of tension and suspicion that pertained to the financial standing of every bank during the Depression.

You approached the manager to state your mission: to close Jack Oakie's account — there and then — and take the money with you. The manager excused himself, had a hasty conference with the owner of the bank, whose desk was also on the platform, and came back to put you off, if he could. This reluctance made Morris apprehensive, but you were quickly assured that the institution was "as solid as the Rock of Gibraltar." Evelyn retorted that she had never seen the Rock of Gibraltar and this was irrelevant. She was only interested in getting the money — not in assurances. Your little group was conducted to an inside office where the money finally was handed to you in greenbacks which you and your mother and Morris immediately stuffed into a safe-deposit box in Equitable Savings down the street.

All this was done punctuated by your impatience to get to the football game at the Coliseum.

Monday morning the lines reached almost around the building, but the Bank of Hollywood never opened its doors again. Yours was one of the very few accounts that wasn't wiped out — sparing all of us a heartbreak that many others experienced, sorry to say.

It is well known that I handled a great number of personalities throughout my career as an agent — before I left it more or less in Morris's hands so as to start producing pictures on my own, and so I think I am qualified to make observations in this area that no one could challenge.

Over and over what I was called on to do as an agent and manager wasn't altogether to my liking. The ego problems of actors and their natural feelings of insecurity often required mollifying with what I'd prefer to call "white" (rather than "black") lies to fortify their courage and confidence, and this was the phony side of personal representation I frankly didn't like.

I can tell you now, if I never did before, that it was refreshing to have a fellow like Jack Oakie in my stable who was legitimately a warm, talented, well-balanced person and whose own honesty and integrity carried him along. You earned what you have achieved — a guy that everybody loved, and those of us who have known you still do. Our association over the years was much more to me than an actor/agent relationship. It was a privilege and within it was a valuable friendship that one rarely finds in a lifetime.

My congratulations on this occasion and my warmest personal regards always —

Sincerely,

Eddie Small

7

"I hope you're satisfied," I said to Ev, and then turned to Morris Small. "You take Mother home, I'm going to the game!" And I ran.

After the game I came home and hurriedly bathed and dressed for a party given by Bill and Ada Ince at the Villa Carlotta. The party lasted all Saturday night and a good part of Sunday, so I didn't see Ev until Monday morning at breakfast. We didn't mention the money; I had decided to leave all that to Morris Small.

"Lewis, will you drive me to the Gotham delicatessen?" mother asked. "I'd like to do some shopping."

We got into my red Packard, drove down Taft Avenue to the corner, and turned right on Hollywood Boulevard. When we got to Gower Street, which is on the top of the slight incline of Hollywood Boulevard, we looked down and saw the crowds jamming the street in front of the Equitable Building at the corner of Vine.

Right out there in the middle of the road were Harry Langdon, Wallace Beery, El Brendel, John Barrymore, and it seemed hundreds more trying to get into the Bank of Hollywood. The guard had locked those doors behind us on Saturday, and they never opened again.

I pulled over to the curb and parked the car. I put my arms around my mother and kissed her. "So you never saw the Rock of Gibraltar," I said. Then I asked her, and I was only the first of hundreds who for years and years continued to ask her, "How did you know?"

"I had a feeling," she said to me, as she repeatedly said hundreds of times for years to come, "I just had a feeling."

STANLEY ADAMS

Dear Jack:

I remember a lot of things but one of the most vivid is the recollection of the first time you set foot on the stage and gave me what later came to be known as the patented Jack Oakie delayed "take." It labelled you a "pro" immediately. So I just sat back and let you direct yourself. You really never tried to steal a scene — you just made an appearance and charisma did the rest.

Those were the days of the Algonquin's round table, but we were so square that we sat around an octagonal table. Of course, that's not entirely true because, as you have proven over the years, you were always worth your wit in gold.

And now you are in the golden years — knee deep in memories and shoulder deep in friends, all of whom, and I among them, are heart deep in love with you.

I don't go for this three score and ten business except for the opportunity it gives to me to tell you how highly I have valued the over 40 years and never a cross word association.

Sam Levenson said that people marry for many things — for money, for prestige, for power, but not for long. Funny, yes, but true, no. When, he said that, I thought of you and Vicki and how beautiful and lasting a marriage can be.

And so, while this is a birthday note to you, it really is a congratulatory line to both of you because as the song says "You can't have one without the other."

Bless you and love from Bambi and —

Stanley

Note: Stanley Adams is President of ASCAP.

Jack Oakie's Mother
Teacher of Clare Luce

When Congresswomen-playwright-war correspondent Clare Boothe Luce was in Hollywood to work on a screen play, she was asked the inevitable question: Was there any player she would especially like to meet?

She said: "Yes—Jack Oakie."

Inasmuch as broad-beamed Oakie specializes in comedy and Miss Luce was in town for a serious drama, the answer rather surprised studio executives. As they arranged for her visit to the set of "Hello, Frisco, Hello," Jack's current picture, Miss Luce explained:

"I've been aching for years to tell him that I know who gave him his insight into human nature.

"I knew his mother. I had her for a psychology teacher at Scudder School in New York, and she was one of the greatest teachers of psychology who ever lived. Quite unwittingly, she exerted a tremendous influence on my life.

"Unfortunately, it's too late now to tell her, but I'd like to tell Jack. Every time I see him on the screen, I think of what I, too, owe his mother." Jack's mother was Mrs. Mary E. Offield.

A DOUBLE PORTION

For a performer there is no reward in the world like applause. And the more experienced and professional the artist, the more beloved is that sound of appreciation for his work. Nothing, but nothing can ever take its place, not even a double portion of cheese! I know, because there was an evening when that gratifying handwork was prohibited and the plaudits preempted by the hands of a clock, and I brought home the cheese.

It was in the early days of radio, before tape was ever heard of, when all broadcasting was live and a show was put on the air right then and there.

I was playing a lot of guest shots with stars like Al Jolson, Eddie Cantor, and Edgar Bergen, and although my mother, Ev, always enjoyed all the broadcasts, it was whenever I was booked for the Kraft Music Hall starring Bing Crosby, that she became the happiest little lady in the world.

At first I thought she favored the show because she loved Bing, but I was wrong. It wasn't Bing, it was the Kraft product. "I'm going to be on the Kraft Music Hall radio show tonight," I told her that Thursday morning, as I left for the studio. I was making the movie, *Florida Special,* at Paramount and, as the radio show went on at six-thirty, I could climb over the Paramount fence to RKO and then go under the RKO fence to the back gate of KHJ, the radio station.

At KHJ the program was broadcast from a studio room that had a stage, a curtain, and seats for an audience of 400, and Bing always played to capacity.

"Oh, Lewis, that's wonderful!"

"Ev, why are you always so happy whenever I do the Kraft show with Bing?" I asked her.

"Because they always give you that great big beautiful basket of cheese," she said. "I love that beautiful basket of cheese."

"Oh? I thought it was because you liked Bing," I teased her.

"Oh, I do like Bing very much," she assured me. "But I love the cheese. So, Lewis, please don't forget to bring home that beautiful basket."

In those days, the Kraft folks always presented their radio guest stars with a huge, handsome wicker basket packed with pounds and pounds of all their cheese products. The variety included soft cheeses, hard cheeses, whips, mixes, and spreads. The jars and packages were tied in place with ribbons and cellophane wrappings. The great basket was placed on top of a heavy wooden cheese platter with more bows and ribbons. Ev was right — it was a very beautiful gift.

"Don't forget the basket," she reminded me again. I assured her I would not forget the cheese.

That night I was standing in the wings with Bing and Bob "Bazooka" Burns. Bob and I were teamed for the show. His slow drawl and my snappy patter were considered great contrast. We were watching Victor Borge at the piano, warming up the audience before show time. He was doing his now famous comedy routine popping explosions from his cheeks as he hit the keyboard.

Suddenly the director of the show, Cal Kuhl, came running over to us. "Listen, Bing," he said. (It was almost show time, and he was pretty flustered.) "Listen, the show's too long tonight. So listen, you gotta go out there and tell the audience that they can't do any applauding!"

"You're kidding," Bing said for all of us. We couldn't believe what we heard.

"I'm not kidding! Now listen, be sure and make'em understand that we can't let'em applaud, especially for that Ossip Gabrilowitsch! Now listen, we know he's going to murder'em and if they ever get started applauding for him he'll louse up our time!" The thought almost stopped his heartbeat as he reverently raised his eyes to the hands of the big studio clock on the wall. "So listen, get out there right now and tell 'em!"

Bing went out and explained the predicament to the audience, and asked those 400 people to withhold all their applause that night until after the show was off the air.

Ossip Gabrilowitsch was one of the most famous concert pianists of that time. He was also the director of the Detroit Symphony Orchestra, and he was married to Mark Twain's daughter, Clara Clemens. As I grew up in Tom Sawyer's country, and my grandmother used to talk about knowing some of Samuel Clemens's kin, I was hoping I'd get to meet the artist that night. My friend Louis Calhern always said that I had been so thoroughly influenced by Ossip Gabrilowitsch's father-in-law that my shenanigans on the screen were the antics of a Huckleberry Capone.

The program had already started when the great artist came into the studio. I watched him remove his soft, black, large-brimmed fedora hat and black, capelike opera coat, and hang them on the

Jack and Bing

Who wants me?

Bob Burns and Jack Oakie.

clothes tree near the door. He was the Maestro! He didn't speak to anyone — sort of kept to himself in thoughtful preparation for his performance. At Carnegie Hall he would have had the plush greenroom for this waiting period instead of having to share a studio room with the rest of the cast and crew. Bob Burns and I felt like peeping Toms as we watched him pace the floor.

When Bing introduced him, he went right to the piano bench, sat down, and charged into his work at the keyboard. The artist gave one of the greatest performances of his career! He played the last notes, lifted his hands, and held them above the ivories in a dramatic pause. But Cal Kuhl's message had got through to the audience! They had "listened!" And 800 hands remained quietly folded in 400 laps. It was so silent you could hear a pin drop!

The man was dazed! He sat there and stared down at the keyboard in wonder as if saying to himself, "I'm sure I just played this thing!" Those silent moments, which must have seemed an eternity to him, must have been one of the greatest shocks in his life. He finally got up. I watched him go direct to the clothes tree in a trance. He put on his hat and coat and left the studio as if trying to get away from a nightmare.

The show was still on, and Bing from the stage got a glimpse of the Gabrilowitsch exit. Bob Burns, who had also seen him go, shuffled over to me and drawled, "What happened to the Maestro?"

"I don't know," I said, and then it suddenly came to me. "I don't think anybody told him about that no applause deal."

As soon as the curtain came down Bing came over. "What happened to Ossip Gabrilowitsch?" he asked.

"Listen, Bing", I said, using Cal Kuhl's by-line. "Did you tell him about the no applause business tonight?"

"Oh, my God!" was all Bing could say. "Oh, my God!"

"Oh, my God!" I gasped right after him. "Oh, my God! Look!" I pointed covetously to the gift baskets set out near the door. "He forgot his cheese!"

Although I came home that night with two beautiful baskets, my mother couldn't get over the heartache the artist had felt because of that cold silent reception. "Oh, my, it's too bad," Ev said sadly as she looked at her double portion of cheese. "It's too bad that the heartwarming sound of applause was displaced by the inhuman hands of a studio clock."

"Man Mountain" Dean, Jack Oakie, Ann Shirley and Johnny Downs.

Jack and Sally Eilers, in *Florida Special*.

YELLOW SILK

I worked on Wall Street during the Bull Market of 1919–1920. I was a runner, a telephone clerk, and a ticket clerk for E.H. Stern and Co., at 56 Pine Street. But I never really got into the rhythm of Wall Street. It was all too fast for me. Every time I made a mistake, my boss made a fortune. Like the time I took a telephone order to buy 1,000 shares and wrote it up on a sell slip. The stock dropped ten points that night. Because of my error, he had sold short!

I was sixteen years old and, although I never learned what it was all about, I loved it. I was living high off the hog. We got big bonuses at the end of the year, and extra time for working late on the month-end statements. We also got a dollar for dinner.

That dollar went pretty far at the Exchange Buffet, where we mostly ate. The restaurant was at the back end of the Exchange building on New Street. It was run on the honor system, and I had fun teasing the spotters. The prices were listed on a large board, and you called out the total cost of what you had on your tray as you reached the cashier. I'd look down at my veal cutlet as I waited in line and say loud enough for the spotter to hear, "Boy, these baked beans aren't worth the dime!"

"Pay for that cutlet!" he'd yell over at me with no sense of humor.

"Sixty-five cents!" I'd shout, and pay for my dinner with the company's dollar.

When I first started, the curb market was still out on the street. Which is why it is called "The Curb." The offices were in buildings on both sides of the street. Clerks sat out on the windowsills, taking their very lives in their hands, to take the orders from the brokers. The brokers worked down below on the street and sent their messages up to the clerks by sign language. They were expert. The transactions were executed as fast as lightning.

Besides working that street hard and fast, they also treated it like a playground. One of the favorite sports was to shower a victim with charlotte russes. The little sponge cake swirls were in paper cups, topped with very rich, thick whipped cream. The vendor came by every day just before lunch, and every broker bought two — one for each hand. We were all targets at one time or another.

When the American Exchange was formed, the brokers came indoors, and all that handwork was a thing of the past. It became illegal to signal transactions by sign language. Those brokers who had been so expert on the street were handicapped. They practically had to be handcuffed to help them break the habit.

At nine in the morning on September 16, 1920, I was watching my boss, Paul Adler, remove his bowler hat and black topcoat. As always, he was dressed immaculately. He wore a dark suit with a white shirt and a stiff white collar. Most brokers wore the jacket of a Palm Beach suit. Never the matching pants — just the jacket. It was like a uniform that said, "I am a broker."

But not Paul Adler. Less than a year before, when the curb was still out on the street, it was a sight to watch him take off all his finery in cold weather and put on an old woolen stocking cap, and woolen scarf and mittens without fingers in them, to go out to work. "Well," I thought regretfully, "those days are over."

Little did I know, at that time of the morning, how lucky we all were that those outdoor days were over.

About a quarter of ten, Paul Adler (who was the Number One broker for our firm) and the other brokers left in time to get to the floor before the ringing of that official ten o'clock bell, which opened the Exchange for the day's business. The Stock Exchange opened at ten and closed at three — for brokers, not for us. We who worked in the office used to say, "Ten to three for them, but ten to three plus three to ten for us."

My friend, Johnny Coleman, who got me my job, also worked down on the floor. He was a page in uniform — No. 13. Paul Adler took a great interest in Johnny. He considered him a genius. In those days before machines, Johnny was a human computer. Today, the John A. Coleman Co. is one of the most prestigious firms on Wall Street. Paul Adler was awfully good to me too. His interest in my singing and dancing and my "Joe Frisco exhibitions" got me my start in show business.

As soon as the brokers left the office for the Exchange, Louis P. Rocker, our cashier and office manager, let us kids go down to the coffee shop in our building. I got into the elevator that morning with Murray Lerner. It was only two flights, but we rode down. "How was your date last night?" I asked him.

THINGS I DON'T LIKE ABOUT MYSELF

BY JACK OAKIE

(As told to Sara Hamilton)

THE gal sits me down to a type-
writer and says, "Now, Oakie,
write down the things you don't
like about yourself."

I give a quick double take and yell,
hey, wait a minute, I'm an actor.
What do you mean things I *don't* like
about myself?

You should have seen that Hamilton
woman wither me with a glance.
"Well, make 'em up," she says and
leaves me flat!

So here I am, an actor with pages
to fill up about why I don't like me.

It's against nature, that's what it is.

Well, now let me see. I gotta put
something down or that dame will
kill me. I could put down I don't like
myself for not wanting to get up in
the morning, I suppose. Yep, I'll start
out with that.

I don't like to get up in the morning
and I don't like it because I don't.

Ingratitude in others is my first and

favorite hate. I don't like it in myself,
either, so right here's a good time to
express my gratitude to a couple of
guys who helped me out of good jobs
and into success. First is Paul Adler,
who worked with me when I was a
telephone clerk on the Stock Exchange. Yep, old Oakie, the Wall
Street tycoon. My antics, especially
the time I got mixed up in a fellow's
order and sold instead of bought (will
I ever forget it) must have tickled
Adler or maybe he was trying to get
rid of me.

Jack Oakie One Of Few

THE BOULEVARD RECORD

Actors Who Never

Friday, May 14, 1937

Suffered 'Mike' Fright

Portly Hollywood Star Says Baseball His Greatest Love

As Youngster, Jack Announced Market Closings Over Michrophone In New York Stock Exchange

BY NEIL AMES

* * *

If Jack Oakie wanted to, he could write a book on "How to be at Home in Three mediums of entertainment." He is unique in Hollywood in that he has never worried about microphone fright.

Mournful Sight

Neil Ames

One of the saddest sights in the show business is to see an otherwise capable actor or actress literally shaking all over.

"Microphones don't bother in a fashion that would drive me," the funny man told your interviewer. "When I was a mere lad of seventeen—a stripling, you might say—and I weighed a good deal less—ah, me, those were the days."

Gently recalled to his subject, Oakie went on to talk of his days in the New York Stock exchange.

"I used to beller out the closings of the market over the loud-speaker system," the comedian reminisced. "My job didn't last long, tho, because I was more interested in baseball than stocks and bonds.

"Even then I had my devoted audience," he smirked, because the floor of the exchange was crowded with business men. They listened to my voice with rapt attention, and never missed a line I spoke.

"I'm afraid those business men had no art in their souls. You know, it happened one summer's day when the bat was on the baseball and my particular athletic hero, "Ping"—they called him "Ping" because when he smacked a ball it always said "Ping"—Ping Bodie was playing.

"I became so excited that I grabbed the microphone and yelled out over the entire stock exchange that Ping Bodie had just completed a home run. Boy, was I happy."

"Don't ask! Please don't ask! She was terrible!"

"Only yesterday you were bragging about how nice she was," I reminded him.

"That's just it. That's just the trouble. She's too nice. You know what?" he asked and explained. "She doesn't let! The next time, before I spend any money on a date, I'm gonna find out first if she lets!"

We sat at the counter having our heavily sugared crullers and heavily creamed coffee. The taste of sugared crullers and coffee, when you're sixteen, is a wondrous thing never again equalled in life. "Say, did you see the yellow silk curtains yet?" Murray asked. He was referring to the yellow silk drapes that had just been hung all along the mammoth windows of the Broad Street side of the Stock Exchange building. We had all been looking forward to their arrival for weeks.

"No, not yet," I said. "But I'll get to see them at three o'clock when I go over for the reports and orders.

"Cost nine thousand dollars!" Murray said in awe. "Some goods! Real silk! Can you imagine, nine thousand dollars for curtains?"

At about eleven fifteen, Louis P. Rocker came over to my cage. "Say, Oklahoma, how about this?" (I grew up in Muskogee, Oklahoma, and my New York friends named me Oklahoma for those geographic traits.) He handed me a complaint slip from the clearing house. It read, "One unstamped ticket." All transactions had to be put on tickets, and every ticket had to be rubber-stamped with our company name, E.H. Stern, and our company number, 412. As ticket clerk, I was keeper of the rubber stamp and responsible for stamping all the tickets for our company. For each omission of this important means of identification, the clearing house fined us five dollars.

"I can't believe it," I said. "I don't know how I could have missed stamping it." And to this day I still don't know how it happened. I was the most careful ticket clerk Wall Street ever had.

"All right, Oklahoma. Just don't let it happen again," he cautioned me good-naturedly. "Here's the five dollars." He gave me the money and sent me right over to the clearing house to pay the fine. I did that at eleven thirty.

Coming back, I stopped and got a good look at those yellow silk drapes. I walked back and forth examining the change they made in the appearance of the Exchange building. The material was beautiful. The color was just right — not too light, not too dark, but bright and sunny. "Must look real cheerful on the inside," I thought. In my estimation, the nine thousand dollars were well spent on those great Broad Street windows. It was

Jack Oakie and Johnny Coleman — tennis in the Poconos.

now about a quarter to twelve, so I started to run to get back to the office before the twelve o'clock rush.

I hurried across the corner of Wall and Broad. There were some people already gathered in the huge, recessed stone window ledge at the J.P. Morgan building. The ledge was so big that as many as twenty people could sit up in there. The regulars, who brought their lunch every day from home, treated the place as if it were their own private club. A horse and wagon was standing in front of the Treasury building directly across the street. Those early lunchers were looking right at that wagon. Well, anyway, they were facing it.

I no sooner turned the corner into Pine Street when I heard the blast! I froze! I stood stock still! It seemed like hours that I stood there motionless! I don't know why, but as I stood there, all I could think of was our storm cellar back home in Muskogee, Oklahoma, where we'd all run to safety from a cyclone. As I stood there, I could even smell the apples my father had kept stored in the cellar. I even remembered I was allowed to eat as many apples as I liked while waiting for the cyclone to pass over.

When finally I had good sense enough to move,

Jack and Johnny Coleman under Johnny's portrait in the Board of Governors' room, N.Y. Stock Exchange.

I took those few steps back around the corner to Wall and Broad where the blast had come from.

Everything was a mess. The people who had been eating lunch in the J.P. Morgan window were sprawled out all over the street. The horse, what was left of it, was dead. A wagon wheel was near my foot.

All at once, as if a still picture had suddenly come to life, people were running in all directions. I became part of the scene. I turned and ran as fast as I could straight for 56 Pine Street. I didn't wait for the elevator; I ran up the stairs to our offices on that second floor. The place was a mad house! Everyone was gathered around Murray Lerner, whose phone had a direct line to the Exchange. He was trying to get the news and relay it to the office force.

Everyone was screaming at once. "What happened? What happened? Did you hear the blast? Did you feel the building shake? What happened?"

"Will ya wait a minute, I'm trying to find out,"

Murray said, trying to quiet them down. "Oh, no!" he said. "Oh, no!" He was talking into the phone and kept repeating to himself, "Oh, no! Oh, no! Oh, no!" He finally turned to us. "Somebody tried to blow up the Treasury building! There was a horse and wagon. The stuff that exploded was in the wagon. A lotta people were killed. The wagon was loaded with window sashes. That's what killed the people — those window sashes!"

"I know, I was just there," I mumbled.

"Oh, geez!, Oklahoma, that's right!" he screamed at me. "You coulda been killed with one of those sashes." (Window sashes were heavy iron bars on pulleys that were used to open and close windows.)

He was right! If I hadn't started to hurry back to the office and if I hadn't turned that corner just when I did, I would have surely been hit. The other IFS that brought grateful thanks were, "what if the curb was still out on the street?" and "what if the explosion had happened fifteen minutes later at the twelve o'clock rush hour?" We all began to thank the good Lord for our lucky stars.

By two o'clock we learned that a lot of people had run down Broad Street and got on the ferries to Staten Island, in order to get to safety. They also told us that it was nitroglycerin that had been loaded in that wagon. They said they knew that because the blast didn't put a hole in the street. (Nitroglycerin blows things straight up and out, and doesn't excavate.) At three o'clock, the streets were cleared enough to get us back on our normal schedules.

"O.K., Oklahoma," Louis P. Rocker called to me, "you can go on over now to the Exchange for the reports and orders."

I went back to the Exchange building. The streets were cleared, and those great windows on the Broad Street side stood bare and broken. Inside the building, the yellow silk drapes were strewn all over the floor, and the material had shattered pieces of window glass all through it. But that didn't stop everybody from tearing away at that yellow silk yardage. Even I got a piece.

That was September 16, 1920. Before the month was out, almost every broker on Wall Street was wearing a yellow silk shirt. Some of us couldn't afford shirtmakers — I had a beautiful yellow silk scarf.

THE RIGHT PLACE AT THE RIGHT TIME

Fifty years ago, on June 13, 1927, I walked into the Ritz Hotel at Eighth and Flower in downtown Los Angeles. I had come to California to try to get into the movies.

The lobby was teeming with groups of men shouting at each other, laughing and exchanging strong handclasps and backslaps. By the time I wove my way through to the desk, I had learned that the Los Angeles Angels always stayed at the Ritz Hotel and that they were all there that day greeting a visiting baseball team. That very first day in Los Angeles I thought that everybody in California was a baseball player.

I put down my overnight bag and registered. "Jack Oakie," I wrote, and "New York City" for my address.

"My trunk is being sent over from the boat by the transfer company," I told the clerk.

"We'll have it put in your room when it arrives," he assured me pleasantly.

I had bought that trunk when I was still in the chorus of the Shubert show, *Artists and Models*. It was toward the end of the run. Lulu McConnell and her husband, Grant Simpson, had put their vaudeville act together again and invited me to join them. The stagehands put the great big HOTEL sticker on it. I never did need a trunk with a THEATRE label on it because I always wore my one suit. I was with Lulu McConnell and Company for over two years. (I was the "Company.") We played spots like Shemokan, Pennsylvania, for a split week and then the Palace in New York. It was the happiest and most instructive time of my career. I stood in the wings and watched those great acts every day and every night.

Then Lulu was asked to star in *Peggy Ann*, the Rodgers and Hart musical. She took me with her, and I went back in the chorus. But in vaudeville I had been learning how to get laughs, and the regimentation of the chorus cramped my style. After months of making my part in the chorus a solo, they finally gave me my notice. But that didn't faze me! Charles Lindbergh had just crossed the ocean, and I felt that if Lucky Lindy could make it, so could I. "Go West Young Man" was the perfect slogan for me, and I decided I, too, could make it by crossing the ocean. So to get to California I left New York on the S.S. President Hayes, of the Dollar Steamship Line, went through the Panama Canal, and arrived in Los Angeles on June 13, 1927.

On the boat I became friendly with Tom Ivey, vice-president of the California Bank. (We continued to be good friends throughout his lifetime.) I asked his advice about a place to stay, saying, "I've never been to California before." In all of our traveling, Lulu had never been booked this far west.

"Well, you just try the Ritz Hotel, at Eighth and Flower. It's a very, very nice little hotel."

"Thanks," I said. "The Ritz?" It sure sounded high-class to me. Well, that first day (and it was, as advertised, a clear sunny day), I got in and out of my room as fast as I could. I was anxious to get out and look for the movie stars.

The ball players were out on the street in front of the Ritz, visiting, smoking big cigars, and being pointed out by passers-by who had come out of their way to see their favorite athletes. As I stood out there on the street in front of the hotel I realized I was all alone — I didn't know a soul. I watched the ball players go in and out of the hotel for a while and then began to wander.

As I walked toward Ninth Street, I looked across the open lot and saw Joe Frisco's name up on the marquee heading the vaudeville bill at the Orpheum Theatre. Suddenly I was not just wandering, I ran right for that stage door. I had found a friend in Los Angeles. I had played on the bill with Joe many times, and we had become very good friends.

There was that time in Portchester, New York, when after the show he took a taxi all the way back to Manhattan and asked me to join him. Taking a taxi all that long way was a very great luxury in those vaudeville days, but Joe was the headliner. He made six hundred dollars and counted his money all the way back to the Alamac Hotel. In his stuttering way, he leaned over toward the cab driver and asked, "Ssay, how much is ten percent of six hundred dollars?"

He also kept asking the time. He had promised to call an actress and didn't want to be late putting the call through. When we got to the Alamac I went right up to his room with him. "Vvery talented," he said to me as he put the call through to Ruby Stevens. Fifteen years later I bought her house in the Valley.

I got back stage of the Orpheum just in time. A lot of the acts were coming out to go to dinner, and I just caught Joe in time. "Ssay, Oakie, what

17

are you doing here?" he asked. Gee, I was so glad to see him.

"Well nothing, Joe. I just came out to try to get into the movies," I confessed. "But I just got here today and I'd sure like to see some movie stars."

"Nnot down here, Oakie. Ththats all up in Hollywood," he explained. "Come on, I'll take you up there."

Once again Joe got a taxi, and we rode all the way up to Hollywood Boulevard and Vine Street to Henry's Restaurant — the most famous restaurant in Hollywood at the time. I had dinner with Joe but couldn't eat. That evening at Henry's I saw one of the most glamorous, most beautiful movie stars in the world. We sat just one table away from Lily Damita, and I stared and stared and stared. She was dressed all in white and was the most graceful, exquisite gal I had ever seen. Even years later when she was married to Errol Flynn and we had become good friends, I always continued to stare.

Joe and I were having our after-dinner coffee, when I had another thrill. "Jack! What are you doing here?" It was Pat Caron, one of the beautiful show girls from *Innocent Eyes,* a Shubert musical I had danced in. I could hardly believe it! Somebody recognized me and knew me in this new world of strangers.

"I'm just here looking around," I said.

"Would you like to come to a party tonight?" The invitation was casual.

"Sure thing!" I accepted, and I was not very casual. "Sure thing," I repeated, realizing how lucky I was that Joe had brought me to Henry's.

Wesley Ruggles

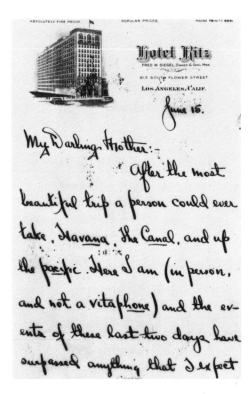

Jack Oakie, Circa 1927

"Meet me at the Hollywood Plaza Hotel at about seven," she said, and was gone like a fairy godmother. Pat was waving her magic wand that night. When Joe went back downtown to the Orpheum, I walked over to the Hollywood Plaza Hotel and waited in the lobby for Pat. Her golden coach was a Cunningham, and she drove us to the party somewhere in Beverly Hills. At the party she introduced me to her boyfriend, Wesley Ruggles.

"What do you do?" I asked him, feeling fresh as paint.

"I'm a director," he said in his mellow rich voice with the patience of a saint.

"Working on something now?" I asked.

"Yes, I'm just starting a picture at Universal," he smiled and looked at me with the friendliest light in his eyes.

"Well, what are you doing for a comic?" I asked, offering my services.

Pat's magic wand really worked that night, because not only did I go to work in his picture, *Finders Keepers,* starring Laura La Plante, but he signed me to a personal contract. And at the party that same first night in Hollywood, he introduced me to Billy Wilkerson, who became my agent and later with some help from Wesley Ruggles started the *Hollywood Reporter.*

I can hardly believe it's been fifty years, but on June 13, 1927, I came to Hollywood to try to get into the movies, and with the help of Joe Frisco and Pat Caron, I got into the movies. On June 13, 1927, I was in the right place at the right time.

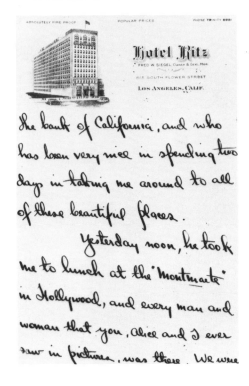

MENU
DOLLAR STEAMSHIP LINE
S. S. "PRESIDENT HAYES"

J. J. CADOGAN, COMMANDER.

—CHOW—

Hard Time Dinner and Dance De-Luxe

Invocation by Rev. Jack Oakie. B.S. B.U.M.

Music by Alex Van-Stratten; Direct from the Tropical Gardens, Havana

Words unfit to be Printed-by Poison Ivey.

Thursday, June 2nd, 1927.

At Sea............Always at Sea...What Goes down might Come Up

Hors D'Oeuvres. Asselta

Young Onions - but strong for their Age   Tasty Olives, Soaked in Axle Grease

Radishes with a Kick

Salted K-nutta. Georgie Hunt

—SOUP—

Pot Luck Dago Style   Poverty Chowder

—FISH—

Singing Snapper, trapped by the White Spot Fox; in Pelham Bay

HONTARYS

Red Hots-Stuffed with Chestnuts

Spoiled Tenderloin of Beef; as tender as a Women's Heart

White meat of Irish Turkey; they are eating it this season

Laughing Duck; Stewed Bees Knuckles

TO ORDER—FROM—THE—GRILL—TEN MINUTES

Saddle Blankets - Whale Bone on Toast—Ostrich Eggs - Elephants Trunks

Creamed Nightingale Tongues in Rancid Butter

VEGETABLES GALORE

Fresh Tomatoes - Right from the Can   Tasty Rice

Suck-a-tash better than Chewing Gum

Hard Boiled Potatoes

Sweet Things

Sash-Weights - Sinkers - Nigger Cake

Apple Pie - N-Every-Thin - Ice Cream

Cheese, that will walk by itself   Crackers, snarred and Bent

Seasonable Fresh Fruit

Re-Boiled Arbuckle Coffee

We thank you: Call Again: Tell your friends: if you have any.

Kindly bring your own!   If not see old Bill Carolin

CAUTION—— No Gun Play

Thursday June 2nd, 1927.   Evan Hughes. Chief Steward

---

me years.

I am living at the above
at present but expect to move
to Hollywood at the end of the
week. Everything is dandy. I feel
like a two yr. old, only one regret
that is that You and Alice aren't
both here to enjoy this too.

Drop me a line at this Hotel
Room 612. Jack Oakie. If I
move I shall leave word here
alright. Now take care of your
self and don't forget that I
love you better than anything in
this world.
From your baby
Lewis.

DOLLAR STEAMSHIP LINE

MENU

Sehguh Nave Drawets Feihc
Neves - Ytnewt - Neetnin   Htneves Enuj Yadseut

Ytriht-Thgie Ta Efac Adnarev Ni Gnicnad

Rion Efac   Stnim Rennid   Stun Dexim
          Nosaes ni Tiurf   Suoirav Srekcarc
Maerc   Aloznogrog   Nacirema Gnuoy—ESEEHC
Setad Naisrep   Snisiar Retsulc   Sgif Aisalac
Maerc Eci Hcnerf   Yllej Nortic   Yrtsap Hcnerf Detrossa
Eip Ecnim Toh   Ecuas Ydnarb & Drah Gnidoup Mulp Demaets

STRESSED DNA YRTSAP

Ecuas Settergianiv Stniop Sugarapsa Dloc

Seotamot Decils—Gnisserd Trofeuqor—Ecuttel Daeh

DALAS

Steeb Ybab Derettub   Maerc ni Spinrut Nedrag Etihw Deliob
Seotatop Werr   Seotatop Nworb Dekab

SELBATEGEV

Ecuas Yrrebnarc Deffuts Yekrut Def Yrelec Mot Gnuoy

Yllej Tnim Bmal Gnilraey fo Gel

Ecuas Hsidaresroh .Feeb Fo Niolris & Sbir EmirP

STSAOR

Eeleg Ua Esiacnarf Steuqennap

Sitor .Esialgna Senissaeb   Esiorgnoh .Leztinhcs Akirpap
          Esioegruob .Nisiar Ua ,Fueob Ed Sodenruot

SEERTNE

Stue Detrossa Eciohc Dloc   Gniddup Saep Htiw Krop Delkeip

DELIOB

Dramoh ,Elos Nomel Fo Telif Deliob

HSIF

Essecnirp Emmosnoc Dloc   Eniacirema Emerc

PUOS

Essur Snotuorc   Sgge Deffuts   Ehcnarb ne Yrelec
Sdnomla Detlas   Sotnemip Htiw Seivohcna   Swarts Eseehc
Sarg Eiof Ed Etap   Sevilo Neerg   Liatkcoc Tiurf Dexim

SREZITEPPA

RENNID

Rednammoc Nagodac Haimerej

"SEYAH TNEDISERP PIHSMAETS"

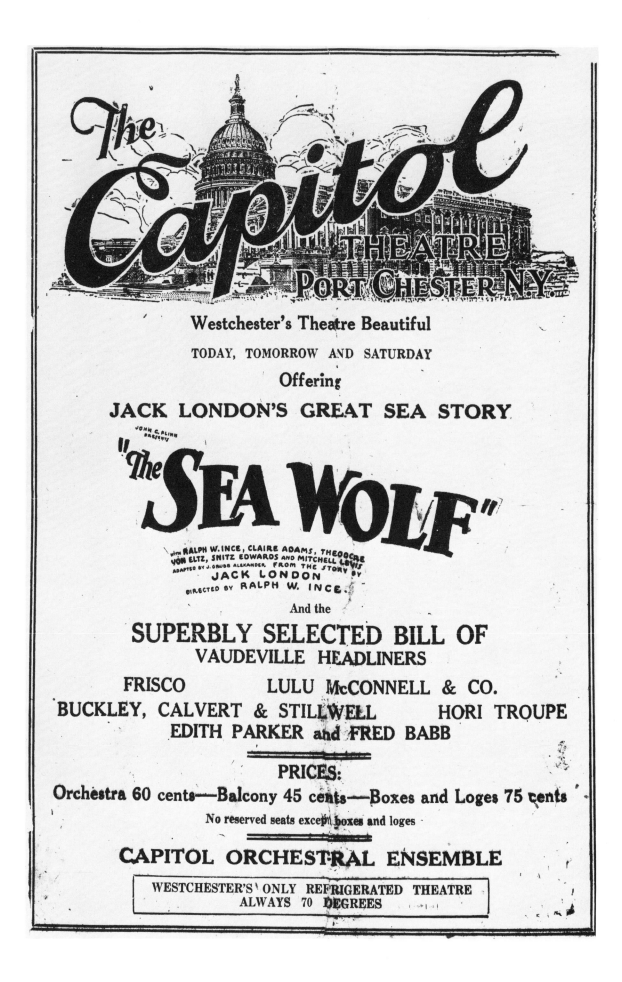

The *Capitol* THEATRE
PORT CHESTER N.Y.

Westchester's Theatre Beautiful

TODAY, TOMORROW AND SATURDAY

Offering

JACK LONDON'S GREAT SEA STORY

JOHN C. FLINN
PRESENTS

"The SEA WOLF"

WITH RALPH W. INCE, CLAIRE ADAMS, THEODORE
VON ELTZ, SNITZ EDWARDS AND MITCHELL LEWIS
ADAPTED BY J. GRUBB ALEXANDER FROM THE STORY BY
JACK LONDON
DIRECTED BY RALPH W. INCE.

And the

SUPERBLY SELECTED BILL OF
VAUDEVILLE HEADLINERS

FRISCO   LULU McCONNELL & CO.

BUCKLEY, CALVERT & STILLWELL   HORI TROUPE

EDITH PARKER and FRED BABB

PRICES:

Orchestra 60 cents—Balcony 45 cents—Boxes and Loges 75 cents

No reserved seats except boxes and loges

CAPITOL ORCHESTRAL ENSEMBLE

WESTCHESTER'S ONLY REFRIGERATED THEATRE
ALWAYS 70 DEGREES

BOWS

There are three stages in the career of a movie actor. In the beginning there is the, "Who's he?" stage. At the peak it's, "There he is!" and finally, the, "My God! Is *he* still around?" For each of the above stages there are bows the actor takes that have peculiarities descriptive of their own eras.

For example, in stage number three (which is the one I have finally reached), I am often asked to get up and take a bow. Invariably at public functions and large dinner parties, a speaker will say, with all good intentions. "Jack, get up and take a bow!" That request, however, is always timed to come at the precise moment that I have managed to mouth some crisp hearts of lettuce. (Have you ever tried to cut that stubborn wedge with a salad fork?)

Then, with a spotlight glaring on me, I try to get up and acknowledge the compliment. The slippery square piece of hotel damask slides off my silk mohair lap. As I remove my eyeglasses so that the audience won't mistake me for Marjorie Main, I don't see the water tumbler until I've overturned it and the contents bring my attention to the incident. Despite all this, I try to rise from a chair that has been pulled up to a table in a nice close fit for eating — even Fred Astaire admits that this kind of agility doesn't go on forever. In this third stage all bows look good from a comfortably seated position while others are taking them.

But during the "There he is!" second stage, bows were varied, there were full arm waves, wrist flicks, head nods, waist bends, and even knee drops. I must say I still recall some of those very thrilling experiences with the same breathtaking emotions I felt in those very agile days.

One of the most memorable was when my mother and I visited a sparsely populated little island called Hawaii. I couldn't believe it but they let school out so that the children could meet our boat, *The Lurline.* Shouts of "Aloha!" "Banzai!" "There he is!" greeted us as we came waving and bowing all the way down that gangplank. The "There he is" stage was not only exciting for me, but it also made my mother and my wife very proud and happy. I shall always be very grateful to the gracious audiences who made that a wonderful period of my life.

It was in the beginning, however, in that "Who's he?" stage over 50 years ago, bows were taken only when permitted with the "and Company"

ensemble that I once took a bow I shall never forget. It was when I was in the chorus of *Innocent Eyes,* A Shubert musical starring Mistinguett, the French chanteuse who had had her legs insured for a million dollars — extraordinary publicity in those days.

We were on tour and were playing the Wieting Opera House in Syracuse, New York, for a five-week run. During our stay S. Hurok booked Anna Pavlova, the great Russian ballet dancer, for one performance at our theatre. She was to appear on a Tuesday matinee and, as our matinees were Wednesdays and Saturdays, all the members of our company (and we were a very large company — over fifty) were given professional courtesy tickets for her performance.

Zeke Colvin, our company manager, was at the stage door distributing the passes. "Oakie," he asked, "how would you like to work with Anna Pavlova this afternoon?"

"You're kidding! Doing what?" (I couldn't quite picture my tap dancing and her dying swan as an entry.) "Remember I'm not ballet, I'm a buck and wing man."

"Well, not dancing," he assured me. "They need a super to look as if he can play the flute."

"Zeke," I reassured him, "it'll take me only a minute to learn to play the flute if it'll get me up on the same stage with Anna Pavlova!" The great artist was the most famous ballet dancer in the world, and our whole company was anxious to watch her work. To get that close to the woman was a privilege none of us had dreamed of.

"She's doing a classic number called 'The Polish Wedding,' and the job pays a buck," Zeke said.

"A dollar?" I jumped at the chance. "I'll take it!"

"OK, see her manager, the little Russian in the grey suit. Tell him I sent you." I went backstage and found my man.

"Zeke Colvin said you need a super for 'The Polish Wedding.'"

He looked me over, nodded his approval, and said, "OK, go get wardrobe to take care of you." He pointed to the rear of the stage where their temporary wardrobe department was set up. "Pays a dollar," he called after me. "See me after the show to pick it up."

"OK, thanks."

They gave me a tent-like robe, a turban, and a flute. I put on the turban and the robe, which completely covered my street clothes, and began to practice playing the soundless flute. "Five minutes!" the stage manager called, and then directed me to a place on the stage where I joined two other supers — fiddle players.

The curtain rose on the set, and the three musicians before Pavlova made her entrance. The members of the cast of *Innocent Eyes* spotted me as the flutist immediately, and applauded the setting, of which I became a very animated part.

As the applause rose I began to give a concert. A real musician would have had to get down on his knees and pray for the notes I blew through that muted flute.

Then Pavlova made her entrance! The tiny lady electrified us all. I was no longer blowing the flute, she took my breath away! I just stood there and watched. I was the best audience she ever had. At the end of the performance, she graciously beckoned to us, her company ensemble, to come forward and take a bow. The members of the cast of my show, all dancers themselves, were very appreciative, so I bowed directly to them, as if the ovation was meant for me.

The curtain came down, and the ensemble left the stage so that Pavlova could take the next bow alone. I stayed. When the curtain went up again, there I was on the stage with Anna Pavlova! She took a deep ballet bow to the floor, and I bent from my agile waist just as deeply. That large block from *Innocent Eyes* rose, and brought the whole house to their feet with them. The applause was thunderous.

When Pavlova rose from her deep bow she looked over at me, so I bowed to her. She was wonderful! She understood the fun immediately! She returned a bow to me, then she smiled and reached for my hand, and then we both faced the audience and bowed together! I shared a standing ovation with Anna Pavlova!

Although I remember it as one of the most thrilling experiences I ever had in my career in show business, I also remember that I never did get my dollar!

TITULAR BISHOPS

I loved Wesley Ruggles, the director who had signed me to a personal contract. He had not only given me my first part in a motion picture, but had also given my career a head start, because I could spit BBs.

My road ahead seemed bright until just one hour before the sneak preview of that very first picture, when I became scared to death that Wes, being a good skate, had mistakenly shoved me in the wrong direction, and those BBs I was spitting suddenly became roller bearings that were carrying me out before I was in.

But that was before I was introduced to "the Bishops." I didn't know that I had already entered their see, and that one of them had thrown me a lifeline. In the silent days of motion pictures there were specialty writers who just wrote titles. They knew how to tell the audience when to laugh, and with their talent they could "make" a picture. A select group of the very best in the business formed a kind of union of their own, and called themselves The Titular Bishops.

Among those I got to know well were Ralph Spence, who worked mainly at MGM, George Marion and Lige Conley at Paramount, and Joseph Anthony and Thomas Reed at Universal. At Fox there was great big fat happy-go-lucky Malcolm Stuart Boylan, and another writer who was called Finis Fox because he was the first ever to use "Finis" at the end of a picture instead of the usual "The End." He was also famous for being the first to write that old standard title, "Came the Dawn." It never missed, because it explained everything by not explaining anything. I called them The Silent Laugh Machine. They were the forerunners of "the sound laugh machine" (the laugh track) that is used on television today, for the very same reason: to tell the audiences when to laugh.

I first became aware of that laugh track while watching one of the very early Lucille Ball/Desi Arnaz "I Love Lucy" shows. Desi put his hand into a drawer and got it caught in a mousetrap. Wham! I never heard such a laugh come roaring out of the television machine. I mentioned it to someone at the station. "Oh, no!" they said. "There's a live audience in the studio theatre watching them shoot the program. That laugh you hear is a live audience reaction!"

Well, I never watched them shoot, but I happened to know their cameraman, Karl Freund.

He was a huge hulk of a man; no audience would have been able to see past him as he shot a close-up of Desi's hand in a drawer.

Those Bishops who controlled the laugh machine in silent movies were very important to the industry, and the studio producers knew it. For example, I remember an emergency call late one afternoon while I was sitting around sharing some gin and mission orange juice with Ralph Spence in his San Fernando Valley home. The phone rang just as Spence was pouring the orange juice. He handed the chore over to me so that he could answer the phone. It isn't good to break the stream of things when you're pouring orange juice over gin — it bruises the liquor. So I picked up right where he left off, and then added the ice quickly to keep the swelling down. I did that job well because those drinks sure were smooth.

THE MASQUERS

November 12, 1973

Dear Jack:

Today is a big day in your life. You reached the happy age of 70. Thinking back, the first time I met you on the Universal lot so many, many years ago you were thin and you looked hungry and you didn't know what the next day was going to bring. I was in the same boat a couple of weeks before I met you. You asked me what I was doing. I told you I was about to start with Wesley Ruggles on a picture called "Finders Keepers" starring Laura La Plant — Directed by Wesley Ruggles — Assistant Director, Joe Pasternak. You made the most wonderful impression on me. During our conversation I made one mistake. I asked you if you needed any money. You asked how much I could spare. I had one $10 bill so I split it in half.

Well, you were a sensation in the picture. Wesley Ruggles put you under personal contract and he made a lot of money for himself and for you, and I am sorry to say you still owe me the five bucks and with interest it comes to about $777.50. The question is how long can I wait for that money? The answer is another 30 years when you will be 100, you pay me back the five if I'm still here. If not, you just forget about it.

Dear Jack, I wish you all the health and happiness in the world for your 70th birthday.

Your #1 fan,

Joe Pasternak

BAD BOY REFORMS

WE don't see so much of Jack Oakie nowadays. Which is rather a pity, because he is so much more entertaining than he used to be.

There was a time when he cropped up on the screen every few weeks, invariably appearing as a bumptious, but in some way likeable, wisecracker, and as often as not shouldering the whole burden of a picture himself.

He made his first film appearance in *Finders Keepers,* in the early months of 1928, and got his first biggish part with Clara Bow in *The Fleet's In,* later that same year.

From then on it was a triumphant progress. His hilarious taxi-driver, Voltaire, in *Let's Go Native,* belongs to this period. He was hailed as a brilliant new comedy find and was put into so many films that he must have needed a bicycle to get from one studio to the next—with the result that we had a little bit too much of him.

To-day, he is the same cheerful, cocksure young man, with a flow of wisecracks from his lips—but there is a certain difference. There is more sympathy in his acting. He is a much more dependable fellow, and many of his more irritating mannerisms have disappeared.

Picture Stealer

He also has the advantage as a rule of appearing in supporting parts, sometimes more or less as himself, and other times in genuine characterisations, stamped, however, with his own personality. He is an outstanding proof of the fact that some players are considerably better in a secondary part rather than a starring rôle.

Without being the star, he has "stolen" nearly every picture in which he has appeared lately.

With such a wealth of talent as Bing Crosby, Burns and Allen, Charles Ruggles and Mary Boland around him in *The Big Broadcast of 1936,* he succeeded in standing out head and shoulders above all the others.

Appearing as a cheerful pessimist in *King of Burlesque,* he made rings round his colleagues, although he was really only a "stooge" to Warner Baxter.

Colleen was primarily a Dick Powell-Ruby Keeler vehicle; but Jack Oakie, with the assistance of Joan Blondell, saved the show and made it quite amusing.

On the strength of these he got top billing,

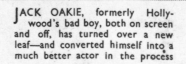

JACK OAKIE, formerly Hollywood's bad boy, both on screen and off, has turned over a new leaf—and converted himself into a much better actor in the process

— says —

LIONEL CLYNTON

without actually being starred, in *The Charm School* and again in *Florida Special.* His latest rôle is as Fred MacMurray's "buddy" in *Texas Rangers.*

Nobody's criticised him for a long time, which is proof positive that he has succeeded in doing away completely with the character who was simply conceited but witty—at the same time, however, retaining his own personality.

And he is essentially a player who, whatever the character he is playing and whatever the situations, must keep his own personality to the forefront all the while. This personality is one of the major delights of Hollywood. Unlike a lot of comedians, he is cheerful at all times. He is instinctively witty, and he's an inveterate leg-puller. There is a boisterous atmosphere on the set when he is working which you will rarely find anywhere else.

"He's never at a loss for a wisecrack," Richard Arlen told me, a little while ago. "Most of his lines in his pictures are his own. He's one of those people who can step on to the set and fire away without any worry and without tripping up."

He grinned suddenly.

"But there was one time when he broke down," he went on. "He and I were playing in a picture with a young newcomer who simply couldn't get the hang of speaking his lines for the mike. He fluffed one scene ten times, and we were about getting tired of the word 'retake.' Then he got his lines right. Jack Oakie was so surprised that he flummoxed his own—and I've never seen him go so red as he did when the other fellow laughed!"

Dick Arlen is one of Jack Oakie's best friends. They have worked together time after time, and have been places together in between pictures.

While we were talking about Oakie, Arlen gave me a vivid character study of him.

"When you see him on the screen, you really know him," he explained. "He's married now, and is a bit tamer than he used to be. But, most of the time I have known him, he has been one of the most inveterate trouble-finders in the world.

"He had a habit of getting into a fix almost every time he went out. I've often waited for him and he hasn't turned up at all because of something or other. I remember waiting an hour for him one day. He turned up, grinning cheerfully. He had been held up on a driving offence, but he'd managed to talk himself out of it.

"That's one thing he can always do—talk himself out of anything. There was a time when the papers were dubbing him 'Paramount's bad boy.' He had disappeared from the studio for three days, and no one had been able to find him."

The Prodigal's Return

"Then he rolled along, as happy as ever. I was watching when he met B. P. Schulberg; but before Schulberg could say a word Jack flung out his hands pleadingly.

"'Please, Mr. Schulberg,' he begged, in innocent tones, 'I'm not your bad boy any more, am I? *Please* say I'm not!'

"He went on in that strain for some time. Schulberg couldn't get in a word. Honestly, nobody can stand up against him. You're bound to give way and forgive him!".

Oakie's marriage was typical of him. He had always denied that he would marry, and it didn't seem very likely that he would, because, everywhere he went, he was seen with his mother.

He took everyone by surprise by marrying Venita Varden on a train. A judge met the train and married them in a reserved compartment, with the train's conductor and engineer acting as witnesses.

It was just the sort of thing he would do. And that is one of the greatest things about him. He always does everything in the way you hope he will.

"Gotta go to work," Spence said when he hung up the phone. "Irving Thalberg's got a stinker on his hands."

"You mean right now?" I asked. It was after six in the evening.

"Yup," he said, "right now. But stay and finish your drink; he's sending the car for me."

Thalberg always sent his car and chauffeur for Spence. He also set up a well-stocked bar in the projection room, and then left him alone with the projectionist. Spence would work all night, having the picture run and rerun for him.

In the morning when he staggered out of the projection room, the car and chauffeur would be right there waiting to take him home, when the salvage work with his fine Spencerian hand was done. Late the very next afternoon, while he was still sleeping it off, Thalberg called, "Spence, it's wonderful! We've got a hit!"

In that picture I remember the scene where Norma Shearer and Gwen Lee come up the steps from a New York basement night club, and stand on the street looking around. "What's that peculiar odor?" he wrote for Norma Shearer.

"Oh, that? That's fresh air." He wrote for Gwen Lee, the comedienne. That was a cue for the audience to laugh, and they howled — and so did I.

Well, that very first picture of mine, a Universal Pictures production, was *Finders Keepers,* written by Mary Roberts Rinehart. Laura La Plante and Johnny Harron starred, and Wesley Ruggles directed. It was a comedy about the First World War, and I played a private fourth class.

During the war, Wesley Ruggles had been in the army with Charlie Sullivan, an actor who could stand right there in front of you and spit BBs in your face while talking to you. He was so expert you couldn't tell that it was he who was driving you crazy, as you tried to brush off the invisible peppering.

"What's the matter?" he'd ask innocently, while shooting at you again and again.

When we started *Finders Keepers,* Charlie was off on location with another picture and, as he was not available, Wes asked me if I knew how to spit BBs. "Sure," I said. "I'm expert." I had been chewing tobacco and spitting ever since I was nine years old. The general store in Muskogee, Oklahoma, had a big sign up on the wall that read: "The men who chew are the men who do!" I wanted to be a doer, so with practice I could spit, and hit a dime on target almost twenty feet away.

Wes cast me in the part of BB Brown, with the running gag of shooting those little missiles at the back of the neck of Eddie Phillips, who played the

shavetail lieutenant. I was good, but I still spent hours practicing in front of the mirror in my furnished room at Mrs. Powell's boarding house, that little white wooden Hollywood cottage on Sunset Boulevard and Vine Street. My tobacco-spitting days stood me in good stead. I never missed.

The night of the sneak preview at the Ritz Theatre on Wilshire Boulevard at La Brea, we were all there. Wesley Ruggles, Laura La Plante, Johnny Harron, and I sat next to Edmund Breese (who played the General, Laura's father). We seemed to be waiting a long time, and I was becoming more and more anxious wondering what was holding us up, when word went around that they couldn't start running the picture because "Uncle" Carl Laemmle hadn't finished eating his dinner yet, and it would be at least an hour before he got there.

To fill in the time, they decided to run a two-reeler that was also directed by Wesley Ruggles. It was called *The Collection* and featured Dorothy Gulliver and George Lewis. I was thoroughly enjoying the campus capers until the camera sorted out Andy Devine to show the audience that he was shooting BBs at one of his unsuspecting fellow collegians.

"Oh, God," I winced, "that's the gag Wesley gave me." I sank down into my seat, squirming as I watched Andy on the screen. "Well, I guess I'm through before I start," I whispered to Edmund Breese. "I guess I'll be heading back East on the next train."

I was so dejected I decided not to stay to see *Finders Keepers* and take the ribbing I was sure I was in for. I leaned over, and said good night to Edmund Breese, meaning it in more ways than one, when the lights suddenly went up, and "Uncle Carl" came down the aisle to his seat.

"Hold on," Edmund Breese said, as he put his strong arm on my shoulder and held me down. The theatre darkened, and *Finders Keepers* came on. Laura La Plante was as cute as the devil. She wore a soldier's uniform that didn't fit, and she kept losing her pants. She and Johnny Harron were established as the lovers, and then I came on and spit my BBs. I hit Eddie Phillips right smack in the back of the neck, and I grinned with satisfaction that my shot was so perfect. Then I had the greatest surprise of my life. The camera cut from my grin to a title that had me say, "It's a great war, ain't it?" All through the picture I kept spitting BBs, and saying, "It's a great war, ain't it?"

Tom Reed was the Titular Bishop who wrote that line for me, and I have revered him ever since. When we were shooting the picture, I no more said "It's a great war" than flew. But for years fans would stop me on the street, slap me on the back, and say, "It's a great war, ain't it? Say, Oakie, that's one of the funniest lines I ever heard you say." When the lights went up again that night at the Ritz Theatre, Edmund Breese very kindly said, "Young man, don't you dare go back East. You stay right here. Hollywood and the movies are for you."

I stayed, and BBs became just as much my trademark as they were Charlie Sullivan's. I was asked many times by producers and directors to use the gag. "Shoot the BBs in this one, will you Jack?" they'd say. I even did it for Lloyd Bacon in *Navy Blues* almost twenty years later. I thought I was an expert until one Friday night at the fights, when I got a taste of what expert BB shooting was really like. I was sitting in my regular down-front seat at the Legion Stadium. Lupe Velez was just to the right of me, shouting, "Geeve eet to heem!" She was rooting for her fighter, Bert Colima, a compatriot of hers. Suddenly I felt a sharp sting in the back of my neck.

"Ouch!" I screamed. I thought I had been bitten by a wasp.

"Geeve eet to heem!" Lupe screeched again, and again I was stung in the neck. It was as if Lupe was cuing the insect. Every time she cried, "Geeve eet to heem!" I got stung. It was not until Colima was lying flat on his back, and Lupe was quietly wiping the tears from her eyes, and I was still getting stung, that I realized the insect didn't have wings. I was on the receiving end of the BB gag.

I stood up and turned around, and there he was just two rows behind me — the Ace, Charlie Sullivan. "O.K. Oakie," he called down to me. "Just wanted you to know that this is the way it's supposed to be done," and he kept those BBs coming while explaining it to me.

Well, I may never ever have been as good as Charlie Sullivan, but Tom Reed's title told the audiences that I was pretty good, and I have been forever grateful that so many have believed him for so long.

Jack Oakie, John Harron, Eddie Phillips and Laura LaPlante — a scene from *Finders Keepers*.

SIN TOWN

On November 12, 1927, I was still young enough to think that, as it was my birthday, it would be nice to have a couple of friends join me and celebrate over a birthday cake with lighted candles on it, so that I could make a wish over the flame. (Besides, in those days I was still skinny enough to eat all the cake I wanted.) But, although I never did spend that birthday with burning candles, I did spend it with another fire, which had me wishing over the flame for the safety of my life as it blazed the way for the birth of one of the greatest wonders of our town.

I was brand new in Hollywood, and had just started working on *Sin Town,* my second motion picture. *Sin Town* was Pathé Studio's "great epic of the West." Our director was Gordon Cooper, and the stars of the picture were Eleanor Faire and Hugh Allen. I played the part of a Westerner.

Because Eleanor Faire was married to Bill Boyd (Hopalong Cassidy), Hoppy was on the set a lot visiting. That night the cameraman let him crank the camera. It took skill to grind the handle of those hand cameras in rhythm, and Hoppy was good at it. During our lifetime friendship, Bill and I often recalled that night, when he photographed one of the most eventful scenes of my life.

After a long hard day at the studio, we were given a call for night shots. "Eight o'clock at the Hollywood Plaza Hotel! We're going out on location," the assistant director shouted. Those were the silent picture days, before the Screen Actors' Guild, when a clock with only two hands didn't have enough help to point to all the hours that moving picture people worked.

After dinner, the Company car picked us up at the Plaza Hotel on Vine Street, and we started west to a wilderness somewhere between Hollywood and the Pacific Ocean. The trip seemed endless, but we finally pulled into a bean field and bumped our way to a stop near a forsaken wooden shack. We were in the middle of the biggest bean field I'd ever seen. Beans no matter which way you looked. All you could see were beans, except for the little wooden shack where all the action was taking place.

There were crowds of people milling around it. Property men were fixing doors and placing wagons loaded with hay in the front of the cabin and in the back of it.

"What's all the excitement?" I asked Freddy Fleck, our assistant. I couldn't figure out why there were so many people there for the night shots. Although I was never given a script, I was told I was going to get locked up in a kind of jailhouse

Sin Town — a silent with Jack Oakie, Eleanor Faire, Hugh Allen and Bob Perry.

Jack Oakie, Frances Langford and Joe Penner — *Collegiate.*

with a couple of other Westerners. "Why such a crowd tonight?"

"Oh, they're not all on our picture," he said. "There's another company shooting here tonight."

"Oh? What's the other company?" I asked.

"Cecil B. De Mille's second-unit camera crew, out here to get some stock shots for *The Godless Girl.*

Cecil B. De Mille's *The Godless Girl* was a big picture, starring beautiful Lina Basquette.

"Why do you suppose they want stock shots of a bean field and a little wooden shack?" I asked. I got the answer to that question later. In the meantime our company was called, and we got right to work. We did some fight scenes between the "good ones" and the "bad ones," in and out of the little cabin. *The Godless Girl's* cameras and people seemed to be getting in and out of our scenes, or most likely it was the other way around. Then the people of both companies were given some torches and matches. I was handed some matches too.

"Now when I say, 'go!,' light up, and start burning!" Freddy Fleck yelled.

"Start burning what?" I yelled back.

"The building!" he screamed. "Some of you hit the hay in the wagons! Burn it all down!"

Well, somewhere during the feverish shooting of fighting and firing, I was tied to some bars so that they could get a shot of me trying to escape from the jailhouse. What we all forgot was that those bars were also made of wood. Suddenly they too started to burn! I tried to untie the ropes that held me, but I was no Houdini. I needed help!

"Somebody get me out of this!" I screamed. But

with two moving picture companies shooting and shouting to get a once-in-a-lifetime fire scene, there was more noise during that burning for *Sin Town* and *The Godless Girl* than anything that has ever been heard on a sound track.

Gordon Cooper was excitedly directing what he probably thought was one of the best scenes of his career. Hoppy was grinding away at the camera, and I almost had second degree burns before they realized I was really screaming for help and needed it fast! I felt as if I were performing for the final chapter of a "Cliff-hanger," serial called "Burned Alive On Birthday." Gordon Cooper finally sent in Bob Perry to untie me. But old Bob was bald, and the heat was too much for his bare head.

"Hold on there, hold on there," he kept saying. He could hardly stay long enough to loosen the ropes, but stay he did, and then we both ran from that fire — two very well-done actors.

"Thanks Bob! Thanks!" I said as we headed away from the heat. We joined a gentleman who was sitting on the running board of his luxury liner limousine. It was parked just far away enough to have a good view of the firey scene and still keep cool.

"Sit down, boys, that was a close call," he said, and moved over to make room for us.

"Thanks, Mr. Janss. This is Jack Oakie," Bob said, introducing us.

"Hello," I said as we sat down. "Now why in the world do you suppose they're burning all that down?" I asked.

"This was the Harold Lloyd Studios," Janss explained. "He used to keep his Great Dane dogs out here."

"Oh? But why are they burning it all down?" I still didn't understand.

"Because we have to clear it off," Janss said. "We're going to build a school out here, young man."

"Oh, I see." I pictured the little red wooden rectangle that I attended in Muskogee, Oklahoma. I thought of the belfry that held the bell, and I remembered that sometimes I was allowed to ring it for latecomers. A little country schoolhouse right there in the middle of a bean field. "A school," I said. "Oh, that's nice."

What I didn't realize was that the bonfire I helped to light that night — on my birthday, November 12, 1927 — was the blazing birthday of the foundation of the walks, the quads, the Lawrence Powell Library, Royce Hall, MacGowan Hall, Pauley Field, and the Medical Center and all that vast beauty that make up UCLA, Westwood, California.

GIANTS THE JACK KILLERS

I started in motion pictures during the silent era, when stealing a scene wasn't just petty larceny, it was out-and-out murder. During those early student days my best instructors were giants who were killers, and just learning to survive their mayhem was the best school of acting a young man could have had.

At that time, although the pictures moved, those big old cameras didn't. Not only were they stationary, but they couldn't see from all the angles and distances that cameras do today. So in those early days, because of the camera's limitations, you had to do two things at once. While trying to get your laughs, you had to keep your performance within the sights of the camera, and anyone who could master that difficult double play was called a "scene stealer."

Each *take* was like entering a contest to see who could get in front of the camera, and then stay there the longest. As in every game, there were some moves that became basic rules. While still making silent pictures, one of the hardest rules for me to learn was the simple one of "keep your mouth shut!" Before talkies, just as soon as you'd open your mouth they'd have to cut away from you to a written title. So to keep the camera, you had to keep from talking. Well, I've always been a naturally talkative fellow, so I had to keep biting my tongue until talkies came in. I'll always believe that talking pictures were invented just for me because they were right down my back alley. Old chatterbox Oakie.

A cut and bleeding tongue was only one of the many wounds I suffered to learn how to stay on camera. One of the greatest giants in show business, Lionel Barrymore, taught me the advantage of being the last one to go out of a door. That lesson was deeply impressed on me when we were making *Road House*. The first day on the set I arrived bright-eyed and alert. I was sure I was going to learn something about classic acting, working with Lionel Barrymore who had such great knowledge of Shakespeare. But I was wrong. I had come prepared for the wrong lesson, and found I was way out of my class. What I really had to learn in order to work with Barrymore was the manly art of self-defense.

Lionel Barrymore was one of the strongest men I have ever known. He had hands of steel. I still carry their deep imprints on the arm he gripped as

"E—1929
TREET GIRL" Prod. by WES RUGGLES

he ushered me through the door of the set when I tried to outstay him in a scene. "This way, young man, this way!" he said, and he sure had his way; I went right through the door ahead of him. Being 'last one to leave,' is a rule I'm very careful not to take advantage of when I'm working with a heavyweight who outclasses me.

Many years later when Lionel Barrymore and I were neighbors in Northridge, we were sitting around one night complaining that it was getting tougher every day to get into the studio. All the streets going into town were being cluttered with Boulevard stop signs. The next morning he pulled into my gate and waited for me. "This way, young man!" he called to me and led me down Balboa Boulevard. He had found the last street that was left wide open.

"At last," I said to myself as I followed him out of Northridge, "I'm finally leaving a scene behind Barrymore!"

News of Radio Pictures

The presence in the audience at the premiere of "Street Girl," Tuesday evening, July 30th, of many prominent men in the world of finance, industry, radio and the theatre, gave a strongly significant note to the presentation of the first production released by Radio Pictures. In the opinion of many who have attended hundreds of motion picture premieres, the opening of "Street Girl" at the Globe Theatre, New York, was an event of historic import inasmuch as it marked the formal entrance of Radio into show business.

While "Street Girl" as a motion picture attraction held the center of the stage and won the unrestrained plaudits of a packed house, the audience itself, composed of world famous figures in business and the arts, lent an atmosphere of dignity and stability seldom observed at a premiere.

Among the invited guests were:

Major General James G. Harboard, president of Radio Corporation of America; David Sarnoff, chairman of the board. R-K-O; Owen D. Young, president of Westinghouse Electric; Paul Cravath of the Equitable Bank; Merlin H. Aylesworth, president of National Broadcasting Co.; Hiram S. Brown, president of Radio-Keith-Orpheum Theatres, Inc.; Colvin Brown, executive vice-president of Pathe; Sam Katz, head of Publix Theatres; Harry Warner; Spyros Skoras; Edward W. Harden, Edwin M. Herr and Edward Hayes, directors of R-C-A; Paul Mazur, member of the R-C-A board; Joseph P. Kennedy, president of Pathe; Joseph Plunkett, vice-president of Radio-Keith-Orpheum Theatres, Inc.; J. J. Murdock; Mr. Dreyfuss, head of Harms, music publishers; Dr. Goldsmith, president, and Mr. Bucher, general manager, of R-C-A Photophone; Richard Currier of R-C-A Photophone; Owen Davis, noted playwright; Frank Craven, playwright and star; Henry B. Forbes, Broadway producer; Miss Ann Caldwell, noted librettist, and Herbert Brenon, noted motion picture director.

JACK OAKIE
One of the Principals in the Radio Picture
"Street Girl"

Now that "Street Girl" has arrived, William LeBaron, vice-president in charge of production, announces that six more of the thirty Radio Pictures listed for production have been finished and will be released shortly.

* * *

September first will mark the formal opening of Le-Baron's own "The Very Idea," adapted from his own stage success of several years ago. Frank Craven both directed and acted an important role in this Radio Picture while Richard Rosson takes credit for assisting in the screen direction. In the cast with Craven, who is well known as both a star and director of the legitimate stage, are Hugh Trevor, Allan Kearns, Sally Blane, Jeanne DeBard, Olive Tell and Theodore Von Eltz.

A week later will find the three Moore brothers—Owen, Tom and Matt—appearing for the first time together in "Side Street," in New York. Broadway is the proper setting for "Side Street" inasmuch as it is whispered that it is adopted from a real story of happenings on one of the streets in the West Forties.

* * *

Fred MacMurray also knows the advantage of being 'last one to leave,' and loves to tell the story of how he tried to outwait me in a scene in *Texas Rangers*.

"I said goodbye to Jean Parker," Fred explains. "Then I stood there and waited for Oakie to say goodbye and leave. I waited and waited and waited, and finally Oakie said 'goodbye honey' and backed out into me, maneuvering me right through the door ahead of him. Well, darn it, as soon as Oakie came through that door I ran right back into the scene before the camera stopped rolling, and said goodbye again. When I went through that door the second time, I was sure I

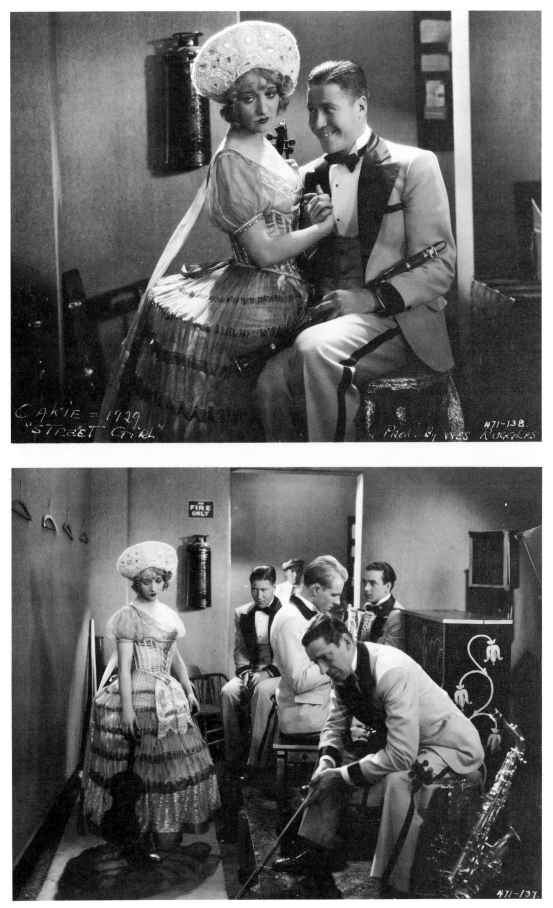

Street Girl — Jack Oakie, Betty Compson, Ned Spark, John Harron.

Street Girl — Ned Sparks, John Harron, Eddie Kane and Jack Oakie.

Jack Oakie and Fred MacMurray in *The Texas Rangers*.

had at last gone through a door after Oakie. But King Vidor yelled, 'Cut! Say Fred, let's take it again, and this time let's just cut out that last goodbye.' See what I mean — nobody ever gets out of a door after Oakie!" I always tell Fred I don't deserve the credit for that one; it was really won by default.

Just staying inside a door, however, was no guarantee that you could hold the attention of the audience. In *Street Girl* I worked with Ned Sparks, another giant who almost killed me, before I learned another very important rule. He stood behind me, firmly planted in his immovable stance, and stared at me with his dead pan, and piercing "fish eyes," as I acted my heart out. The harder I worked, the harder he stared. I was fighting a losing battle.

"Ned Sparks is killing me!" I almost cried as I told Wesley Ruggles, our director, that I knew he was murdering me. "He's killing me! I don't know what to do! He's just killing me!"

"Where are your hands?" Wes asked quietly.

"Oh! My, oh my, oh my!" I understood immediately! I knew exactly what he meant! The very next *take* I went right up to Ned and pushed him with both my hands. I kept right on pushing him all during the scene.

"Keep your hands off me!" Ned warned me in his monotone.

"This is the way I work," I explained pleasantly, pushing him a little more to demonstrate I never let him get "set," and you can't "fish eye" when you're off balance.

One of the greatest examples of a "fish eye" stealing a scene was Lewis Stone staring at Mickey Rooney in the "Andy Hardy" pictures.

Having survived a great many giants I was finally murdered by one of the greatest giants of all, "the gentle giant," as his wife Margaret calls him. Victor McLaglen had earned his Masters in scene stealing long before I began to take lessons. The first day on the set of *Murder At The Vanities,* Vic said, "Oakie, old boy, they tell me you're quite a scene stealer. Guess I'll have to keep my eye on you, eh?" Coming from the master, that was a nice compliment, but I knew it was I who had better keep an eye on him. I also remembered that Vic was a very strong man. On March 10, 1909, he fought a famous exhibition match with Jack Johnson, who had at that time just won the heavyweight title of the world. As Margaret says, "Victor remained perpendicular the full six rounds."

Having set my heart on remaining perpendicular on *Murder At The Vanities,* it was a foregone conclusion that I was the first one to go through every door on that picture. Only once did I try to take advantage of him. As we were leaving the chorus girls' dressing room, I bowed to him as Alphonse and Gaston would, to allow him to pass through first. But he took hold of my sore Barrymore arm, and threw me through that door so hard I kept right on going until I almost left the stage through the wall! But it wasn't with the power in those strong hands, which resembled catchers' mitts, that he murdered me; he did it with sleight-of-hand so delicately I didn't know I was dead until the next morning when we viewed the daily rushes in the projection room.

The scene was in the chorus girls' dressing room. I was the stage manager and, although a murder had been committed backstage, it was the opening night of the Vanities, and I was trying to explain to Vic, the detective who was there to investigate, that he shouldn't stop the performance.

"The show must go on!" I kept trying to convince him. Vic sat behind me at the traditional wall-length mirror that served about twenty dressing tables. I kept walking back and forth, acting out my long monologue in forceful terms, but I kept my eye on him as I talked and walked. He seemed to be just sitting there listening to me. However innocent he looked, I kept watching him like a hawk during each *take*. I was prepared to counteract anything he might do, but he wasn't doing anything but listening to me, and letting me take the stage.

Mitch Leisen was directing. "All right, cut!" he called. "Let's just take it once more." Well, with

Vic behaving so well, I got careless. I began to act just for the camera, and with my back to him I gave my all to the lens.

"Cut! Print!" Mitch shouted. And then the roof fell in! All the members of the crew were hysterical! The stage shook with the roar of their laughter.

"I knew it!" I said. "Mitch, what did he do?" I asked.

"Wait till you see the rushes tomorrow morning," was all he'd say. Next day we were all there in the projection room at nine o'clock. Mitch Leisen signaled the projectionist. The lights went down, and the work we had done the day before came up on the screen.

There I was, full-face to the camera, giving an Academy Award performance. Vic was sitting at a dressing table in the background, listening to me with the patience of a big old Saint Bernard dog, when suddenly he noticed his face in the chorus girls' mirror. He looked around carefully to be sure he wouldn't be caught, picked up a powder puff and, without removing the derby he was wearing or the cigar he had in his mouth, he very daintily powdered his nose, got closer to the mirror to admire that ugly face of his, happily re-

Earl Carroll's *Murder at the Vanities* — Victor McLaglen and Jack Oakie.

placed the powder puff, and turned back in time to assume interest in what I was talking about.

"Touché!" I called to Vic across the projection room.

"Righto, old boy," Vic called back.

That's what we used to call stealing a scene, or in this case what *I* call "murder at the vanities."

Once in a Lifetime — Jack Oakie, Sidney Fox, Gregory Ratoff, Aline MacMahon and Russell Hopton.

WHEN WE LEARNED TO TALK

During the year that I made silent pictures, all the publicity stories that came out of New York carried warnings to us here on the West Coast. "Motion pictures are soon going to talk," they predicted, "and when they do, those film actors out there in Hollywood will be silent forever!"

Broadway stage actors, who got their messages across the footlights with their trained, well-modulated voices that could easily be heard way up in the second balcony of the theatre, were sure that we who did all our acting with our hands and our faces and our body muscles were "unspeakable"!

I was on location down in Chino, California, making *Someone To Love*, with Charles "Buddy" Rogers and Mary Brian, when the word reached us! It spoke up loud and clear in the form of a mimeographed letter from the front office of Paramount Pictures Studio. A copy was handed to each of us, and Buddy read his aloud. "You will upon completion of your present assignment, report immediately to the studio to make a talking test."

"Well", said Bud, as he reached over to shake my hand in a dramatic farewell, "see you and Mary in the actors' home." I don't know why Mary and I laughed; Bud wasn't a comedian.

We finished making *Someone To Love* with none of the enthusiasm we had had when we started it, and I did what the notice told me to — I reported to the studio to prepare for a talking test. As I entered the main gate of Paramount Studios, Harvey Pugh, head of the mail room, dashed out to meet me. "Say, I've been watching for you," he said, and handed me a sealed envelope. "See Roy Pomeroy over on stage 5, he's expecting you."

"Thanks a lot," I said gratefully, and took the envelope. The typed instructions on the front of it read, "You will please learn the enclosed script and report to Roy Pomeroy." I put the unopened envelope into my pocket, turned right around, walked out of the gate, crossed the street, and entered that haven known as Oblath's Coffee Shop. I sat in the corner of a back booth. I wanted some time to evaluate the situation. Margaret Rogers, our motherly waitress, brought me some coffee.

"Have something to eat, Mr. Oakie," she urged. Margaret always felt that some food could settle all problems.

"No thanks, Margaret, just some coffee." The fear that was eating at me that morning needed no nourishment. I took out the envelope, set it before me, and read the instructions again. "You will please learn the enclosed script and report to Roy Pomeroy."

We had heard that they were using scenes from Shakespeare's plays for test material. Although Hamlet was a favorite role of mine, I didn't think the prince would have sounded quite right using my Oklahoma drawl. More frightening than Hamlet was Roy Pomeroy. He had become the bogeyman we were all scared to death of. He was considered the genius of sound at Paramount, and his word was law.

It wasn't until years later, when *Talkies* grew up a bit and we with them, that I learned from Gene Barrett, the sound man on most of my early sound pictures, that he and Roy Pomeroy had been telephone splicers. Gene told me that he and Roy used to work underground splicing telephone wires. They both burrowed their way into the new wide-open field of talking pictures, and kept the

Charles 'Buddy" Rogers and Jack Oakie.

rest of us in line with fear. "But in the beginning," Gene said, "our guess was as good as anybody's in finding out how to record the human voice."

It was a guessing game, because nobody knew what was expected of them, and fear was the major reason so many were inundated by those soundwaves. The long casualty list finally included some of the screen's greatest stars. Clara Bow, who had wrung more tears out of an audience with one-syllable words, was suddenly given lines written by Lloyd Sheldon, an Oxford graduate. In *The Wild Party* she had to say, "I'd like to meet you perpendicularly!"

"What the heck does that mean?" she asked on the set. "Somebody look it up!" She had to keep rewriting her scripts so that the words wouldn't interfere with her great talent.

John Gilbert's story was the greatest heartbreak in the history of talking pictures. His voice recorded in an unattractive high pitch. Those high notes broke his heart, and so he himself broke his contract. At a quarter-of-a-million dollars a picture, the studio bosses were very glad to have him break that agreement with them!

ZaSu Pitts couldn't remember lines; she kept reaching for them with her hands as if she could pull the words out of the air. Luckily for her, those frustrating gestures became an amusing style of delivery.

Hugh Herbert, another fine actor, was also at a loss for words. His "woowoo" and nervous fingertip touching pulled him through. "Nobody is listening to what I say," he always explained to the dialogue director.

Gary Cooper, who could only say "yup" even when you asked him a simple thing like the way to the men's room, was given a Shakespearean test to take. We were all worried about Coop at the time, but Clara Bow said, "Don't worry about Cooper talking; he has something in his eyes that talks for him!" Time proved her to be right.

Tom Mix, one of the most important stars in the motion picture industry and one of the highest paid (he was getting twenty-five thousand dollars a week at Fox), had the studio very worried about their investment. They weren't sure that he would be able to make the transition from silents to sound. "What are we going to do with Mix?" they kept asking each other for weeks. Finally, the decision-makers decided to call him in and discuss it frankly. "Tom," they asked him bluntly, "can you talk?"

"Well," he said, after thinking about it for a moment, "I've been asking for whiskey for over forty years, and I always got whiskey, so I must know how to talk!" That assured the front office, and Tom began to talk. But there were some things that he just couldn't say.

He was making *Destry Rides Again,* in which Claudia Dell was his leading lady and Benny Stoloff was his director. It was the last day of shooting out on location in Santa Fe, New Mexico. Benny told me they had spent the whole day trying to get Tom to say "I love you" to Claudia. But he just couldn't. "Come on, Benny," he said, trying to toss away his embarrassment, "You can't expect me to say that."

It began getting late, and the late afternoon light was turning yellow, a cameraman's nemesis, but they had to get the shot and they had to try to get it before the sun went down altogether. No matter how hard Tom tried, he could no more say those three words than fly.

"I finally got an idea," Stoloff told me. "Tom," he said, directing him, "you look at Claudia. Look right into her eyes. Now very slowly take your gun out of your holster. Hold it out a moment. Now very slowly put it back into the holster again."

When the company got back to the studio in Hollywood, Stoloff had that expert trick shooter, Pardner Jones, shoot the letters, I LOVE YOU, into a wooden fence. After the film was edited and released, the audience saw Tom take out his gun as he looked into Claudia's eyes, they saw a cut to the fence as bullets wrote the words, I LOVE YOU,

"Prepare for a treat," says "Buddy" Rogers to Jack Oakie — *Someone To Love.*

and then they saw Tom put the gun back into his holster, still looking into Claudia's eyes. When the picture opened in New York the notices said it was the most beautiful love scene the screen had ever produced.

But that morning as I sat in Oblath's in a cold sweat with a cold cup of coffee, and with feet too cold to open the envelope, I didn't know that that day was going to be the second luckiest day of my life in motion pictures. I always consider the first one the day that Wesley Ruggles, needed a soldier who could spit BBs accurately.

Well, I had put it off long enough. I left Oblath's and started back across the street to the studio to stage 5. I put the unopened envelope back into my pocket, feeling sure that if Shakespeare was in it, it did not hold the right key for me to open the door to this great new Pandora's box. I went through the gate, and just as I turned the corner at the writer's building I bodily bumped into Robert Milton, the New York director, who wore pink hair.

"Hello," I said. He had directed my last Broadway show, *Peggy Ann,* at the Vanderbilt Theatre on Forty-eighth Street, starring Helen Ford and Lester Cole.

"Hello!" he said excitedly, and grabbed my arm in a kind of semi-embrace. "You here?"

"Yes, I am," I admitted.

"What are you doing here?" he asked, and held on to my arm for dear life.

"I'm under contract to Paramount," I explained. What I hoped wouldn't show was the worry I had, wondering how much longer I could make that statement.

"Good! Good! You're just the man I want," he said, and his grip on my arm tightened.

"I am?" I asked.

"I've got a terrific part for you! Come along with me right now and pick up the script."

I went along with him to his office — I had to, he never let go of my arm. He gave me the script. It was called *The Dummy.* "We go into production tomorrow," he said. "So get right on it, Lester." Those predictions from New York were coming true.

For *The Dummy,* Robert Milton had brought in

"Buddy", Jack and William Austin — *Someone To Love.*

Jack and the "It" Girl, Clara Bow — *The Wild Party*.

ZaSu Pitts and Oakie — *The Dummy*.

Jack Oakie, Hugh Herbert and Joan Blondell.

Roscoe Karns, Jack Oakie, Joyce Compton and Gary Cooper — *If I Had A Million*.

Cooper, Oakie and Karns — *IF I Had A Million*.

Fredric March, Ruth Chatterton, and John Cromwell, three great Broadway stars, and he thought he had a fourth as he called me "Lester" all during the shooting of the picture.

I played the part of Dopey Hart, and teamed with ZaSu Pitts we were a couple of lovable crooks. After each scene we went into an adjoining sound room to hear the playback. Even Fredric March thought about opening a hamburger stand after listening to his efforts. But *The Dummy* was a hit at the box office and advertised as "a comedy-melodrama 100% all-talking picture."

At the premiere, Robert Milton took me aside and asked, "What's this new name the studio is giving you? Lester Cole was good enough for the marquee on the Vanderbilt Theatre, wasn't it?"

"Oh," I explained, "the studio likes 'Jack Oakie,' because I come from Oklahoma." That seemed to satisfy him.

I would have loved to have thanked him, but I had no way of explaining that he once took the place of a sealed envelope. To this day I shudder to think that if it had contained the soliloquy from Hamlet, "To be or not to be" would have been questionable. I never did open that envelope!

FAST COMPANY

Oakie Goes to Bat.

When Paramount bought *Elmer The Great,* they thought they were taking a big chance. It was the first time the motion picture industry ever made a big baseball picture. The very successful and wonderful Ring Lardner/George M. Cohan play starred Walter Huston on Broadway. And to insure their investment, Paramount also bought the star when they bought the property. But as is usual in movies, they made changes. First, they were so afraid that ladies wouldn't buy tickets to a baseball picture that right off the bat they changed the title from *Elmer The Great* to *Fast Company.* Although changing the title was an error, the picture batted in a hit from every corner of the park, including the gate. Will Rogers wrote a letter to *The Los Angeles Times* and complained about the title change.

"I planned to take my family to a movie, but I drove right by the Paramount Theatre. I wouldn't dare take my wife and children into a theatre showing a picture with the title *Fast Company.*

But, luckily, as I passed the front of the theatre I caught a glimpse of the name of my old pal, Ring Lardner, and turned around and came back. Why it was sacrilegious to change the title of that great play. Of course we went in to see the picture. It was the most enjoyable entertainment we ever had."

Then they took a good look at Walter Huston when he got to the Coast and decided that by Hollywood standards he was too old to play the role he had created in the theatre. I was the kid under contract, so the part of Elmer Kane was given to me. I fell in love with that ball player and he has always been my favorite part. They then gave *The Virginian* to Huston, which he also made very successful.

Although they replaced Huston with me, the studio did put some real fast company in the picture. Evelyn Brent, "Betty" to us, was a very big star, and when they offered her the part of Evelyn Corey we were all afraid she might turn it down because she might not want to play the sweetheart of a baseball player. But she thrilled us all. She took the picture and was wonderful in it and very wonderful to me. Skeets Gallagher played my pal, and Sam Hardy played the manager. I was working in fast company, and the picture put me in the major league.

Before coming to movies Sam Hardy had been Ethel Barrymore's leading man in the theatre for many years. Whenever they would go out on tour with a play, he would go directly on arrival to each new town's major newspaper office and declare: "Right here and now I want it denied that I am going to marry Ethel Barrymore!" The statement *always* brought a headline which *always* sold tickets at the box office.

"You know," Sam used to say, "nobody ever thought to ask me, 'Who the devil ever said that you were going to marry Ethel Barrymore?'"

Sam Hardy was a very sweet guy and a very funny man. He had a dry wit that even his best friend W.C. Fields couldn't dilute. Those two men mixed well, and it was always stimulating to be with them when they were stirring. It was a blow to us all the morning we heard that Sam Hardy had died. I ran right next door to W.C.'s dressing room. "Bill," I asked, "What happened to Sam?"

"Awwwww .." he drawled in disgust, "he quit drinkin'!" And then Bill brought out his jug of *Four Roses* and poured a drink to keep both of us going.

I loved everything about *Fast Company;* I even enjoyed the hardships we suffered while making it. We started shooting in 1928 — it was one of the very early talking pictures at Paramount. And at that time all the stages were still merely three-

JOSEPH L. MANKIEWICZ

August 16, 1973

Dear Jack:

Maybe it's the result of all those hysterical parts she played for so long, but it seems to me that your good wife Vickie is pretty confused. How the hell can you be seventy?

FAST COMPANY — our first — was 1929, right? And you were 16 at the time, right? (You had been on Broadway in INNOCENT EYES in 1925 — which made you the only 12 year old chorus boy the Shuberts had ever hired — right?) And, in 1929, I was the only 10 year old dialogue writer in Hollywood, everybody knows that. So that makes me 54 — and you must be close to 60, at the most. So let's start by straightening Vickie out on her arithmetic. One of the many things I found out about actresses over the years is that their acting talent is usually in inverse proportion to their ability to add.

And how the hell can I pick any one or two or twenty memories to write about — when so much of your life was my life back then? We worked a lot and laughed a lot, there was a lot of work — and a lot to laugh about then. I am quite sure that you and I were young at the very best time that ever was for being young. And that we lived the best years that show business ever knew. Those years are gone — they won't be back — and the great joy of living them will never be recaptured from watching scratchy old films or reading faded scrapbooks. That joy remains in our remembrances. Yours, and mine, and the village of show people working at — no, not "film," not "cinema," not an "art form" — just making "movies."

How can anyone "reconstruct" what it was like? The crazy innocence of a crazy life — "soundproofing" the old silent stages by hanging carpets on the walls — starting shooting at 5 p.m. and finishing at 5 a.m. to keep the traffic noise from the microphones — and then knocking off a fifth of brandy with "Iron Man" Sutherland — and then you and he'd go play golf while I wrote the next day's work.

Two quick memories. First: you and Gallagher are walking down the street. You've been in a fight. (You were always in a fight — which Gallagher always started with a stranger who beat you up.) You are holding a raw steak on your eye. You say to Gallagher: "What do I do with this piece of meat?" Gallagher says: "Hold on to it. There'll be a dog along in a minute." I thought — I still think — it was one of the funniest lines I ever wrote.

It first appeared in FAST COMPANY. It got yawns at the Glendale preview — and out it came.

I used it again in THE SOCIAL LION. It bombed again at the preview — and out it came again.

I put it in JUNE MOON. Sutherland said: "I have a strange feeling that I remember this line of dialogue from somewhere. You said — and I shall never forget the loyalty of your lie — "I think it's a funny line. Let's try

it." We previewed JUNE MOON — and out it came. I want you to know that I have no intention of letting you down. Whatever else I do between now and the grave — that line will appear — and keep appearing — until it gets a laugh.

Probably my most vivid — and certainly most tender — memory of all, you will not be surprised to know, has to do with one of the most remarkable women I have ever known. Your mother. The same Mrs. Offield who is known to the multitude as having given to the world Jack Oakie — but who is known only to a very few as probably the greatest financial wizard, in her sex, since Hetty Green — and the only financial wizard who, singlehandedly, spat in the eye of the Great American Depression.

You can't possibly remember the number of times I came to your house for dinner. Nor can I. But I shall never forget one night in particular.

You and I were seated at the table, and your mother was bringing in the food. She was chatting about having gone shopping that morning — and then she mentioned that, carrying her market basket over her arm, she had gone into the Bank of Hollywood. She said that she had walked up to the teller, and he had greeted her very pleasantly and asked what could he do for her. Your mother said to him: "I would like to withdraw all of the money in my son's bank account." The teller smiled indulgently and said of course — but was there any particular reason? "No particular reason," said your mother, "I just have the feeling that this might be a good day to take all of Jack's money out of the bank." The teller, you will remember, gave her all of your money — in cash — and she put it into her market basket and took it home.

You made no particular comment, as I remember. After all, she was your mother — and you were a well-behaved dutiful son. But I also remember that I commented that there was no need for her to behave so rashly. That, after all, the Bank of Hollywood was an institution of great repute — that I, too, had all of my money in the Bank of Hollywood — that while our country was struggling through a Depression, there were great economists and financial geniuses at work in Washington who would straighten everything out — and there was really nothing to worry about. Your mother merely said that she felt better about having all of your money where she could keep an eye on it.

The next morning the Bank of Hollywood did not open its doors. Nor did hundreds of other banks in the United States. Together with thousands of other Americans I was wiped out. For quite a while, eating at your house was more than a pleasure — it was a necessity.

Your mother, my friend, was — on or off the stage and screen — your greatest achievement. Having known her is one of my most cherished memories. Having been — and being — your friend is another. It can't be otherwise, really, when the lives of two people for so long a time were indistinguishably part of the same life.

Yours ever, Joe

sided walls with no tops on them, and the studio had only just begun to rebuild them for sound. As the construction crews building the new stages worked all day, we actors had to work all night. Just as soon as the carpenters went home, we came to work.

Not only were they trying to·sound-proof the

old stages, but the experts were trying to sound-proof the old cameras. The noise of the camera was one of the greatest problems during that period of transition. One of the devices invented to subdue the camera's noise was called "The camera booth," and after just a short session in the air-tight contraption, the great cameraman, Harry

Jack Oakie and Richard "Skeets" Gallagher — *Fast Company.*

Eugenie Besserer, Jack Oakie and Chester Conklin — *Fast Company.*

Merlin, found that *he* was being more successfully silenced than the camera. He came out of that booth and swore he'd never get back into one again. He never did.

Another innovation was "The horse blanket." Our cameraman, Eddie Cronjager, wrapped his machine in a great many of those heavy swaddling clothes, and we'd constantly hear his call for "Blankets! Come on, get me some more blankets!" The walls were always covered with them. You'd get on a set and get lost, because all means of ingress and egress were covered with horse blankets.

Early one morning after a very hard night's

43

work, Sam Hardy, "The Skeeter," as I used to call Skeets Gallagher, and I were lying on some narrow wooden benches trying to rest while waiting to be called for the next *take*. Dawn was just beginning to break, and so were we.

The camera had been noisier than usual and our director, Eddie Sutherland, and sound man, Gene, were waiting for Cronjager to quiet it down.

I had just begun to doze when Sam muttered, in that resonant voice that could be heard in the second balcony: "Fellers, hey fellers, look."

The Skeeter and I raised our heads to look, and Sam, with only one eye open to show us how sleepy he was, pointed to the property man, Neely Wheeler, and a couple of his helpers. They were all bent over double carrying a great load of horse blankets.

"It won't be long now," Sam predicted in his rich monotone, "They're sending the horses home!"

Our laugh swept through the company, and Eddie Sutherland swept us out. For the first time on the picture we actually went home that morning before the construction crew came in. But, "They're sending the horses home" was a quote

that stayed in the industry until those horse blankets became a thing of the past.

For me Elmer Kane was an athlete who was exceptionally good at his job and knew it. I played him with simple honesty and with all my heart.

At the showing of the first preview, Walter Huston put his arm around me and said: "Kid, you *are* Elmer — and you're great." It was the most beloved praise I've ever had. Except, of course for the time I marched down Fifth Avenue in the Saint Patrick's Day parade. I was dressed in my military uniform and kept in step with my schoolmates from De La Salle. When I joined my mother who had been watching all those thousands and thousands of marchers, she put her arm around me and said: "Lulie, you were the best one."

The other night I saw the picture again. The showing was made possible through the courtesy of the UCLA film archives. It was gratifying to find that the audience knew I had given my heart to Elmer Kane almost fifty years ago and I, too, as I watched the young man's performance, found that my heart was still there.

Elmer The Great as *Fast Company* is still my favorite picture.

CALL OF THE WILD

In the course of all the many pictures I've made, I've been on locations where the temperature reached 110⁰, and locations where it dropped to 10⁰ below zero. But of all the Fahrenheits I have known, my fondest memory of a location goes back to 1935 to the temperature I loved best on Santa Catalina Island, only twenty five miles away from home. In those days the island was mostly inhabited by wild goats, and by some cubs known as the Chicago National League Baseball Team (owned by Phil Wrigley, who also owned the island). It was also inhabited by George Burns, Gracie Allen, Wendy Barrie, Henry Wadsworth, Lyda Roberti, and me, who were there on location for *The Big Broadcast* for Paramount. Our first morning of shooting was to be outdoors, halfway down the coast at White's Landing, and my very early call got me up with the sun.

Only a month before, I had had the feeling I'd never see that sun again, that I'd never again feel its warmth. So that morning I got up and leaned out of the window of my top floor corner suite at the St. Catherine Hotel and let that early morning warm sun beat down on my face. "Hit me some more!" I said to it as I leaned as far out over the windowsill as I could, sopping up that sunshine.

The view of the bay was magnificent in that early morning quiet. I could hear the silence as I took some good deep breaths of the clean warm air. (There was no smog in those days anywhere.) Suddenly, there he was! That walk was one in a million and I couldn't mistake it. Clark Gable, "the King," was taking long strides, strutting briskly in the direction of the pier. He was the only person on the street. I thought of how the crowds would jam the place if they knew he was down there.

"Hey, Moose!" I hollered at him from the window. He stopped and turned around. "Hey, Moose! Up here! It's Oakie."

Gable smiled and looked up. He knew darn well who it was. I had named him "Moose" when we were making *Call Of The Wild* up north with Loretta Young and Buck, the St. Bernard dog who was really the star of that Jack London story. I called him Moose with affection and he loved it. "But Oakie, you're the only one in the world who can call me that!" Gable had said. And I *was* the only one; everybody else took "the King's" warning seriously.

We made that dog story near Mount Baker, in

Jack Oakie and Loretta Young — *Call of the Wild.*

the state of Washington. It was the coldest location I have ever known. All the time we were up there, the temperature hovered below zero.

"Hi, Shorty!" Gable waved up at me. "Have you thawed out yet?" he asked.

"I'm working on it," I said. "What are you here for?"

"Something called *Mutiny On The Bounty.* What are you here for?" he asked.

"Something called *The Big Broadcast,*" I told him.

"Shorty, did you ever take off those woolen drawers?" Gable laughed, remembering I wore two pairs of longies under my woolen pants when we were up in that snow.

"Sure did! Stay right there and I'll show you." I threw up my robe, backed up to the window, and "mooned" at him to prove my dressing habits had changed with the weather. "How'm I doing?" I asked as I modeled for him.

"In the pink! Shorty," he called up, "In the pink!" With that OK, we waved, and he hurried on out to the pier to meet an arriving speedboat, which took him to the isthmus where they kept the *Bounty* boat they were working on.

As he strutted away that warm morning, I thought again of the icy stabbing winds and flurries of snow on that frozen north location we had just returned from. We had stayed at the Mount

Baker Lodge, in Heather Meadows just below Mount Shuksan, north of Bellingham. All the time we were there, the winds piled snowdrifts up as high as thirty feet. We were always having to be dug out. But that weather didn't keep the ladies away. They braved all hazards to get a glimpse of "the King."

One night, when we stopped over at the Leopold Hotel in Bellingham, Washington, the path to the entrance was jammed with ladies who had been standing in the cold so long, their smiles were frozen on their happy faces. Gable waved at them with his gracious charm, grabbed my arm, and whispered, "Hold on to my arm, Shorty, and let's get straight on up to our rooms."

So we walked arm in arm, and I played interference for him as we made our way into the hotel and through the lobby to the elevator, with "the King" nodding and smiling as we hurried along.

Suddenly we heard a woman cry, "I touched him! I touched him!" We looked back and saw a little lady screaming hysterically. She practically went into a faint as she swooned into the arms of another woman. I held the elevator door for our director, "Wild Bill" Wellman, as he caught up with us and demanded to know, "What's she screaming about? Who'd she touch?"

"She touched Gable just now as we got into the elevator," I explained.

"Oh," mumbled Bill. (That wasn't the kind of electricity that would get a spark out of Wellman.)

I think that in all the history of Hollywood there have never been any two who attracted the ladies both on the screen and in person as did Rudolph Valentino and Clark Gable. All during our stay, in near-blizzard conditions, no matter where we were shooting, hundreds of women came out just to get a look at "the King." But it was one afternoon, when we were doing a scene together in a kind of round shallow pit, that I learned that the Moose had his own evaluation of womanly beauty.

The ladies surrounding us were on a raised ridge, where they had a good view of us and we had a good view of them. I nudged Gable. "Get a load of that beautiful little girl in the tam-o'-shanter," I whispered, and pointed with my elbow to a very pretty young girl.

"Shorty, you want to see some real beauty?" he asked. "Look at that woman up there to your right, in blue."

The lady Gable pointed out had very soft features and the most beautiful white hair I had ever seen. The Moose was right, she was a real beauty. But I would have guessed the woman was in her middle years and older than he was, because on February 1, 1935, he was only thirty-four. We celebrated his birthday huddled under a tarpaulin trying to keep out of the wind. We were waiting for the cameras to line up a shot, when a property man found us and handed Gable a surprise package. I helped to tear it open. It was a big box of homemade cookies sent up from Los Angeles by his wife, Ria.

"Happy Birthday!" I shouted as I helped my-

Jack Oakie, Loretta Young and Clark Gable — *Call of the Wild.*

Gable and Oakie — *Call of the Wild.*

Young, Gable and Oakie — *Call of the Wild.*

self. (I must have wished him happy birthday fifty times that day, taking a cookie each time.)

I gained a lot of weight on that picture, but the Moose didn't put on a pound. Besides giving me most of his cookies, he also worked hard at keeping in condition. One of the exercises he was expert at was cracking those bull whips that were used in the picture to reach the lead dog of the pack pulling the sled. The whips were at least twenty feet long, with leather handles. Gable would hold one in each hand and whip them out their full length in rhythm like a fighter jabbing away at a punching bag. The crack-crack, crack-crack, and his light footwork made it look easy; I couldn't even hold on to one of them with both hands, the darn things were so heavy.

It took longer than scheduled to make *Call Of The Wild;* not only were we continually fighting the unusual weather conditions, but we also lost time over what I called "the snowshoe rabbit escapade."

Wellman ordered about fifty snowshoe rabbits. He wanted them to run through the background of a scene. The rare, sensitive little animals, named for their feet which are webbed and look just like snowshoes, were very hard to catch. It cost a fortune to send out a special crew to set nets for them. The men kept complaining that it was almost impossible to gather them, and that fifty

was out of the question. Wellman finally agreed that the few they had collected would have to do for the scene.

"Action!" Bill called. "Let 'em go!" The rabbits were let loose. The dogs, with their mouths wired to protect the rabbits, were sent to chase them, but the scared little things wouldn't move. "Scoot!" Wellman shouted, trying to get them to act for the cameras, but they wouldn't budge.

The property men fired guns at them, but they wouldn't take Wellman's direction. They gave the little things some Spanish fly, but even that wouldn't rouse them. They just wouldn't run through the background of the scene. Wellman tried every trick he knew and finally gave up. "Those aren't snowshoe rabbits!" he screamed. "They're fireside rabbits!"

The following day the crew went into town and rounded up all the stray cats they could find. They glued rabbit ears on the alley cats and when the dogs were let loose to chase them they did just as Bill directed, they scooted!

One night at the lodge, Gable, Loretta Young, and I were sitting around the table after dinner. It had been one of the coldest days we had had during the shooting of the entire picture. We had to be dug out that morning, and the path leading to the street where we were shooting was flanked by snowbanks at least ten feet high. The Moose

Clark Gable, "Buck", Jack Oakie and Sidney Toler — *Call of the Wild*.

and I were having some brandy, trying to thaw out, when "Wild Bill" came in with a blast of icy wind.

"Would you mind coming back out on to the street for just one more shot?" he asked. We couldn't believe it!

"You're kidding!" Gable said. It was now colder than ten degrees below, and at the last report there was more than fifteen inches of newly fallen snow.

"Look, the crew is all set up. The lights are on. We're ready to go!" Wellman pleaded. "I promise ya it won't take more than five minutes. Come on, help me out. Just this one shot. I'm telling ya, it won't take five minutes." Gable and I looked at each other. Here we were, still trying to thaw out, and we sure hated to leave that good brandy.

"Shorty," he asked me, "what do you say?"

"It's OK with me, Moose," I said. "If you go, I'll go."

"All right." He turned to Wellman. "Oakie and I'll give you five minutes."

"Good!" Wellman said, and then put his arms around Loretta. "How about you?" he asked her. "It'll take only five minutes."

"Now wait a minute!" Gable and I both pounced on him. "Not Loretta!" She was so tiny, I don't think she weighed ninety pounds.

"Loretta'll never be able to stand the cold!" the Moose objected. But Wellman won her over.

"I'll come too," she said. "If you two can take it, so can I."

The three of us bundled up in all our wardrobe of furs and extra woolens, and huddled together as we stomped our way through the snow to the "Skagway Outpost," at the end of the street where we had been working that day. Sure enough, Wellman had the lights on and the crew was ready. We stomped into the direct line of the camera, ready to work. We kept right on stomping to try to keep warm, but nothing happened.

"Come on! What are we waiting for?" Gable called to Wellman. "Let's go before we all freeze to death!"

"Aw, nuts!" Wellman swore. "We're waiting for the dog! The dog's in the shot. Will somebody get that dog!" he yelled.

"He'll be here in a minute, Mr. Wellman," an assistant's voice answered.

"Well, you'd better get him up here fast!" Gable warned.

"My God, Moose," I whispered to him. "Look at Loretta." She was turning purple!

At last Carl Spitz, the owner and trainer of our star, "Buck," arrived with the dog. Gable, more or less to keep warm, started to play with him.

George Burns, Gracie Allen, Wendy Barrie, Henry Wadsworth, Jack Oakie and Lyda Roberti
— *The Big Broadcast.*

Wendy Barrie, George Burns, Gracie Allen, Jack Oakie, Lyda Roberti — *The Big Broadcast.*

The Nicholas Brothers, Henry Wadsworth and Jack Oakie — *The Big Broadcast.*

Jack Oakie, Bing Crosby and Lynne Overman.

"Come on, Buck," Gable said, scuffling with him. The dog didn't move. "Come on, Buck!" Gable coaxed him, and tried to wrestle with him. But the St. Bernard just stood and growled. "Buck!" Gable scolded. "Don't you growl at me!" And he began to pull gently at the dog's jowls.

"No, no, no!" the trainer warned. "Watch out! Don't do that! That ain't Buck!"

"That's not Buck?" Gable asked.

"Oh, no! That ain't Buck!" Spitz explained. "I brought up Buck's double; it's too cold up here for Buck!"

"What!" Gable screamed. "It's too cold up here for Buck!"

I'd never seen the Moose that mad. He picked up that St. Bernard dog, lifted him over his head, and threw him into a snowbank. Then we both picked up Loretta, and got back to that brandy as fast as we could. They never did get that shot!

In the original script, I died pretty dramatically

after being tortured by our villain, Reginald Owen. But after the first preview nobody ever again saw my demise. Some people thought that this scene marked the end of the movie and started to walk out, so Darryl Zanuck, head of Twentieth Century-Fox, had the ending re-written, and called me back for the retakes.

But his timing was bad; he wanted me at the studio the afternoon I had to be at my dentist's office.

"Oakie! You be here, damn it!" Zanuck said over the phone. "The camera crew is waiting, and Gable has to be at MGM in the morning! You be here!"

"No, darn it, I won't! I have to keep my appointment with my dentist because I have to be at Paramount, darn it!" And I kept my appointment with the dentist.

I was in Dr. Nechtow's chair with my mouth wide open when Zanuck marched in with Bill Dover, Big Ben Silvey, and Bill Goetz. It could have been a scene that Mack Sennett directed, but it got me back to the studio facing the cameras. Jimmy Starr, the Hollywood columnist, headlined it, "Zanuck Kidnaps Oakie!"

It was worth it. The new finale had Gable embracing me as I returned to the cabin, and the Moose gave me some of the best hugging and loving I ever had on the screen, even though I had to be tested for broken ribs.

That early morning on Santa Catalina Island I dressed for the scene and, with the warmth of the sun and all my ribs intact, I got on down to White's Landing and started work on a fun picture and on my favorite location.

UNSUITABLE

"Rebate Spurs Sale," was the headline in the *Los Angeles Times* that spurred the next story. It reminded me that if you live long enough, you learn that nothing is new and it's all been done before. The only difference is that other people are doing it and calling it by another name. Today it's called "rebate," but I remember when we just called it "bait"; and how hard it was sometimes to keep from being sold a bill of goods.

One of the most vivid recollections I have of fighting that hook was the time Paramount tried to sell me a suit that didn't fit. This happened before the days of the Guild, when actors never had set hours; we worked day and night, Saturdays and Sundays and holidays. I had been under contract to Paramount Studios for about two and a half years and hadn't had a single day off. I had just finished making *The Sap From Syracuse* with Ginger Rogers at the New York Paramount Long Island studios. On the way back to California they booked me for personal appearances, and I no sooner got off the train when I had to report to work on *Sea Legs*, with Eugene Pallette and Lillian Roth.

In the meantime we all heard about the studio's preparations for *Paramount On Parade*, which was going to be the prestige picture of the year. Every contract player in the studio had been spending weeks and weeks preparing for his or her sequences in the picture. They were all carefully fitted for wardrobes that would suit the elegance they were to represent.

The star-studded cast included such names as Richard Arlen, Clara Bow, Mary Brian, George Bancroft, Evelyn Brent, Clive Brook, Maurice Chevalier, Nancy Carroll, Ruth Chatterton, Gary Cooper, Leon Erroll, Skeets Gallagher, Mitzi Green, Helen Kane, Dennis King, Fredric March, Zelma O'Neal, Bill Powell, Buddy Rogers, Ginger Rogers, and me. But the studio had kept me too busy to allow time for me to be fitted for the picture. Anyway, they were so used to keeping me in a sweat shirt, it never occurred to them that of all the thousands of garments hanging in their mammoth wardrobe department not one suit of clothes had my name on the inside of the pocket.

When I arrived in Hollywood I had had two suits of my own, and whenever I started a new picture the orders were simply, "Oakie, wear the other suit for this one."

It was a Saturday night, Gene Pallette and I had just finished shooting the last scene of the day; I was tired, and anxious to take off my sailor suit and get into my sweat shirt. Leonard Goldstein was waiting on the set for me. Leonard, who later became a very successful producer, was a man of all chores at the studio in those days, and one of my most constant companions.

The assistant director of *Paramount On Parade* was also waiting for me. As soon as he heard our director, Victor Heermann, shout, "Cut! That's all for today," he came over with his message.

"Oakie, your call for *Parade* is nine tomorrow morning."

"I thought I was going to have this Sunday off." I was so tired, and this was sure a disappointment.

"Nope, 9:00A.M. it is." And he started to go.

"Wait a minute," I called to him. "What am I supposed to wear?" I knew everybody was wearing beautiful clothes for *Parade*, and I was looking forward to being dressed up myself, as I was to be master of ceremonies for some numbers and introduce some of the stars.

"Whattaya mean, whattaya wear? Ya wear your tails, of course."

"Tails! I don't have any tails!" I reminded him.

"Oh? Oh, yeah." He was remembering that this was Oakie he was talking to, the kid with the two suits and a sweat shirt. "Well, ya better go on up to wardrobe, they'll find something for you. See you in the morning."

"I've got to go up to wardrobe," I explained to Leonard, who had heard the orders.

"Come on," he said, "I'm right with you." And he always was. On the way to wardrobe I veered over to the administration building. Jesse Lasky, the big boss, was back East in New York, and Mike Levy was running the store, so I went in to see him.

"Mike, I'm supposed to wear tails in *Parade* tomorrow morning. I don't have tails," I reminded him.

"I know you don't," he said. "Just go on over to wardrobe, and they'll find something for you."

"I don't want them to find something for me." I felt like crying. "I want a suit that's made for me and fits me."

"Come on, Jack, stop making a fuss. Wardrobe will fit you."

"Listen, Mike, everybody in the picture has had their clothes especially made for them. Why can't I have a suit that's made for me?"

"Come on, Jack, there's no time. You're working in the morning."

"Everybody else had time. What's the matter with giving me a little time?" I asked. He wouldn't

say. He got up and walked me to the door.

"Come on, Jack, get on over to wardrobe." Leonard and I went over to wardrobe.

"I'm supposed to wear tails in the morning," I told the little tailor who was waiting for me.

"Yes, I know. I got some things ready for you. So, at last they're going to dress you up, huh, Jack?" I was too tired to appreciate his enthusiasm. "At last they're going to let you look like a movie star." He went off to get the things he'd put aside for me.

I looked at the racks of clothes. There were all kinds of tuxedos and tails in beautiful rich woolens and silk grosgrain, made for everybody in the world but me. There were even suits with Imboden Parrish's name on them — dozens of them. His father was the head of the Health Department in Los Angeles. There were even more with Jack Luden's name on them. His family made cough drops.

"Here, try these on, Jack." The tailor handed me a pair of Richard Dix's pants that he must have worn in some old Civil War picture. He gave me one of Gary Cooper's old swallowtail coats, and then he handed me a beautiful custom-tailored vest with Jack Luden's name on it. It had the only class in the outfit; I would have preferred to wear it on the outside of the coat. I pointed to one of the beautiful suits hanging on the rack.

"How much would a suit like that cost?" I asked the tailor.

"Oh . . . about seventy-five dollars, Jack. That's

Jack Oakie, Mary Brian and Gary Cooper — *Paramount On Parade.*

custom-made." I stood before the full-length mirror as the tailor put pins into folds of cloth, and with his mouth full of those weapons he kept explaining, "See, we'll take this in here, and let this out here . . ."

I looked at my sorry, forlorn reflection, and remembered another time my heart was broken because of a badly fitted suit, and I wanted to cry again. It was when we lived in Muskogee, Oklahoma. My mother told me to get ready to go into town because she was going to buy me a "union suit." As I put on my hat and coat I pictured myself in the blue uniform of the Union army with its visored cap, and I began to rehearse marching and saluting. All my friends were going to be pretty envious when they saw me so tall and straight and military. The storekeeper brought out a long-sleeved, long-legged, one-piece set of underwear, and held it up under my chin to show my mother how well it was going to fit. I was the most dejected five-year-old in all of the Oklahoma Indian Territory.

Then the little tailor stuck a pin in just the right place and the injection worked. "Come on, Leonard," I called to him, as I stormed out of the wardrobe department and practically ran back to the administration offices. I just wasn't going to let Paramount put a "union suit" on me again!

In those days we all believed that the career of a motion picture actor was good for only five years. So I was not just fighting for a suit of clothes, I was fighting for those other two-and-a-half years left of my professional life. If I looked that bad in the mirror, I knew I would look that much worse on the silver screen, which was famous for exaggeration. I had to get Paramount to spend the seventy-five dollars! After all, I was going to be introducing the biggest stars in the business, and that sure wasn't the right time to get laughs with funny clothes!

"All right, Mike!" I said as I walked right into his office without knocking. "Is this the way you want me to look?"

"Come on, Jack, forget it." He was unmoved.

"It'll cost seventy-five dollars. Buy me a suit that fits. Please, Mike, buy me a suit."

"No, there's no time, and besides you'll probably never wear it again. We're not throwing money around."

"I can't work in this. Mike, buy me a suit." I was begging.

"You can work in it. Be on the set in the morning, because that suit will be there ready to work." He was adamant.

"Well, then, put the suit to work," I said, "because I won't be there!"

I left the suit at wardrobe and got back into my sweat shirt. As Leonard and I walked to his car, I

Jack Oakie and Zelma O'Neal — *Paramount On Parade.*

could hardly keep from crying. Maybe it was because I was so tired, but when Leonard said, "Let's get out of town for a couple of days," I knew I had to. I wasn't the first actor who had had to run away in order to stay alive.

"Where can we go? You know they'll come right after us." And the studio henchmen did just that. They knew all the hiding places from Santa Barbara to Palm Springs.

"I know just the place, and they'll never think of looking for you there," said Leonard. He drove, and we went directly from the studio to the Casa De Mañana, in La Jolla. That was Saturday night. I slept all day Sunday, and it wasn't until Monday morning that Leonard checked in with his cohorts at the studio, by telephone.

We learned that the studio's men were up in Santa Barbara and Palm Springs looking for me. We also learned that besides holding up Leon Errol, Skeets Gallagher, Fredric March, and Zelma O'Neal, I was also holding up Abe Lyman and his orchestra ... and that was expensive! Sammy Bricker, the property man, kept kicking at Lyman's big base drum insisting that I was hiding in it. "Come on out of there, Oakie," he'd say, getting a laugh. The whole town knew I was missing, and

why I was missing. I was still tired so I rested on Monday, and then Tuesday Leonard called my agent, Eddie Small, to tell him where we were.

Eddie, with his good sense, very calmly told us he would get back to us that day. When he called us back late that afternoon, he spoke to Leonard and said, "All right, you and Jack come on home. Jack is going to have a new suit. Jesse Lasky is back and wants Jack to know that Paramount is not running a five-and-ten-cent store. Jack will have the best suit that money can buy."

Leonard and I were back at the studio that night. I was given a card that read "Complete white tie and tails," and I was sent to Alexander and Oviatts to be outfitted. Nat Deverich kept the store open that night and waited on me.

"Well, Oakie, the studio told me you are to have the best. Now let me see." Nat was wonderful! He went overboard! Besides the most elegant tails in the shop, I brought home two hats, two canes, six pairs of white gloves, six silk scarves, two pairs of patent leather pumps, about twelve pairs of silk shorts, at least two dozen pairs of silk socks, twelve shirts, a gold chain, and twelve ties. My seventy-five dollar suit cost about $750, plus the $200,000 for the three-day delay, totaling $200,750.

Wednesday morning I showed up bright-eyed and alert. I was well rested and well dressed, and suitable for *Paramount On Parade.*

Whether "rebate" or "bait," when it comes to a sales pitch I always go back to the philosophy of my good friend, Sid Grauman. That great little showman always said, "Buy it, folks! All I lose is a dollar on every one I sell, but I sell so many I can afford to make a profit!"

Ginger Rogers and Jack Oakie — *The Sap From Syracuse.*

SWEAT SHIRT

A white sweat shirt was my "open sesame" to some of the most wonderful experiences I ever had in Hollywood. I started to wear it in the late 1920s and kept on wearing it all through the 1930s. When Paramount Studios put me in so many college pictures, they finally ran out of titles. *Collegiate, Touchdown, College Rhythym, College Humor* and *Sweetie* — I was the all-American college boy, and my sweat shirt identified me with that form of higher education.

At the studio, whenever a new Oakie script was discussed, the prevailing joke was, "Why bother with Oakie, just get the sweat shirt." The pictures were a joy to make, and the audiences seemed happy to see them. The publicity departments, which had been advertising Charles "Buddy" Rogers as "America's Boyfriend," now publicized me as "America's Joy-friend."

I played football for "State" for over ten years. During that time, there were periods when the studio decision-makers felt that I was getting too old to play football, so they'd take me out of the game and make me a coach, or have me inherit a school, as I did in *Collegiate*. Then after a few pictures of keeping me off the field, they'd change their minds again, and put me back in the action. Once more I'd be the greatest football player "State" had ever had, as I was in *College Humor,* with Bing Crosby singing "Learn to Croon."

But on the field or off, they kept me in my sweat shirt, and so did everybody in Hollywood. Both on and off the screen, my sweat shirt was my trademark.

Jimmy Starr, the Hollywood columnist, wrote in his advice to tourists, "If you see or smell an old sweat shirt walking down Hollywood Boulevard, be sure to take a second look; it's sure to be Jack Oakie." I was always expected to wear it.

One time at a housewarming party that Clark Gable and Carole Lombard gave, that sweat shirt got me in safely, and then got me out safely. It was at a great mansion they were renting in Beverly Hills, just before Gable bought the Raoul Walsh place in Encino. Gable and Lombard stood right outside the door, greeting their guests as they arrived. He was in white tie and tails, and she wore a long,black, tight, slinky thing that showed-off her very beautiful figure.

"Oakie! What the devil are you doing here in white tie and tails?" Lombard shouted.

"Your invitation requested this monkey suit," I said.

"Not for you, Shorty!" Gable towered over me as he blocked the doorway. "Go on home and get your sweat shirt!"

"OK, OK, I was only fooling!" I said, as I removed the jeweled studs and opened my shirt. "There you are!" I exposed the sweat shirt I was wearing under my formal clothes.

"Well, that's better!" Gable approved. "OK, you can go on in." He passed me through the door to a waiting butler, who ushered me into the huge living room. The room was already filled with guests. They were all standing up and milling about, visiting with each other. They had to stand up! There was no place to sit down. The room was totally bare. There wasn't a stick of furniture anywhere!

I removed all my finery and spent the evening in my comfortable sweat shirt. A very formal dinner was prepared, and we were instructed to sit down on the floor to be served. None of us had the physical prowess to find the position comfort-

able. Norman Taurog, who was directing the picture I was making at the time, no sooner put his palms down on the floor so that he could stretch his leg muscles when the heavy foot of a waiter stepped right on his hand and broke his thumb.

We all came to his rescue. Somebody devised a splint, and we bundled some wrappings around it. Norman was in great pain and decided to go home and get in touch with his doctor. I offered to drive him. When we got outside the front door, we met Louella Parsons and her husband, Doc Martin. They were just arriving after having been to another party first, and we could see that Doc had had a good share of celebrating.

"Hey! Where you going?" he asked us. "Party isn't over yet, is it?"

"No," Norman said, "but this is pretty painful." He held up his badly bandaged hand.

"Say! What happened there?" Even through his dulled vision, Doc could see that the bandaging was a pretty clumsy job.

"A waiter stepped on my hand," Norman explained.

"Let's take a look at it." As Doc reached for the hand, he suddenly realized what Norman had said. "Oh, a waiter stepped on your hand, eh?" Doc said sarcastically.

"Yeah, a waiter stepped on my hand and broke my thumb," Norman repeated. "Come on Oakie, let's go." He was in pain, and wanted to get going. But Doc became indignant. Somehow his medical ability was affronted.

"Wise guy, eh? So a waiter stepped on your hand, did he?" He reached for Norman's hand again. "Let's see!" I quickly stepped between them and blocked his way.

"Honest, Doc, Norman's thumb is broken," I explained. "I'm trying to get him home."

"Come on, Docky Wocky," Louella urged. Doc quieted, and suddenly smiled. He was looking at my sweat shirt. Then affectionately he rubbed his hands over it as if appraising the material.

"See you're wearing that good old sweat shirt, Oakie. OK, boy, you go ahead, take him home." Doc and Louella finally went on inside, where they found out what Norman was talking about.

Another "must" for my sweat shirt was a black tie affair that Jeanette MacDonald gave to honor me. We had just finished *Let's Go Native,* a musical interlude between colleges. This was long before Jeanette was teamed with Nelson Eddy, and she thought my Oklahoma drawl sounded pretty good.

As the honored guest, I didn't take off my tuxedo. I tried to prove that I could be as well-dressed as the next man, but I didn't stand a chance. All that night, John Gilbert and Ginger Rogers opened my shirt for each new guest as they arrived and pointed to my sweat shirt under it.

Maurice Chevalier, a newcomer to Hollywood, was intrigued with the sweat shirt. He couldn't understand why Ginger Rogers and John Gilbert were so anxious to display it. He wanted to know if he too was expected to wear such a shirt under his dress clothes. When I saw him in Paris some years later, he still asked me to explain the significance of it to him. I couldn't. The very last time he was out here in California, I met him on the Paramount lot. It was more than thirty-five years since we had both been under contract to the studio.

"Oh, Jacques, you are still here?" he asked.

"No, Maurice, I've come back just to be in *The Rat Race,*" I told him.

"Yes? Oh, of course. But what picture are you doing?" he asked.

"I'm in *The Rat Race,*" I said.

"Oakie, I know, for sure we are all in the rat race. But the picture? What is the name of the picture?"

"Maurice, the name of the picture is *The Rat Race,*" I explained more carefully.

"Oh, now tell me, Jacques, what about the undershirt? You still are wearing it?" he asked.

Once again, I couldn't explain it. The symbol was just too foreign for the Frenchman.

My sweat shirt was welcome not only on land but also at sea, and my good friends George Converse and his wife, Anita Stewart, often had me bring it aboard their yacht, *The Dorsal,* for many wonderful cruises. George was commodore of the Newport Yacht Club at the time, and as *The Dorsal* was one of the largest boats in the harbor, they were hosts to many large and lavish parties. George had flags for all occasions; he raised and lowered them himself and worked hard at it all day. The flag I loved best to see go up was the one with the cocktail glass on it.

Anita, who was one of the screen's most beautiful actresses, was also one of the best cooks I ever knew. After every visit on the boat with George and Anita, the studio had to force me back on a diet. I was always hungry and thirsty out on the Pacific and, between Anita's cooking and George's flag with the little glass on it, I used to swell with the ocean.

One afternoon while relaxing and swelling on the deck of *The Dorsal,* George and Anita both shook me out of the cradle of the deep.

"Come on, Jack," George said. "Some people are very anxious to meet that sweat shirt." We rode over in the dinghy to *The Serenade,* Jascha Heifetz's long, sleek, white yacht, since sold to the son of Jacques Cousteau, the famous oceanographer.

"Welcome aboard," Mrs. Heifetz greeted us. She was Florence Vidor, another great lady of the screen. There was a Stuff Smith jazz record being played below, and we were led down to where the music was coming from. There he was, the great artist, bowing his violin off rhythm with the record. We waited for him to finish the number.

"Here's that sweat shirt," Anita said, as she introduced me.

"Welcome aboard, Mr. Oakie," Mrs. Heifetz repeated.

"Thank you for having me," I said, and realized this was the second time in my life that Florence Vidor didn't know me. Before my sweat shirt days, when Jascha Heifetz was courting Florence Vidor, I had worked in a picture with her called *China-*

Jack Oakie and Howard Jones, famous USC coach of the Trojan Champions (undefeated and untied in 1932) — *College Humor.*

town Nights. She and Wallace Beery were the stars. I played the stuttering reporter. It was started as a silent picture and at the very last minute they added sound, thinking it would do better at the box office. It didn't help. Billy Wellman was our director. The night I worked with Florence Vidor, Wellman was perched up on a parallel with the cameraman. The scene was in a theatre in Chinatown, and about 300 Chinese extras filled the house. When she came onto the set, Billy called down to her from the parallel, "Now, Miss Vidor, when you enter the theatre from the rear, there'll be a gunshot; you grab Mr. Oakie's arm and both of you run down the aisle to the first row."

"Oh? Just a minute, Mr. Wellman," she called back to him. "Tell me which one of these Chinamen is Mr. Oakie?"

Now my sweat shirt and I were invited to *The Serenade.* "Welcome aboard," Heifetz said. Then after all the proper nautical hellos, he asked, "What would you like?"

"I like everything," I said, thinking he was offering some liquid refreshment. But the fiddler went back to the machine, turned the record over, and started playing again. He was fascinated with that offbeat rhythm. I wondered what Carnegie Hall audiences would have given to hear the great Heifetz and Stuff Smith in concert.

Another time that my sweat shirt led me to a concert on a boat was aboard the *Joby R,* Dick Arlen's yacht, named for his wife, Jobyna Ralston. We cruised from the Wilmington Yacht Club to Catalina. There were four of us — Dick Arlen, Dick Mook, a writer, Gary Cooper (whom we used to call Long-tack Sam), and me and my sweat shirt. Coop drove us all down to the harbor in his yellow and green Duesenberg, but even that oddity didn't take the play away from my sweat shirt. As we pulled out, there were shouts of warning from the shore, "Don't let Oakie get that sweat shirt wet, it'll take all the starch out of it!"

We were well out in the middle of the ocean when Arlen, Mook, and I heard the harmonica. It was being played very, very well. Good enough for Carnegie Hall. The music was something we didn't know, sort of folklorish. I started to try to hum the tune, but Arlen shushed me. "Wait, let's look." We looked down below and saw just enough of Long-tack Sam's crossed legs as he lay on a cot, playing and swinging his foot in time to the beat.

"Did you ever hear him play that thing before?" I asked Arlen.

"No," said Dick, shaking his head and shrugging his shoulders in disbelief. Well, we had a musician with us, and he was good! So we

George Murphy, Linda Darnell and Jack Oakie — *Rise and Shine.*

started below to join the musicale.

"Sweet Sue!" I called down, requesting my favorite number. When Coop realized we were coming to join him, he hid the harmonica in embarrassment. (Gary Cooper's shyness was not just a publicity stunt.) I never, ever, heard him play it again. But what I did hear of his inhaling and exhaling that day was so good, I have never forgotten how impressed I was with his musicianship.

After I made *The Great Dictator* with Charlie Chaplin, I thought I could graduate myself from college and give up my sweat shirt. But I was wrong. Darryl Zanuck sent for me to do the Mark Hellinger story, *Rise and Shine,* for Twentieth Century-Fox, and that started the football rolling again right from the beginning. We made *Rise And Shine* more than twelve years after Paramount decided that I was getting too old to play college football. Yet here I was cast as Boley Bolenciecwcz, a freshman.

Rise And Shine was another of my favorite pictures; I loved the music and the comedy. Boley was the greatest football player of all time, and we kept telling the audience so, in the immortal words and music of the Leo Robin and Ralph Rainger song, "On the bench he never sits, Boley Bolenciecwcz, the one-man blitz!" Linda Darnell had her hands full helping me with my studies and such tough examination questions as "Who's buried in Grant's tomb?" George Murphy, who later became our U.S. Senator, played her boyfriend and my pal. It was a good musical with a good cast, and good dance numbers by Hermes Pan. It made my sweat shirt more popular than ever. Again it was invited to and expected at all events.

The sweat shirt had made so many touchdowns that Camel cigarettes decided to get in on the play. Their advertising agents felt that my greatest following was to be found on college campuses, so they hired me to teach the students to smoke. They gave me my own radio show, called it "The Oakie College," and made me president of it. The sweat shirt and I were now called "Pres." It was always fun to hear Dr. Rufus Bernard von Klein Smid, president of USC, call across a room at some public affair, "Hello, Pres!" Of course I always returned the compliment and addressed him as "Pres," too.

In those days, none of us knew how harmful cigarettes were, so I kept telling the people that, "Camels are made from more of the finest tobaccos, both Turkish and domestic, than any other popular brand." Although my announcer, Bill Goodwin, professed, "I'd walk a mile for a Camel," I personally must have disliked walking, because I always carried a pack of Chesterfields in my pocket.

My regular sign-off for the show was, "Non compos mentis, which means, keep in touch with me, and I will leave you know!" But on the evenings that F.D.R.'s "Fireside Chats" followed "The Oakie College," I'd address him personally and sign off with, "All right Pres., you can take over now." And I'd turn the air over to President Franklin Delano Roosevelt.

When the folks in Sedalia, Missouri, honored me, they had a Jack Oakie day, and for the parade I was assigned to ride with Senator Stuart Syming-

Oakie and Darnell — *Rise and Shine.*

ton. He greeted me with his warm handshake as I got into the car, and then jokingly he threatened, "Just a minute, Oakie, don't you get up into this buggy with me unless you're wearing that sweat shirt!"

I wish I had worn a sweat shirt under my suit that day. We sat up on the folded hood of an open car and it rained all afternoon. To designate my birthplace, a marble and bronze plaque was placed in the landscaping in front of the house where I was born. As our car passed the big brick house at 522 W. Seventh Street, an elderly lady very graciously handed the senator and me an umbrella.

"Jack," she said, "do you see that room up there?" She pointed up to the second floor front window. "I used to tie diapers on you up there in that bedroom."

"My dear, you used to tie diapers on me up there in that room?" I asked.

"Oh, yes!" she shook her head proudly.

"Well, honey," I advised her, "you wouldn't recognize the old place now!"

"Haw!" Senator Symington shrieked with laughter, and almost fell off the car as he took the umbrella and thanked the lady for once again trying to keep me dry.

During that week of celebrations, I was asked to

Murphy, Darnell and Oakie — *Rise and Shine.*

Jack Oakie and Dick Arlen.

speak before the students of the Smith-Cotton High School. The young people had been shown a double feature of my college pictures the night before, to familiarize them with my work. As I entered the auditorium, I started to sing, "Fight on for old SC." The students got up in a body. "What a song!" they cheered. They thought I'd brought them a new song for Smith-Cotton.

"Sorry, that old fighting song belongs to USC," I explained, "so we can't give it to Smith-Cotton. But how lucky you all are, to be going to this beautiful high school," I commended them. "I envy you! I never had time to go to high school," I said, downheartedly. "I spent all my time in college." I think that baffled them, and I'm sure they're still trying to decode the message.

The fame of that good old sweat shirt has worn well. Just recently Al Wesson, the public relations man for the Hollywood Park Race Track, gave me a press pass pin, to wear in my lapel buttonhole. The little green and gold disc was so beautiful, I asked him to give me another so that I could have the pair made into a set of cuff links.

"All right, Oakie," he said, "here's another one, but tell me, since when do you wear cuff links with a sweat shirt?"

Although I have now put that sweat shirt out to pasture and only wear it around my ranch in Northridge, it still attracts invitations and frequent requests to bring it before the cameras.

"Come on, Jack, put that sweat shirt back to work again. What do you say?"

I always say, "Yes! I'll be glad to make a movie again, just as soon as I'm sure there is a demand for a white-haired, seventy-year-old football player!"

IT'S A FASCINATING BUSINESS!

In all of my motion picture career, I have never used makeup. That makes me something of a freak, because in show business one of the very first and basic rules is that a performer learn how to put on a good makeup.

I know that Stein greasepaint and pancake is very important. I've seen miracles performed with it. Some of our most glamorous stars, both men and women, report to the studio looking like bad embalming jobs until the makeup department goes to work on them. In *Little Men,* I saw false eyelashes and a full stage makeup transform an ordinary milk cow into Elsie, that world-famous, alluring heifer. The billions of dollars that grease the coffers of the cosmetic companies are proof that most people in the world do know the value of using the product, and have known it for thousands of years. But I am the freak exception that occasionally breaks a rule.

My lifetime habit of using a well-scrubbed face started over on the Universal lot on my very first picture, *Finders Keepers.* It was a silent picture. Nobody talked to me about makeup and, as I didn't have any, I didn't use any. Virgil Miller, the cameraman, and Wesley Ruggles, the director, came out of the projection room after viewing the first day's rushes, looking pretty pleased. Virgil Miller took me aside. "Young man," he said, "we liked what we saw. Now you listen to me. Don't you ever use makeup!" He patted my high cheekbones and tapped on my freckles. "You're very lucky," he said. "You have no beard line. You have what we call a natural puss for the screen. Don't you ever let them even put a powder puff on those cheeks of yours!"

I listened to him, and for over forty-five years I've followed his advice. There were times, however, when to keep that well-washed look, I got into some pretty hot water.

Like the time I was on loan out from Paramount to Warner Brothers for *Colleen,* with Ruby Keeler. The very first day of shooting, Tony Gaudio, the cameraman, came out from behind the horseshoe of lights that framed his camera, and asked, "Where's your makeup, Oakie? We're ready to shoot."

"Tony, I don't use makeup," I explained. "I'm ready, so come on, let's go right ahead and shoot."

"No!" He couldn't believe it. "I-don't-a-shoot-

you-without-a-makeup," he warned, in his musical Italian lilt.

"Well, then you don't-a-shoot-me," I said, imitating him. "Because I don't use makeup."

"It's-a-impossible!" he insisted. "Everybody uses makeup! You stand next to Ruby, she has a makeup. How can I shoot you without a makeup? You have to put on a makeup!"

"Tony, I never use a makeup," I repeated.

"Oakie, I can't shoot you without a makeup. You have to use a makeup! I tell you I don't shoot you without a makeup!"

"You know, Tony," I said, "this sure is a fascinating business. Why is it Paramount can shoot me without a makeup and Warner Brothers can't. Can you tell me why?"

He didn't tell me. He just looked at me and mumbled, "Oh, at Paramount they shoot you without a makeup." And then as if he were accepting a challenge, he got behind his camera with that horseshoe of lights, gave some instructions to his gaffer, and we went to work.

About a week later he came to me. "Oakie," he said, "don't-a-you-worry, I gotta you looking beautiful!" He gave me the OK sign with his circled fingers and grinned. "It's a Fastinating Business," he agreed with me. "Oakie, it's a Fastinating

Business!" Ever after that, "It's a Fastinating Business" became our own private code to explain anything that happened on the set that was unusual, and he pronounced that "st" in fastinating with gusto and loved our joke.

On *Hello Frisco Hello,* Ernie Palmer, the cameraman, put me through the same routine. "Oakie, you have to use makeup!"

"Why?" I asked. "Ernie, I never use makeup."

"But Jack, this is technicolor," he explained. "You have to use makeup with color."

"Why?" I asked again. I had made *Hit The Deck,* the very first picture in which one sequence was experimentally made in color, and I didn't use makeup for that.

"Why?" He couldn't believe I'd asked him such a stupid question. "Oakie, how can you ask me why? This is technicolor. Think about it. When you get mad, for instance, your veins will stick out and you'll be red all over your face!"

"Oh now listen, Ernie. Look at me. When did you ever see me get mad on the screen?" I asked.

He looked at me and shook his head. "OK, OK, no makeup!"

In *Hello Frisco Hello* and *Tin Pan Alley,* I worked in scenes right between Alice Faye and Betty Grable, and my veins photographed in technicolor looked just as good as theirs. When I worked on *Touchdown,* Harry Pringle was in charge of makeup. He couldn't see how the cameraman could photograph me without his handiwork on my face, and kept insisting that I use makeup. Harry had a know-it-all attitude, not just because he was an excellent craftsman, but because he was the uncle of John Gilbert, the great MGM leading man.

Pringle was on the set every day demanding that I use makeup. "Mr. Oakie, my department is responsible for the way you photograph. You have to use makeup!"

"Harry, you can't make a racehorse out of a mule," I told him. "That's why I don't use makeup."

One morning he took the problem to our director, Norman McLeod, with a final warning. "There's still time for me to get Oakie to look right for you, Mr. McLeod, but this is the last time I'm going to tell you."

Norman, who always loved fun on the set of any picture he made and was hoping that Harry would leave me alone, pointed to Jim Thorpe, "the Indian from Carlisle," the greatest all-around athlete and football player of all time, and said, "Pringle, I want you to make that man up to look like an Indian." This was the first day on the picture for Jim, and Harry (who had never seen Jim Thorpe in person) thought he was just another actor sent out from central casting to play football.

"Sure, sure, just leave it to me," he assured Norman in his cocky way. That was at eight o'clock in the morning. About an hour later he and Jim came back from the makeup department. "How's this?" Harry asked McLeod proudly, and he had Jim turn his head from left to right to model the makeup job.

"Come on, Pringle, what the heck are you doing?" Norman turned away and winked at us. "I didn't say make the man up to look like a Hindu, I said an Indian — an American Indian."

"Yes, yes, I see what you mean, I know exactly what you mean," Harry said, and Jim Thorpe, who had a bit of the Irish humor in that great heart of his, loved going along with the gag.

George Bancroft, Charles Esmond, "Elsie", Kay Francis and Jack Oakie — *Little Men.*

Kay Francis, "Elsie", Jack Oakie and George Bancroft — *Little Men.*

By four o'clock in the afternoon, Norman had turned down the look of a Chinese, a Mongolian, and three or four others. "Pringle, I want this man to look like an American Indian!"

It was quitting time when Harry and Jim came back to the set. Jim's face was freshly scrubbed clean of all traces of greasepaint and powder. "Mr. McLeod," Harry said, taking Norman aside and letting him in secretly on an idea that had come to him, "I want to show you something. Now, take a good look at that man's face. Do you know something, I don't think he needs a makeup at all. He looks like an Indian."

"You're right, Harry," Norman agreed. "He does look like an American Indian. He should! He

is an American Indian! Come on Harry, let me introduce you to Jim Thorpe."

"Jim Thorpe!" Even Harry Pringle knew that famous name. "You see! What did I tell you?" Undaunted, he took credit for making the discovery. "I told you he didn't need a makeup!"

On *Touchdown* there were two of us from Oklahoma who made the picture without makeup.

On *College Humor,* I watched the makeup department make a leading man out of "the Groaner" (a name I hung on Bing Crosby in our Malibu days, long before he made movies). First they glued his ears back to his head. The glue took two hours to dry so they wrapped a bandana round them to hold them in place. (Many's the time Dick Arlen and I flipped those ears loose to get off early.) Then they put a girdle on him to hold his stomach in, and padded his shoulders to build them out. They built lifts on his heels to give him height and attached a toupee to his scalp to supplant his thinning locks. On that picture I nicknamed him the "Robot of Romance." The day

Lillian Randolph and Jack Oakie — *Little Men.*

Bing realized he could sing just as well with his ears out, and a hat on, he joined my club and spent very little time in the makeup department.

Because of the expressions I loved to use on the screen, like *"the double take"* and my *"triple with the fade,"* it was important that I always work with my face uncovered. It would be impossible for me to make football pictures today, what with all the hardware the players now wear to protect themselves. I used to run that field without a mask or a helmet.

There was one time, however, when I had to work with my face covered. And although Nor-

man McLeod was the director again, even he couldn't get me out from under, because everybody in the picture was masked. I played Tweedledum and Roscoe Karns played Tweedledee in *Alice in Wonderland.* I was making another picture at the time, so our scenes were scheduled for Sunday shooting.

Our masks were about two feet wide, and completely covered our heads and faces. They had fringelike hair, topped with beanie caps, and ear-to-ear smiles that rested on double chins. The makeup man used pots full of heavy black glue to attach them to our faces. "Hey, fellers, that hurts!" I kept complaining. My skin is tender, and the weight of the heavy mask pulling away at my face was painful. It was pretty hard to live up to that broad happy smile the mask was wearing. After hours of torture, we finally got down to the set just as the company was breaking for lunch.

"Good," I said. "I'm starving. Let's get this thing off and get something to eat."

"Right," Rocky agreed. "Hey, get us out of these," he called over to the makeup men.

"Don't touch those masks!" they screamed at us. "It'll take four hours to put them back on again."

"Well, what the devil are we going to do?" we screamed back. "We're hungry!"

Just then the property man came up to us with some extra-long glass hospital straws. He stood back, looked at us, and, not knowing which was which, just spoke to both of us at once. "Mr. Oakie, Mr. Karns, you're supposed to use these to have some soup. That's what all the others have been doing." And he gave one to each of us.

"Well, just how do you use this?" I asked.

"Oh, let me show you." He peered into the

Jack Oakie and Alice Faye — *Hello, Frisco, Hello.*

smile of my mask. "Now where's your mouth?" he asked, and pushed the glass straw through the mask, looking for my mouth.

"Just a minute!" I had to back out of the experiment — he was putting my eye out.

"Sorry." He handed me the straw again. "Well, that's the idea. You're supposed to have a liquid lunch."

"OK, thanks. Come on, Rocky." We took our straws and went back to my dressing room. Cracker, my stand-in and understanding pal, was standing by.

"Say Oakie, which one is you?" Cracker asked, as he stared at our identical masks with their broad grins.

"Cracker," (he recognized my voice) "we're supposed to sip some soup through these straws; will you go out and get us some real nourishment to suck on?"

"Gottcha!" Cracker understood, and was back in no time at all with the proper bottles and ice. Although Rocky and I sucked on those straws for an hour, it didn't change the expression on the masks one iota. They kept right on smiling from ear to ear.

"You're wanted on the set," an assistant advised us. Somehow we got to the set and into the lights, and stood before the camera.

"Just a minute," the makeup men called, and came running in to powder the happy masks.

"All set?" the assistant called. The makeup men were happy, the cameraman was happy, the director was happy, so he called, "Action!" I don't know what happened to Rocky — he was on his own — but I walked right into a lamp standard and knocked it over.

Jack Oakie and Frances Langford — *Collegiate.*

"Cut!" Norman yelled. The crew stepped in and replaced the light and apologized. After all, the lamp must have been misplaced, because from where the crew, the cameraman, and the director sat, Tweedledum and Tweedledee looked fine in their great happy smiling faces.

"All right, let's take it again," Norman directed. "Action!" I must have been tilting in that direction because somehow I knocked over the same lamp.

"Cut," Norman called again. The cameras stopped rolling, and he came up to find out what was wrong. "What's the matter, boys?" he asked. "The set too small for those big heads of yours?" Then he got a whiff of what was behind those smiling masks. "OH!" he said. "Breathe right in my face, boys. I can't drink it right now, but I love to smell it. That's all for today!"

Somehow I didn't feel a thing as the makeup man yanked and pulled on that thick glue and removed half my face. The following Sunday, when Rocky and I came back and used the hospital straws for sipping soup, they got the shot.

Lily Pons was another who never could understand my shiny face. We made two pictures, *Hitting A New High* and *That Girl From Paris,* and in both she lovingly tried to help me. "Jackie," she said, "you always have two electric lights coming out of your cheeks. You should puff with some powder."

"Lily," I explained, "this is the way I work. You

Betty Grable, Jack Oakie and Alice Faye — *Tin Pan Alley.*

Tweedle-Dum (Jack Oakie), Tweedle-Dee (Roscoe Karns) with Alice (Charlotte Henry)
— *Alice in Wonderland.*

Jack with Tweedle-Dum mask — *Alice in Wonderland.*

wouldn't want a powder puff to tamper with my livelihood?"

But Lily couldn't understand it. Being a native of the country that stands head and shoulders above all others in the knowledge of cosmetics, she believed in that basic theatrical rule. "Jackie, you are a good actor," she said. "You should put on a good makeup." But even that top-line canary of the Met didn't sway me.

When I worked with Charlie Chaplin in *The Great Dictator,* although it was pretty well established that I didn't use makeup, I was afraid the great man might have other ideas on the subject, because makeup was such an important part of the era in which he grew up. The first day of shooting, Charlie was on the set in front of the long makeup table with its wall-size mirror. He was fingering a hank of hair about two feet long.

"Come on, Muscles." He nicknamed me Muscles and invited me to sit beside him. "Karl Struss tells me you don't use makeup." (Karl Struss was the cameraman on *The Great Dictator* and knew me well from our Paramount days.)

"That's right, Charlie. I never use the stuff." I was worried; I thought, "Here it comes."

"Well, on this picture I want you to do everything your own way, just as you always do," he said.

I couldn't believe it! From that moment on, it became the most comfortable picture I ever worked on. As Charlie spoke to me he was combing through those two feet of hair with the fingers of his left hand. "What made you decide not to use makeup?" he asked. I watched him as he seemed to caress and rearrange each hair of that long hank.

"I got some good advice, on my first picture,

from that great cameraman, Virgil Miller. He told me to keep my face clean or I'd lose it."

While we talked Charlie put some glue on his upper lip and some glue right in the center of the two feet of hair. Then he pressed the hair into place right under his nose. When the hank was firmly fixed so that he had a foot of hair on each side of his face, he picked up his left-handed scissors, the longest pair of scissors I have ever seen, and snipped about a quarter of an inch off the left side and then an equal amount off the right side. He snipped alternately in tiny amounts.

He kept snipping as he talked, until there was nothing left of the two feet of hair but that famous smidge right under his nose. It was the most fascinating operation I had ever watched. The professional makeup man stood by and watched with his hands in his pockets; he too was hypnotized by the magic of Charlie's performance. I asked him about the black rings he used to draw around his eyes. "Not on this picture, Muscles," he said. "I'm not using the rings on this picture."

I didn't use makeup on *The Great Dictator,* but I got to the studio early enough to watch Charlie

Joan Blondell and Jack Oakie — *Boulevardier from the Bronx, from Colleen*

67

The great All-American, Jim Thorpe with Jack Oakie and Mrs. Norman McLeod.

perform at the makeup table every morning, and he always started with that great long hank and worked it down to that little bit of hair centered right under his nose.

It was Leon Shamroy, the cameraman at Fox, who finally threw some light on the unpopularity of my makeup habit.

"Sham, you'd think everybody would be happy," I said to him one morning. "I'm saving time and work."

"Oakie, you're wrong," he laughed. "What you're doing takes more time and extra work." I couldn't believe it.

"Sham I don't understand, how can that be possible?" I asked.

"Well," he explained, "after spending hours lighting up a scene, the cameraman then has to go to work to take the light off you."

"Oh." Although my appreciation of all those good cameramen rose, it didn't change my delivery one iota; I still continue to work without makeup. On T.V., the cameraman's objection usually includes the argument, "The President of the United States uses makeup on television. You have to use it!"

I merely say, "Come on fellers. I know it's work, but take the light off me."

"Who told you?" they ask, and go about the business of taking the light off my shiny face.

One of my most fascinating experiences was in 1961 when I got a call from Nellie Marie Manly. "Jack," she asked, "will you please be king of the makeup men and hairdressers' ball at the Palladium?"

"Nellie" I reminded her, "I never use makeup, so maybe they'd better get another boy for king."

"No, Jack, we've all voted and you're our choice."

When my mother, Ev, died, Nellie, our number-one hairdresser at Paramount, called and asked for the privilege of dressing my mother's hair. "I want Ev's beautiful hair to be done right," she said.

I couldn't refuse that gracious Nellie Marie Manly anything, so I was king of the makeup men's ball and Spring Byington was queen. Together we ruled for the evening and judged the "debs" of motion pictures, heavily made up for the occasion.

"Nellie," I said, still wearing my well-washed look, "it's a fascinating business!"

That well-washed look still provokes some pretty baffling experiences. My wife, Vickie, and I were walking along the pathways up in the quiet of the hills of Northridge, when a car with Texas license plate passed us, then screeched on its brakes and backed up. "Say, aren't you Jack Oakie?" the lady on the passenger side called over to us.

"I'm not his brother," I said. (That sometimes gets a laugh.)

Jack Oakie, John Payne, Betty Grable and Alice Faye

"No . . . no kidding! Are you really the movie star Jack Oakie?" she asked.

"That's the name I'm using," I said. (Still no laugh.)

She scrunched up a quizzical face, looked at me a little harder, and said, "Well, my husband here says he's sure you're Jack Oakie."

"Well, my dear, you tell your husband he's right; I am Jack Oakie." Now she looked at me as if I were the proverbial side dish she hadn't ordered and started to laugh.

"You can't be Jack Oakie!" she screeched, enjoying the joke. "You look too natural!" Her embarrassed husband pulled away.

As the car sped off, my wife explained, "She just can't believe that your clean face can look exactly like the one on the screen. People must believe that the face they see on the screen looks as it does because of a good makeup job, and they can't identify your off-screen likeness with your motion-picture appearance."

I have never understood that woman in the car with the Texas license plate, and I am still trying to understand my wife, the psychiatrist, whenever she comes up with her explanations of what I call, "A Fascinating Business."

The Great Dictator — Jack Oakie and Charlie Chaplin.

CHAPLIN

It was my thirteenth year in Hollywood. It was also the thirteenth Annual Awards Dinner of the Academy of Motion Picture Arts and Sciences.

Along with the four others, Walter Brennan, for *The Westerner*, Albert Basserman, for *Foreign Correspondent*, William Gargan for *They Knew What They Wanted*, and James Stephenson for *The Letter*, I was nominated for Best Supporting Actor for the role of Napaloni, in Charlie Chaplin's *The Great Dictator*. I didn't hold out much hope that I could possibly be the winner, because no comedian had ever been presented an award in all the twelve ceremonies before.

Although thirteen was a lucky number for me — after all I arrived in Hollywood on June 13, 1927, just thirteen years before, and always felt it was the luckiest move I had ever made — I still felt that one dozen Awards had set a pretty firm precedent, not to be laughed at, and being just as superstitious as the next, I couldn't make myself believe that number thirteen was going to change things for this comedian. The evening of the Awards dinner, Alice Faye, Johnny Payne and I were running late at Twentieth Century-Fox, where we were working on *The Great American Broadcast*.

I don't know how we ever got through that heavy day's work because everybody on the lot came by our set to wish me luck. Alice handed me a lucky charm. "Oakie," she said "This is the thirteenth Academy dinner. It has to be lucky for you!"

"Thanks Faysie," I said. It's pretty tough to say very much more than "thanks" through a dry mouth with tongue and teeth sticking to the hope that your friends are right. I had my tuxedo brought from home to my dressing room so I could change and go directly from the studio to the Biltmore Bowl in downtown Los Angeles.

While changing into my dinner clothes I decided to remember that, although the statuette was a coveted honor, I had already had one of the greatest honors of all: I had worked with Charlie Chaplin, who gave me the chance to play the part for which I received the nomination.

It all started through the grapevine. Although the whole town heard that Chaplin was going into production soon, nobody knew what he was going to do. In a way I had more of a clue than most, because just a few months before I had come home from Europe on the *Ile de France* with Charlie's brother, Syd.

"Charlie's working on an idea for a picture about Hitler," Syd said. And in afterthought I remembered that he used to look me over as if he were trying to guess my weight. Never dreaming that he would ever send for me, because I wasn't German and felt sure there was nothing in a Hitler picture that I could play, I cheerfully joked about the idea.

"Sounds good to me, Syd. After all, Hitler's been trying to imitate Charlie wearing his moustache."

So when Charlie did send word that he wanted to speak to me, I could hardly believe it. I began guessing that perhaps with my rotund build he was considering me for a character like Goering.

"Oakie," he said, "I've been watching you, and I hear that you have a reputation for being a pretty good wise cracker. How would you like to be in a picture about Hitler?"

"What would I play, Charlie?" I asked. "Goering?"

"No! Oakie, I want you to play Mussolini," he said.

"Mussolini!" I couldn't believe it. "Charlie, you must be kidding."

"No, Oakie, I'm not kidding. I want you to play Mussolini." "Charlie, I'm Scotch-Irish," I protested, almost talking myself out of the job. "You want an Italian to play Mussolini."

"What's so funny about an Italian playing Mussolini?" he asked.

I looked at the little man and realized again how big his genius for comedy was. He was going to get his first laugh just with the casting. I knew right there and then what Charlie wanted, and knew I could play the part. I had seen Il Duce strutting around in the newsreels almost every day.

"Charlie," I said as fast as I could, "I'm your man!"

"Good, good," he said. He could see how thrilled I was. "Good!" he said again, and meekly raised his left palm, Nazi fashion, and saluted me. He kept his elbow tucked into his waist and held his hand below shoulder level. It was the sheepish salutation he used all through the picture. I returned his greeting with an energetic right hand raised high above my head. It was just what he wanted — a blustering Mussolini in contrast to his

Alice Faye with John Payne, Cesar Romero and Jack Oakie — *The Great American Broadcast*.

spineless Hitler.

"Do you want me to shave my head?" I asked. Mussolini had started that bald fashion long before Yul Brynner, or "Kojak's" Telly Savalas.

"No, Jack, I don't want you to shave your head," he said, looking at my full head of thick reddish-brown hair. "Keep the hair in." I must say I was always very grateful for that. Wearing a lot of hair had been a lifetime habit.

Charlie was not a spendthrift and, although he called me in to have lunch and talks with him many times, the job wasn't really mine. It was weeks and weeks before my agent, Morris Small, finally called to say, "All right, Jack, at last! The deal's made!" I could hear his deep sigh of relief over the phone. "It's all set. You're in. You're now working with Chaplin!" I silently stopped holding my breath and began to feel light-headed. For the first time since I told Charlie that I was his man, I inhaled a goodly supply of oxygen. "You're working with Chaplin," Morris repeated, as if I hadn't heard him.

"Thanks, Morris." That was another time when "thanks" seemed to be all I could say.

The news that Charlie was talking to me spread from the very first day that I went in to see him. The word went through the studios like wildfire. I was driving a big blue Darrin in those days. I had just bought the custom-made car from Donald Meek, and everybody in Hollywood knew it was mine. The Chaplin Studio was on the Southeast corner of LaBrea and Sunset Boulevards. The old house and tennis court were still on the lot. The

house, which had once been the home of ZaSu Pitts, was now being used for dressing rooms and, although Chaplin still used the tennis court, it was wide open and, combined with the back yard which fronted on Sunset Boulevard, was now the parking lot area.

So just by driving into the Chaplin gate on La-Brea and parking out there in front of the tennis court, my robin-blue sports car was practically sending up smoke signals. Through the chainlink fence it called attention to all to witness the fact that I was talking to the great man. Before Morris even made the deal with Charlie, his phone began to ring with offers from producers who had never before thought of me.

"What do you have in mind?" Morris would ask.

"Well, we'll find a property to suit him," they would advise Morris over and over again. "There's a part that can be tailored to suit him just fine." He was told about scripts that were already in production.

"Why change your script?" Morris asked many times, and was told, "Because if he's good enough for Chaplin, he's good enough for me!" At Twentieth Century-Fox, I signed a term contract with Zanuck, and RKO got my signature on the dotted line for *Little Men*. I was in demand!

Right after the Chaplin picture everybody wanted me to do another part like Mussolini. Arnold Pressburger called me. "Oakie, this is going to be a kind of Mussolini character. Dudley Nichols is writing it just for you, and René Clair is coming in from Paris to direct." He was selling me the part of Cigolini which I played in *It Happened Tomorrow*.

Casting directors and agents began to take credit for getting me the job with Charlie. But no agent, not even my own, Morris Small, had anything to do with Charlie's calling me. It was his brother Syd and his good friend A.C. Blumenthal who put the Oakie bug in his bonnet, and I have always been very grateful to them for influencing him, especially as Charlie had never in his life been easily influenced.

Working with Charlie Chaplin was the highlight of my career. He also made it one of the happiest periods in my life. All through our association he kept telling me not to change my ways. He harped so much on forbidding me to break any old-time habits while on the picture, that I thought it only fair to warn him that among "my ways" I had a reputation for getting drunk.

"Sometimes the Irish in me takes to scotch, Charlie," I confessed.

"Oakie," he said, "listen, if you want to drink go

Jack Oakie — *The Great American Broadcast.*

right ahead and drink. I don't want you to change any of your ways. If you get drunk, just don't come in. We're shooting this picture leisurely. We're not in any hurry."

He was so gracious I never took advantage of his offer. Even that New Year's Eve, 1939, at the *Trocadero* I wouldn't take a drink. I was with my Paramount pal Dick Arlen, and his date, beautiful Virginia Grey, and Boris Morros. Boris had a bottle of champagne that he put my name on trying to get me to toast the evening.

"Come on, Oakie, take a drink. It's New Years."

"Go away!" I said as he kept pushing the glass of wine into my mouth.

"Come on, let's have a drink and make a resolution." I think the only resolution he made that night was to try to get me drunk.

"Go away!" I said. "Stop trying to get me drunk!" I'm a pretty stubborn Irishman. When I drink, I go all the way. When I don't drink, I also go all the way. Well, after signing with Charlie, I wasn't drinking. I wanted to be sure that when I reported to that Chaplin studio, I wouldn't miss a move the man made. From the moment Morris Small set the money and made the deal and said I was in, I became a student again. I was working with the greatest comedian of all time.

Although he didn't realize it at the time he started *The Great Dictator,* Charlie, who demanded perfection of himself and took his time achieving it, made a mistake by shooting this picture leisurely.

"Muscles," he said one morning. He nicknamed me Muscles and called me that all

through the shooting of the picture. "You see what's wrong with this business of ours?" he said, showing me an article in the trade papers which listed the advance schedule of pictures to be made at one of the major studios. "They make 100 pictures in one year, I make one picture in five years."

Although Charlie didn't take five years to make *The Great Dictator,* he still had trouble trying to keep up with the news headlines. By the time the picture was released, Hitler was no longer a funny little clown to be laughed at. By 1940 he had already become a heavy, and was greatly feared. The little man was doing exactly what he said he was going to do: he was going right through all those countries like a dose of salts.

When the picture was released at the end of the year, Chaplin's Hynkel and my Napaloni found it rough going to get laughs. If Charlie could have made this one in six months instead of what he considered a quick year, the timing would have been better from a comedy point of view.

All during the shooting of the picture, as the news about the two dictators changed, Charlie tried to follow suit to cover the unpredictability of current events. For example, when we started the picture my original name was Benzino Gasolini, and I thought it was a helluva good title. But Charlie came in one morning worried about it. "It's too broad, Muscles," he said.

"But, Charlie," I protested, hoping he wouldn't change it, "Benzino Gasolini is a terrific burlesque on the man's name."

"No, Muscles," he explained. "Mussolini hasn't

Alice Faye, John Payne and Jack Oakie — *The Great American Broadcast.*

joined the Axis yet, and nobody can tell what move he's going to make. For all we know he may even join the Allied forces.''

So he picked a name that he thought would be less offensive, and still get a laugh. I became Napaloni, the dictator of Bacteria.

The Great Dictator was Charlie's very first talking picture, and he wanted to break the news in his own way, so from the very first day I spoke to him he asked me not to discuss the picture with anybody. But the folks in the industry and the newspaper columnists were very curious. "What's he doing?" I was asked hundreds of times, and Sidney Skolsky, who was always so good at getting Hollywood news, was one of my most frequent questioners. "Go ask Chaplin," was my standard answer.

As we got deeper into production the question changed from "What's he doing?" to "Does he talk?" I was asked "Does he talk?" not hundreds of times but millions of times. Everybody working on the picture was asked "Does he talk?" so often it became a password among us. For years after the picture we would still greet each other with "Does he talk?" I'd repeat "Go ask Chaplin," and Charlie handled the mystery. With all his other talent, he also sure knew how to stir up interest.

Besides his extravagance with time, Charlie was also extravagant with film, exactly the two items that major studios always pressured us about. I had got into the habit of working fast in order to get in a good tag at the end of a scene. If I didn't go right into a *take* or *double take* or my *triple with the*

fade, I might very well hear "Cut!" before what I believed was a good lick for a finish.

The only producer in the major studios who ever realized there was value in an Oakie tag was Darryl Zanuck. He always came down on the set the first day of shooting on any picture I was in at Twentieth Century-Fox and gave orders: "Don't anybody say 'Cut' when Oakie's working. He'll let you know when he's finished with a scene."

Sometimes, even after getting in my licks, they were lost on the cutting-room floor. I was sitting next to the director, Alfred E. Green, at our preview of *Colleen.* I watched Ruby Keeler, Dick Powell, Joan Blondell and Hugh Herbert go through the door in a scene and heard absolute silence in the theatre, as the picture went right into another sequence. "Where's the shot of me

looking around the bed as they go out?" I asked Al.

"That's right," he said. "Who left that out?" Rudy Fehr, who cut the picture, didn't think it was needed. The next time the picture was run, the shot was put back in. With a shrug and a *double take* I look into the camera and tell the audience that the four who just left had had a silly ruckus. You never heard such a laugh in the theatre.

The first bit of shooting I did with Charlie was a kind of screen test. He had a very, very low stool set in front of his enormous desk. I was to sit down on the stool and not realize it was so darn close to the floor. I sat down expecting the stool to be normal chair height and let the long distance down to get to it shock me, and then did a *surprise take*. I was showing Chaplin I knew how to get in a lick. Charlie didn't say "Cut!" and the camera kept right on rolling. Finally I heard his voice. "All right, comedian," he said, "What do you do now?"

He was a great teacher! I knew exactly what he meant! That was his way of telling me to "milk it." "Oh!" I said, realizing that I didn't have to worry about time or film. I got back down onto that stool and this time I was so bewildered I practically took the thing apart examining it. I milked the situation so long they ran out of film.

"OK," Charlie called to me. "Take it." So I did my *triple with the fade,* and he said, "Cut!" "Good," he said, making me very happy. "You see, Muscles," he explained, "I always try to get three or four laughs where most comics just get one."

Besides suddenly having an abundance of time and film to work with, I was also very pleasantly overfed. I had been on diets so many times in my career, because studio executives were always after me to reduce, that I wouldn't be surprised if the statistics proved I'd taken off as many pounds as elephants weigh. I was still on a kind of prolonged diet when I came in to see Charlie.

"Oh no, Muscles," he said, "you're not going to lose weight on this picture!" He was adamant. He wanted as much contrast as he could get between his meek Hitler and my blustering Mussolini.

"You're the boss, Charlie," I said, and couldn't have been more pleased.

"Muscles, you're going to have lunch with me every day!" It was an order. So all during the shooting of the picture, Charlie and I lunched together every day. He had a wonderful Japanese cook who planned delicious meals, and Charlie insisted that I eat everything he served. Whenever I felt I had eaten enough, Charlie'd disagree and force the food on me. He and his cook stuffed me daily. Being cooperative, I went along with the

luxury and ate enormous amounts of the tastiest cooking ever, relishing every bite. My weight kept going up and up, and Charlie and I kept getting happier and happier.

Although Charlie also ate a pretty big lunch, he never gained a pound. He worked it off, acting, directing, and writing the script. (This was the first time his script had been on paper. It had always — before *The Great Dictator* — just been in his head.) He also helped light the set, and worried about the sound, and wrote the music. And everything he did came right up out of his heart — well, his left side.

Charlie Chaplin was the most left-handed person of all the left-handed people in the world. Sometimes he even confused the right side and the left side of the camera when looking through the lens. Karl Struss, the cameraman, had to keep reminding him that what he was looking at was on the side he meant it to be.

While writing music for the picture, he'd often try out some passages on the set. I loved to see him pick up his violin, put it under the right side of his chin, hold the bow in his left hand, and with that left arm of his going up and down play the most wonderful melodies.

At lunch I used to tease him about being on the wrong side of the fork. Right after lunch one day, with food still on his mind, we went onto the set of the large banquet hall. This was the scene where Hynkel and Napaloni were to have their special private meeting. Chaplin directed that as we two dictators entered the banquet hall, his cabinet members were hurriedly to usher all the guests and waiters out of the room. We rehearsed the scene of our entering the room and the guests leaving.

Charlie directed one of the young actresses, a dress extra and a very attractive young lady, to pick up a plate on the run, fill it with food from the magnificent buffet table (which was laden with plates, silverware, napkins, and extra-large platters of salads, meats, cheese, fruits, spaghetti, breads, cream dressings, and condiments), and take it with her greedily as she quickly left with the other guests.

"See," he said, and demonstrated what he wanted her to do. He picked up a plate, filled it with some cheese and meat, hurriedly reached for some slices of bread, and then rushed through the doors before they were closed by the guards. We started the scene and the girl picked up the plate exactly as Charlie had done. She tried to fill it with some cheese and meat, but the slices kept sliding off the plate, and the bread tray seemed far out of her reach. She was too late getting to the doors

This still was taken on November 12, 1943, Jack Oakie's fortieth birthday — *It Happened Tomorrow*.

before the guards closed them.

"No, no, honey," Charlie called to her. "Be quicker. Pick up the plate just as I showed you. Put some cheese and meat on it, reach for the bread and don't stop for anything else. Go right out of the doorway."

"Yes sir," she said. The poor girl was becoming nervous.

"That's all right," Charlie said kindly to give her confidence. "Let's try it again." This time the food slipped and slid more than ever. Nothing stayed on the plate. Charlie stopped the rehearsal and tried to put her at her ease. He went through it again and showed her exactly what he wanted her to do, and then called for another run-through of the whole scene.

We entered the room, the members of the cabinet shooed everybody out, the guests and waiters all left, and the young actress was still at the table trying to get the victuals to stay on the unbalanced plate. This time Charlie asked the other extras to leave the set, and asked her to try it again, hoping that being alone on the stage would help her concentration. He pulled up his director's chair next to mine, and we watched her go through the action again.

"How can anybody be so stupid?" he mumbled to me. He liked the girl and didn't want to take the little piece of business away from her. She seemed such an attractive, graceful girl, I too wondered how she could be so clumsy.

Charlie joined her at the table. "Now," he said, "do exactly as I do." He stood beside her and had her follow him and imitate each gesture as he went through the scene. He picked up a plate, she picked up a plate, exactly as he did. But she didn't seem to be able to hold on to it. He reached for the cheese and put some on his plate. When she did exactly as he did, the plate seemed unbalanced with the weight of the cheese. He put some meat on his plate. She put some meat on her's, but it wouldn't even stay there with the aid of the fork. He picked up some slices of bread, but she couldn't manage that because she was holding on to the meat and cheese.

He then led her to the doorway and let her leave the room. As I watched them I began to realize that the more the girl tried to please Charlie by doing exactly as he did, the more awkward she became. Then suddenly it dawned on me! I knew why she couldn't handle the plate and food business. Charlie sat down beside me.

"Muscles, what am I going to do?" he said. "Have you ever seen anybody so stupid?"

"Charlie," I said quietly, "that girl isn't left-handed."

"Oh?-Oakie, you're right!" He got right up and went off to talk to her privately. The very next *take* she picked up the plate with her left hand, and with her right hand she filled it with plenty of cheese and ham, and reached for the slices of bread and got to the doorway for her exit just as Charlie wanted her to.

Although Charlie was extravagant with film and time, he sure watched his purse strings in every other way. The National Labor Relations Board had just been set up, and *The Great Dictator* was the first picture Charlie made on which he had to deal with their rules. Every production had to have so many grips, so many makeup men, so many property men, so many cameramen, so many sound men, whether needed or not, and so on right down the line. Charlie had never seen so many people crowding his stage.

"Who are all these people?" he'd ask, looking around at the hustle and bustle. He just couldn't get over the shock of having them around. "Who are all these people?" he'd turn to me and ask over, and over, and over again.

"You have to have them, Charlie," I told him.

Day after day his brother Syd explained the necessity. "It's the law, Charlie. If we don't have them, they'll close down production."

When we worked out on the street it was considered being on location, and it murdered him to see that long, long line of workmen being served at the lunch counter at his expense.

"But we don't need them!" he complained. "What's a makeup man?" he said, putting his finger up to his little moustache. "I've been putting this on my face long before he was born!" he said, pointing across the road at the young man sipping coffee and trying to stay out of Charlie's way.

On *Modern Times,* the picture he made just before *The Great Dictator,* the only crew he had was his cameraman, Roland Totheroh, and one property man. Not even a script girl, because the script was in his head. While talking about the terrible cost of things and the necessity of watching the purse strings, Charlie painted the blackest picture ever about *Modern Times.*

"I should have made that one a talkie," he said. "I made a big mistake. Lost a lot of money on that one." I felt terrible. It seemed awful to me that Charlie should have suffered such disappointment with such a great picture.

"I can't believe it, Charlie," I said. "It's such a wonderful picture." I was trying to tell him that I didn't think that anything about *Modern Times* was a mistake.

"Yes," he said, "but a big mistake." I thought he was going to cry, remembering the tragic error that was breaking his heart.

"I made only ten million dollars on that one." He shook his head. He believed that if it had been a talkie he could have doubled that figure. But that ten million-dollar disappointment was nothing compared to the disappointment his purse strings felt because he hadn't tied up an apron on *The Great Dictator.*

We were shooting out on Hollywood Boulevard near Highland, about half a block from a brand new Woolworth store that looked like an elaborate department store. One morning he looked Paulette Goddard over and decided that the rag she was wearing needed a little help. "Get a cotton apron," Charlie told her. Paulette told Teddy Tetrick, the wardrobe man, what the Boss wanted, and the apron was there before the first shot of the day. It looked just right, and Charlie was pleased.

The apron worked for about two weeks, and then Charlie went on to other things; it was over a month later that he decided on some retakes and asked Paulette to wear the apron again. "They don't have the apron," Paulette reported when she came back from wardrobe.

"What do you mean, they don't have the apron?" Charlie couldn't believe the girl knew that she was talking about. "It's that little, old-looking, cotton apron! You wore it in this scene," he reminded her.

"I know, Charlie. But the wardrobe department doesn't have that apron any more," she explained again.

"Get that wardrobe man over here!" Charlie was trying to control himself. "How can an apron disappear?"

"Yes, sir?" Teddy came running. *The Great Dictator* was early in his career, and he wanted to do a good job.

"I want Miss Goddard to wear the little cotton apron she had on in this scene," Charlie said.

"Oh, well, we don't have that apron, sir," the young man explained. Charlie couldn't believe it.

"You did have the apron," he said slowly as if he were trying to understand.

"Yes, sir. We did have it. But I thought you were through using it so I sent it back," Teddy said as if there should be no problem understanding that.

"Sent it back?" Charlie screamed. "What do you mean you sent it back? Where did you send it?"

"To Western Costume, sir. It belongs to Western Costume." He repeated the name as if Charlie had never heard of the famous motion picture costume company.

"Western Costume!" Charlie screamed louder. He very well knew the company and how costly their things were.

"Well, they were so good about sending it over by special messenger when we needed it, I thought it would be nice to send it right back just as soon as we were through using it." He expected Charlie to see how well he meant.

"Western Costume!" Charlie screeched again. "Western Costume! You could have walked across the street and bought an apron for fifteen cents!" he said waving his arm over at the beautiful new Woolworth's. "For fifteen cents the apron would have belonged to us, not to Western Costume!"

But it was too late for that kind of Chaplin economy. The apron had to match the scenes that were already shot.

"Well now, wait a minute, Mr. Chaplin. I'll call up Western Cosume and see if they've still got it over there." The helpful young wardrobe man made the phone call, and Western Costume thoughtfully sent it again by special messenger. The cost of renting the apron and having it delivered by special messenger twice came to four hundred dollars. I wondered if the young man's wardrobe career was going to be at loose ends, until I learned that he had strings that tie much tighter knots than those of a purse or an apron. Teddy married Betty Chaplin, Charlie's niece.

All through the picture, Charlie encouraged me to do anything that came to mind. Like the day Charlie and I, in full military dress uniform, were sitting in the bleachers watching the parade of Hynkel's military might. As if at the circus, Napaloni was eating peanuts out of one of those familiar little paper bags. I kept tossing my empty broken peanut shells over into Hynkel's lap. Chewing away and with my mouth full, I finally offered him the open sack.

"Would you like some peagoobers?" I asked.

"Cut!" Charlie called to the cameraman. "What's that?" he asked me.

"What's what?" I asked, thinking I'd gone too far by throwing all those peanut shells at him.

"Peagoobers?" he asked, "what are peagoobers?" The Englishman had never heard of my Oklahoma expression for peanuts.

"Peanuts, Charlie. That's what we call them down South. 'Peagoobers.'"

"Oh?" He thought a moment and then asked Karl Struss, the cameraman, "Ever hear of peagoobers?"

"Yes, Charlie. That's peanuts," Karl convinced him.

"Good. Keep that in," he said. Once again he seemed to like my nonsense. He especially liked my expression, "good shape," which I used all through the picture. Whenever he'd ask me a question, I'd always answer with "good shape, good shape." But there was one day that I thought even "good shape" couldn't help me. I honestly thought Sir Charles was going to fire me. Even his brother Syd took him aside and asked, "Do you know what that guy is doing to you? Watch him, Charlie!"

The scene was set in the barber shop. Charlie and I were sitting in adjacent barber chairs. I said my line and then cranked my chair up a bit so that I was sitting a little higher than he was. The Charlie said his line and cranked up his chair so that he was sitting a little higher than me. We kept saying our lines and competing for position to top each other, until the springs gave way and both chairs dropped to the floor at the same time.

Charlie never allowed anybody to tell him anything. He always wanted to figure things out for himself. Like the time he bought his first car, a Rolls Royce. He told me he wouldn't even let the salesman show him how to start it although he had never driven a car before in his life.

"When I finally got it started," Charlie said, "the darn thing was heading right for the side of the

building. I put my hand out of the window to try to push the wall away, and then took some driving lessons."

Although this was his first talking picture and he knew very little about the mechanics of sound, he still wanted to do everything his own way. For instance, he got hold of a celluloid card and a small electric fan and tried to simulate airplane noises. He held the celluloid card into the spinning blades (it's a wonder he didn't lose his hand) and listened to the change in the whirring sounds as he slowed the fan down and then speeded it up.

"Percy!" He called over to the sound man, "how's this?"

"What's it for?" Percy asked.

"For the airplane sounds."

Percy politely said that it sounded pretty good. But he knew that it couldn't be used as they were going to dub in the real thing later. Well, after the first *take* in the barber chairs, Charlie called over to Percy, "Play that back." I watched his face as he listened to the sound track. The scene was exactly as he had written it. He heard his lines and mine, but somehow they weren't quite right.

"All right, Muscles," he said, "let's take it again." We started from the floor and did the scene again exactly as we had done it before. We spoke our lines and cranked our chairs. When we hit the floor again, Charlie called over to Percy, "All right, now, play that one back."

Again I watched him closely as he listened to our voices, but he still didn't like what he heard. He knew something was wrong, but he wasn't going to ask anybody what it was. I knew exactly what was bothering him. I was using a trick I had learned from that Russian expert, Gregory Ratoff, who had pulled it on me when we worked together in *Once In A Lifetime*.

We spent the whole morning going up and down in those barber chairs, and he stopped to listen to the playback after each *take*. We broke for lunch and, when we came back to work, we started the process all over again. Toward evening, when it seemed we had hit the floor for the hundredth time, he turned to me.

"All right, Muscles!" he said. "What are you doing to me?" He had to be pretty disturbed to be asking anybody a question. "Come on, Muscles," he repeated. "What are you doing to me?"

"I'm taking your lines away from you, Charlie," I said, as I thought, "Here it comes, I'm going to be fired."

"Oh?" he said, thinking a moment. "How do you do that?"

"I just hop on top of your lines before you finish talking, and take your lines away from you.

Jack Oakie, Linda Darnell and Dick Powell — *It Happened Tomorrow.*

That's all," I explained. Then, just as I expected him to tell me I'd never have the chance to hop on his lines again, he reached over and shook hands with me.

"Good, Muscles, good!" he said. "That's just what I want you to do. Good." He said it again and again and made me feel good.

"Percy!" he called over to the sound man. "I like it. That's what I want. Print it!"

One night when just the two of us were working late after the crew and everybody else had gone and we were alone on the stage, Charlie felt a bit sentimental and wanted to talk about comedy on the screen. The man worked so hard he was always damp. So his habit was to put a white turkish towel around his neck and over his head of beautiful, thick, sopping wet hair. "Muscles, get a chair," he said, wrapping himself in his towels. "Come on, sit down."

We sat down in a couple of odd directors' chairs and felt dwarfed in the center of that lavish mammoth banquet set. "Muscles, you've been in pictures a long time," he said.

"Oh no, Boss." (I had started calling Charlie "Boss" the day of my first interview with him.) "Not all that long," I said.

"Oh yes, you have," Charlie insisted. "I've been hearing about you for a long time, and they tell me you know a lot of tricks."

"Honest, Charlie, I'm just a student and I'm still learning." What else is there to say when you know you're speaking to the master?

"Come on, Muscles," Charlie said. "Tell me about the tricks you use, because you know I invented them all." Charlie was not a modest man, and there was no reason for him to be modest, because he was right. He was only stating a fact. As far as I was concerned, Charlie did invent every worthwhile trick in comedy. Anyway I didn't have a chance to tell him anything. He felt like talking, and I was smart enough to listen to his gems.

"You know, Muscles," he said sadly, "I miss the click, click, click, of those good, old-fashioned, hand-cranked cameras. I could hear the beat of the camera and time every one of my movements to its rhythm." (When talkies came in, the cameras had to be silenced, and in *The Great Dictator,* his first talking picture, the silence of the camera threw him off balance.)

"You know," he began to reflect, "how those Keystone Cops used to run into a scene swinging their clubs in every direction so fast you couldn't tell whether they were coming or going?" Charlie demonstrated their thoughtless, hurried actions by waving his arms around every which way, and said, "Well, I slowed all that down. I gave it tempo. First I'd find the target, like the villain's head, then I'd take off his hat and, picking a good spot, I'd aim before hitting it with my club."

Charlie's pantomime was so precise, I could see the head as he held it under his open right palm and hit it with his policeman's club held in his left hand. "Then I'd turn the head a little and hit it again, then turn it again to an even better spot and hit it again." I could just see the head as he explained the maneuver and hit it over and over again slowly and carefully. "I would get four laughs with the one gag," he said, "just by slowing it all down with deliberate timing."

Getting more laughs than any other comedian was a science with him. I realized that night that Charlie's great performances were carefully calculated, that he was a master mathematician of comedy. Just like in music, for Charlie there were always just so many notes to the bar. There was never any guesswork; for him, two and two always equaled four and perfection. We sat quietly for a moment, and as I looked at his passive face I realized how active the clockwork was inside that beautiful head. I don't think he'll ever know how much I wanted to thank him that night for showing me an example of the Chaplin multiplication table for increasing laughs.

Suddenly Charlie sighed. "Muscles," he said as if he were the greatest failure in the world, "nobody is such a great actor that he can do everything. You know, when you get into a spot where you're not sure how dramatic you can go," he said sadly, as if what he did was a very poor solution to the problem, "just turn your back on the camera." He paused as if once again he were trying to find another answer to the riddle. He shook his head and said with resignation, "I don't know why, but with your back to the audience, they'll watch you, and then do the acting for you." I guess Charlie hated to turn any of his acting over to anybody else, but he was right.

I, too, was the audience many times watching that lonely little figure with his back to the camera recede into the distance. And I, too, cried many times.

Besides being an actor, director, and musician, Charlie was also a great dancer. He loved the ballet, and was practically a ballet dancer himself.

When the Ballet Russe de Monte Carlo was in town, we went down to the Shrine Auditorium for almost every performance. Eglevsky was the star he was most interested in. His leaps and elevation thrilled Charlie, who from my point of view was almost as good.

Charlie and I attended many social events as the pair of dictators, but the most exciting for me was the party at Pickfair that Mary Pickford and Buddy Rogers gave to honor the British admiral, Lord Louis Mountbatten. I was standing at the fireplace under Mary's beautiful, full-figure painting with the tall, stately Mountbatten, who was very graciously laughing at one of my jokes, when he suddenly stopped. He looked across the great living room at Charlie. "Well, well," he said, "here I've got both Hitler and Mussolini with me in the same room." That was 1940. I wonder if world events would have taken a different turn if what he said that night had actually been true.

Well, that night when I got down to the Biltmore Bowl to attend the thirteenth annual Academy Awards dinner, I was a little late and I don't remember what was served. What I do remember ingesting was the knowledge that I was right — once again no comedian was honored with an Oscar — once again it was given for "dramedy."

Alfred Lunt, the presenter for Best Supporting Actor, came to my table after giving the Award to Walter Brennan. I can still hear his full, rich, beautiful voice. "I wanted with all my heart to give it to you," he said as he sat down. "I saw *Tin Pan Alley,* and I know you'll get it for that one."

I never did. I have, however, never forgotten the warmth of his hand on mine and, if good wishes from fellow actors are honors, I've been greatly honored, a multitude of times.

THE REDHEAD

Clara Bow was a "natural." She was one of the most colorful stars the screen has ever known, with natural untrained talent and natural brilliant beauty. Her thick, wavy, flaming red hair framed her face and set off her huge amethyst-colored eyes. When those enormous gems looked up at you, you looked into the biggest pair of purple glims that anyone has ever seen.

But the little girl's magnificent red hair and purple eyes were lost on the screen. During the time that Bow was the biggest star in the motion picture industry, the silver screen was limited to black and white films. "The Redhead," as we all called her, photographed like a brunette with dark eyes. Artists all over the world who painted her portrait from publicity pictures always painted her eyes dark brown or black, and her hair brownish. Technicolor and Kodacolor were not yet invented. But although the limitations of the old nitrate film subdued her vibrant coloring, it did not subdue her fire as a performer, both on the screen and off.

I first met "the Redhead" on *The Fleet's In* at Paramount Pictures Studio. The launching of my part, Salty, in *The Fleet's In* started when I was still in vaudeville with Lulu McConnell. Toward the end of 1926 we were playing in Kansas City, and one of the acts on the bill was called "The Battling Butler" with Ted MacNamara. We had just finished the first matinee, and a couple of us were sitting around in Lulu's dressing room when Ted came in practically crying.

"Just got a call from the coast!" he said. "Lu, it's a helluva offer. They want me to play this part in the movie *What Price Glory* with Victor McLaglen and Eddie Lowe, at the Fox Studio. What'll I do?" He kept walking back and forth in that tiny dressing room and talking without waiting for Lulu to answer. "What'll I do? It's a chance in a lifetime! I want to take it, Lu, I sure want to take it!"

"Take it!" Lulu shouted at him. "Take it!"

"What do you mean, take it? How can I take it? How can I get out of this vaudeville contract?" It was pitiful to hear him. He was so anxious to break into movies.

Lulu looked right at him, shaking her head as if Ted were the stupidest man in the world, and assuming one of her best drunken expressions she said, "Get drunk!" Then in all soberness she repeated it for him, "Get drunk! You know they'll

Jack Oakie, Clara Bow, Maurice Chevalier and Eugene Pallette.

fire you right now!" Ted stood still, and as he looked at her I could see Lulu's wisdom lighting up his face.

Well, Ted took her advice. We were playing three shows a day then, and he didn't show up for the next matinee or the evening performance. The next day he missed all three shows. The following morning, less than forty-eight hours after Lulu said, "Get drunk!" the manager posted his notice on the call board. Ted MacNamara was fired right there and then. But he hadn't wasted any time; Ted was packed, had his ticket, and was on the train to the Coast before the ink on his notice was dry.

In *What Price Glory*, Ted was a hit. They teamed him with Sammy Cohen, and Ted and Sammy became an established team like Beery and Hatton. In fact, they were sort of the start of "The Cohens and Kellys."

The studio got their top-line writers to write stories for them. Malcolm Stuart Boylan, one of the very best in the business, prepared the script *Plastered In Paris* for them. They were ready to start shooting the picture, Benny Stoloff was set to direct, and Sam Katzman, Benny's assistant, had everything ready to go, when Ted MacNamara suddenly died. I'd been on the Coast about six

Jack and "The Redhead," Clara Bow — *The Fleets In.*

months then. I'd made *Finders Keepers,* my first picture, and was just finishing my second picture, *Sin Town,* when I heard about Ted. We had kept in touch with each other, and his passing like that, just when he was enjoying such a successful career, was quite a shock.

When Ted died, Billy Wilkerson, who was my agent at that time, heard that they were trying to keep the team going. So he took me over to Fox to see if I could replace Ted and work with Sammy Cohen.

Three of us showed up to be interviewed for the part — Puddles Hanaford (a famous circus clown and bareback rider with Barnum and Bailey), Joe E. Brown, and I. Sol Wurtzel took one look at Brownie and dismissed him immediately. "Your mouth is too big for the part," he told him. They then tested Puddles and weren't satisfied. By the time they finally looked at me, they decided they wouldn't even bother with a test, because they wanted a comedian and they were sure I'd make a good "heavy" for another picture that they were starting right away, called *Road House.*

Road House starred Lionel Barrymore, Warren Burke, and Maria Alba, with Richard Rosson directing. We shot the whole picture up at Santa Cruz, and while up there on location Richard Rosson had a visitor whose insight helped me get back to getting laughs on the screen again. Lige Conley, a comedy writer (who was really called a comedy constructionist in those days because he didn't write dialogue, he created situations), spent a few days with us at Santa Cruz and decided I was not a good "heavy" for the screen.

Lige was also a good friend of Wesley Ruggles' and had seen me in *Finders Keepers.* He told me that he knew that Malcolm St. Clair was getting ready to cast *The Fleet's In* for Paramount, and that there was a good part in it for me. Lige got back to Hollywood before we did and spoke to Mal St. Clair for me. Then Wes sent Billy Wilkerson out to sell me, and when I got back to town from Santa Cruz I was sent out to see Mal, who seemed to take to me immediately. I was in like a burglar.

Working with both Clara Bow and Mal St. Clair was one of the biggest thrills in my life. Their kindness made *The Fleet's In* a training ground for me. They taught me some of the important basics of acting for the screen.

I had just come from Vaudeville and Broadway, where we sang and spoke to the second balcony. But on the silent screen actors had to show the audience what they were thinking and feeling. Emotions had to be acted out, not talked about. "Watch this," Mal St. Clair said to me one morning. Bow was tearing up a picture of Jimmy Hall and throwing the pieces into a wastepaper basket. She was wonderful. Nobody on the screen ever tore up a picture with so much feeling. "Now!" St. Clair called to her, and the next thing you knew she was down on her knees, taking the pieces out of the wastepaper basket and trying to sort them out like a jigsaw puzzle to put the picture back together again.

"See," Mal St. Clair explained, "'that' tells the audience that she really loves the guy no matter how much of a heel he is." The Redhead was one of the greatest emotional actresses ever. When a scene called for tears she could flood the place, and she did it naturally. She didn't need the help of that onion juice that the property men used so regularly for other performers. She could turn it on as easily as a faucet, cry buckets from those purple eyes at will, and then just as readily turn it right off again.

I also learned about heroes and villains from Mal St. Clair. I was doing a scene in which Jimmy Hall was supposed to pick a fight with me. Just as Jimmy hauled off to hit me, I started to defend myself. "Cut!" Mal cried out. He took me aside. "Oakie, when Jimmy throws those punches keep your hands down at your sides. Don't lift your hands at all. Just let him hit you," he directed.

When we did the scene, I did just as Mal told me to — I let my arms hang limp at my sides. At the showing, when I saw the scene on the screen, Jimmy looked like the heavy and the audiences sided with me.

Bow was exceptionally good to me on that picture. She encouraged Mal St. Clair to give me every advantage. Mal told me that when she learned I was under personal contract to Wesley Ruggles, she went up to the front office at Paramount and spoke for me. "Get that boy," she said. "Don't let him get away." Although there were a lot of other factors involved, I know it was her strong influence that finally got me my contract with the studio. Paramount bought my contract from Wes soon after we finished *The Fleet's In.*

The Redhead included me in many of her social functions. I remember some early visits at her house when she lived in Hollywood at 7675 Hollywood Boulevard. I thought it was a wonderful little house. Then she soon moved to her larger house at 521 Bedford Drive, in Beverly Hills. But no matter how small or large the house, Bow always found a spot for a Chinese den. She furnished the room with red-lacquered Chinese furniture, where she always kept some incense burning in a Chinese pot.

I was a frequent visitor at Bow's. Many, many times after I'd have dinner at Henry's Restaurant, I'd call her. It could sure be lonely in Hollywood after leaving the studio. "Stay right where you are," she'd say. "I'm sending the car for you." I'd wait right there at the northwest corner of Hollywood and Vine, and looking toward Highland Avenue I'd watch for her great big black Packard. It never took very long before I saw it coming down Hollywood Boulevard, practically making a solo appearance. The chauffeur would drive me back to her house on Bedford Drive, where there was always something of interest going on, with interesting people from all over the world and

every walk in life, from extras to great stars like Sessue Hayakawa, the famous Japanese leading man.

In those days we thought we were living high off the hog whenever we were lucky enough to get a little gin. We'd mix it with our favorite Bireley's mission orange juice, which came in black glass bottles then, and the *pièce de résistance* was squeezing some anchovy paste out of a tube like toothpaste onto a saltine cracker.

Gin was all we ever could get to drink until we went down to San Pedro on location while still shooting *The Fleet's In.* At San Pedro we were all treated to some drinks by some Navy personnel — it's a wonder we lived to finish the picture. Those boys mixed Coca-Cola and pure alcohol. They got the alcohol from the supply that was used to fire torpedoes.

Bow was a good name for the Redhead. She allowed everyone to loop strings around her and tie knots in her good nature. She was always helping somebody. For example, she decided to sponsor Jimmy Dundee, an ex-fighter turned stunt man, who told her he wanted to get back in the fight game. To help him she converted her entire back yard into a gymnasium. She rigged all the necessary equipment for training a fighter, including a full-size professional boxing ring. Dundee worked out hard, but more and more we all realized he had no chance of ever fighting again. In fact, one of the hardest workouts he ever had was when

James Hall, Jack Oakie, Clara Bow, Malcolm St. Clair, and others — *The Fleet's In.*

June 24, 1950

Hi! Jackie Boy, How's everything with you these days? Busy now or taking it easy? I've been back here at the Institute of Living for eight months. It goes without saying that I'm mighty lonesome for my boys and Rex, also my old Dad. I came here to see if they could do anything about the chronic insomnia I've been suffering from for so many years. As yet, no success but I have not wasted my time. I've taken and passed with all A's a four year course in Remedial English. I'm also taking drawing and painting lessons, plus a course in speed typewriting — the touch system. I may take either French or Spanish in the future. I've become very ambitious in my old days. I expect to stay here until at least the end of the year. What ever became of that long promised letter of yours that Vickie said you were going to write me? Better get busy and write your old red-headed pal soon — I need a little morale boosting. I thought you might get a kick out of a copy (over)

of my first oil painting — I know I'm no genius but I don't think it's too bad for a first attempt. I'm now working on a portrait of Tony from a very small snapshot — it's tough sledding but I believe it will be passable when finished — Write when you have time Jack I'll love hearing from you

Love to you and Vickie —

Clara

12214 Aneta St.,
Culver City, Calif.
Dec. 10th 1961.

-2-

Dearest Jack;

I hope my telegram reached you in time for the Masquer's dinner honoring you. I've seen you on T.V. quite often and you are still tops with me, as funny as you were in my pictures long ago at Paramount Studio. Those were the days of hard work and laughs, too. The stars of today are more fortunate money-wise than we were. It amazes me how they can pick best selling stories, be their own producers, directors, command tremendous salaries they do, and be able to travel vast distances for location scenes and if they choose be hours late on the sets. Of course T.V. is a wonderful medium for them, too. I must say I envy them at times, but actors, God bless them, have at long last gotten the breaks we actors of yesteryear never had. Hollywood, I'm afraid, has lost the glamour of old and most of its really great personalities have passed on.

In these terrifying times of the H. Bombs, etc. perhaps they are really the lucky ones after all.

Rex is well and as busy as ever with his many interests in Las Vegas, Reno and Carson City. I'll see him Christmas. Tony is not well, I saw him Thanksgiving Day and for all of his 6 ft. 5 inches he only weighs 165 pounds. He works in Reno, so don't see him too often, but he writes me often. Georgie has been married for a year and a half to a lovely Vegas girl of twenty and works for her Dad there. "Yup", as old "Coop" used to say, I am a grandmother of 54 with a handsome, healthy, fat and intelligent grandson of 10 months.

The reason for these typewritten sheets is because of an injured right hand which I can not use at present but perhaps my friend, Estella Smith told Vicky this over the phone recently. I do hope you and Vicky enjoy the happiest of "Holidays", and I wish you could get a series on T.V. I know how talented you were and still are!

Well, old dear think I will sig off for now, I'm growing tired.

Give Vicky my love and when you find time write and tell me all the news on your homefront, and I'll see you again on T.V. I hope soon.

I hear from Gilbert Roland and Dick Arlen often, they seem well and both are still handsome. Fans still write me from all parts of the country, amazing isn't it? You know, Jack, there are persistant rumors that reach me, some that I am an alcoholic which I have never been, as you welll know, and others that say I am confined in a rest home which is also untrue, these stories upset me no end. I am enclosing a snapshot of yours truly, taken on my 54th birthday this last July 29th in the living room of my modest little home in Culver City. Ye Gods! What an "It Girl" Write soon- Bye for now.

Clara

85

One night while out in the back yard watching Dundee train, Bow decided he needed more supervision with his exercise. So she got into her bathing suit, a one-piece Annette Kellerman sleeveless model, which in those days we thought was very revealing. Today it would be considered a Mother Hubbard costume. Bow watched him closely, concentrating on all his moves. Then every once in a while she'd stop him and point to one of her own muscles to illustrate just which muscle he needed to concentrate on in order to develop it more. She left him with a muscle to concentrate on and went into the house to answer the phone.

Suddenly she came running out. "Come on everybody! We've got tickets!" she said. "We're going down to the Biltmore to see *Dracula*." She was so excited she didn't stop to dress. She just threw a great long mink coat over her swimsuit, and we all got into her chauffeur-driven black Packard limousine. Bela Lugosi was starring in *Dracula* on the stage of the Biltmore Theatre downtown.

Bow had read about it. "I want to meet that man," she said. "Do you know he doesn't know how to speak English." She couldn't get over the fact that he was on stage for two hours perform-

Bow sent both of us out one night to forage for her new pets.

Some fans had sent her a couple of bears she called "honey bears" from Australia. We all thought they were as cute as the devil until that night. Dundee and I got to Bow's at the same time, and she stopped us at the door. "Wait a minute," she said. "Before you come in, will you both go out someplace and bring back some eucalyptus branches?" We thought the Redhead had lost all her good sense until she explained that eucalyptus was all the honey bears would eat.

Dundee and I got into the limousine with her chauffeur and drove for miles until we found a row of eucalyptus that was put in as a windbreak for a grove of orange trees. We tore away at those trees and drove back with the doors of the car wide open, dragging ten-foot-long branches with lots of bark and leaves for miles. Her house looked like a jungle. Bow finally gave the bears to the zoo, because their diet took up too much of her living room.

Pastel portrait by Henri Sabin (circa 1929-30) hung in Henry's Restaurant for many years.

ing in a language he couldn't speak. Bow kept her mink coat on, and we watched Bela Lugosi in his monstrous makeup with his teeth sticking out, chewing on gals' necks all evening. Then we went backstage.

He couldn't speak English, but no language barrier could hide his thrill at meeting Clara Bow. He was overwhelmed with the Redhead. "How do you know your lines?" Bow asked him immediately. We finally understood the Hungarian's explanation. He told us that he memorized each word from a cue and, if by mistake another actor should ever give him a wrong line, he would be lost for the rest of the night. Bow invited him to her home, and they became very good friends.

The Redhead's father, Bob Bow, whom she loved very much, never grew up. Clara usually gave him everything he asked for, including a restaurant. Bob came up with the idea that he could run a restaurant, and the one he wanted very much was on Beverly Boulevard, near La Brea; so she gave him the money, and he gave her the promise that he'd work hard and make a success of it.

But the only thing he worked hard at was giving her the bills. He gave everything away, he never gave anybody a check, and he invited everybody to be his guest. Bow put up with it, thinking it kept him out of mischief, until the night he called her screaming in terror. I was standing near the phone with her and could hear him. "Clara!" he was yelling at the top of his lungs, "Clara! The stove is burning up and the water pipe broke and it's flooding the whole damn place! What'll I do?"

She slammed the phone down, got a group of us into her car, and we drove down to the restaurant. We put out the fire, stopped the flood, and, after turning off the stove, the water and the lights, she put everybody out of the restaurant — the chef, the waitresses, and the nonpaying customers — and locked the door. She brought the key and her father back home, and the restaurant never opened again.

Although my wife, Vickie, and I were in touch with Clara all her life, the last time we saw her was on her birthday, July 29, 1949, when we took her a huge Frieda Schroeder birthday cake. She was in Los Angeles before going East.

"Oakie," she said, "can you believe it, I haven't slept for years." She looked very beautiful, and her great big purple eyes were bright and alert and had no tell-tale signs to show that they hadn't closed often enough to give her some rest.

We kept in touch with each other through the years and on July 29, 1965, we sent her a telegram.

Jimmy Hall and Jack Oakie — *The Fleet's In.*

She answered: "Thanks for remembering my birthday. I spent the day in the dentist chair. Oh boy what fun. See you one of these days. Keep well."

We never did see her again, because just two months later, on September 27, she died.

Her son, Rex Bell Jr. called me: "Jack, will you be a pall bearer for mother? She especially asked for you."

We put the little girl to rest at Forest Lawn, where she was entombed in the Freedom Mausoleum next to the body of her husband, Rex Bell, former lieutenant governor of Nevada. I enclose a couple of the Redhead's notes so that she may speak for herself.

Editor's Note: Jack never forgot "The Redhead's" birthday. Following is one press account illustrating his antics in this regard:

Los Angeles, California
To celebrate Clara Bow's birthday, July 29th, 1929 the studio planned a surprise party, and had a huge birthday cake wheeled onto her set.

Just as she was about to cut the cake, Jack Oakie quipped:
"Be careful Clara! You know you can't eat your cake and have "IT" too!"

DANCE PEP

Helen Kane and Jack Oakie give the boys and girls something new to spring on the gang at the next collegiate hop. It's called the "Prep Step," and is introduced by the pair in "Sweetie," Paramount's picture of college life. The routine is shown in the following series.—Photos by Dyar.

PREP STEP PING

HELEN KANE, baby voiced singer, who has a featured role in "Sweetie," Paramount's musical romance of campus life, has sung over the radio, in vaudeville, in night clubs, in sound pictures, in musical comedies and has made over three million phonograph records.

SWEETIE

I had been doing Al Jolson imitations all over town. At the drop of a hat I'd go into his *Mammy* number at parties. So when we were making *Sweetie*, Richard Whiting and George Marion, Jr. wrote *Alma Mammy* especially to give me the chance to do my impersonation of Jolson on the screen. *Sweetie* was advertised by Paramount as an "All talking, all singing, all dancing picture," with Nancy Carroll their new star and Helen Kane, the "Boop-Boop-a-Doop" girl. Frank Tuttle was directing, and on the first day of shooting the *Alma Mammy* number everybody on the lot gathered round to watch.

Nathaniel Finston was the orchestra leader, and when he gave me the music I was told to sing just one chorus as Oakie, then stop and say: "And now I'm going to do an impersonation of Al Jolson." Then go into the second chorus singing it as Jolson would. I stood up on the platform and sang full voice with the full orchestra, stopped after the first chorus, looked right into the camera and said my line, explaining to the audience that I was going to sing the second chorus in the Jolson manner. The music came up again, and I went down on my knee and gave a Jolson rendition of the second chorus.

When we stopped for the orchestra's break (they got considerations no actor ever did), Helen Kane, who had been watching, took me aside. "Jack," she said. "Don't stop to explain to the audience what you're going to do. Go right into the second chorus with your Jolson impersonation without stopping; the audience will know what you're doing. You don't have to tell them."

I went over to Frank Tuttle and, without explaining that Helen Kane suggested it, I asked him to let me do as she advised. (In pictures, changes mean trouble, and if anything went wrong with the song, it would have to be my responsibility.) "No!" he said immediately. "You can't do it that way, the music is orchestrated for you to stop and say your lines before you go into the second chorus."

Those were the days before prerecording, and with the full orchestra right there on the set I asked Frank to ask Nathaniel Finston, who had arranged the music, if he could rearrange it so that I could go right into the Jolson impersonation without stopping.

Well, we called a special meeting and Nat said

he could rearrange the music. But Frank was still not sure that it was the right way to shoot the scene, and became adamant. "No, Oakie, you have to stop and say your lines before you go into the second chorus!"

I became adamant. I knew that Helen Kane knew how to deliver a song, she had been doing it very successfully for a long time and was expert, and I had to have the chance to try it her way. We worked on that number all day and finally late that night Nat came up with the new orchestrations. We compromised and shot it both ways, first

---

BUDD SCHULBERG

November, 1974

Dear Jack:

How warmly I remember you from those good old days at Paramount when you were working for my old man, B.P., in such films as "The Fleet's In," "Sweetie," and all those happy college movies. I can still remember B.P.'s saying what a joy it was to have you in his pictures, lighting up the lot. There were some big names who would play up to me because I was the boss' son but when you would give me that open, happy and usually funny hello, I could tell even then that it was the real thing, that you were glad to see me, and that making me laugh sprang from a genuine sense of humor and love of people.

I remember how you made my mother Ad Schulberg laugh, the first time she went in to see Manny Cohen who had succeeded B.P. as head of the studio, and was then in that big office sitting behind the desk that we still felt belonged to my father. She must have had a chip on her shoulder because she stood in front of that great desk and said, "Mr. Cohen, it seems to me that the least you can do when I come to see you here for the first time is to stand up." To which the diminutive Mr. Cohen replied, "Madam, I am standing up." When she came out of the office you were the first person she told that story to. You roared with laughter and then, sensitive to her feelings at having B.P. replaced, pointed down to the ground as if you were admonishing Tom Thumb and said, "That's right, Ad, whenever I have to talk to him I wave my finger at him like this and say 'Now look here, Mr. Cohen!'" Ad remembers how you peered at the ground as if trying to locate this almost invisible little figure. I know that the image of your cheering her up has stayed with her as something vivid, loyal, and engaging to this day.

With fond memories and affection,

Budd Schulberg

Frank's way and then the way Helen said it should be done.

I sang the first chorus and then, without any hesitation, I went right into *Alma Mammy* just as Jolson would. When the picture was previewed, the audience proved that Helen Kane was right. Thanks to Helen I got very good notices and also made some unusual motion picture history, which I accredit to her good judgment — and to Al Jolson's popularity.

Show World, October, 1929

Jack Oakie, in *Sweetie*, while not an old timer whose name has become firmly planted in the public mind, is never-the-less making rapid bids for that kind of desirable fame. He is a new type of talking comic. He has a great voice and he knows how to use it for maximum laughs.

Motion Picture Herald, April, 1930

To Jack Oakie goes the distinction of being the first talkie star to take a recall.

When *Sweetie* was first shown at the Paramount in New York, the audience applauded Jack's singing of *Alma Mammy* so strenuously that they stopped the show. The management rewound the film and had the song repeated before they would allow the picture to continue.

Variety, April, 1930

Whole-hearted applause is remarkable in this advanced day of sound pictures.

For the first time in the annals of the Paramount Theatre, an actor in a talking picture stopped the shw. This happened when Jack Oakie sang *Alma Mammy*. The crowds went wild.

Editor's note: To this day no other actor in a motion picture has ever played an encore during the showing of a performance on the screen of any theatre.

LET'S GO NATIVE

In 1929, when we had been making Talkies for about a year and a half, some of us were already considered veterans of the sound era. But with all our experience, none of us could figure out why it was so hard to record a song. Whenever we made a musical picture, we had to sing every number over and over, time and time again. It was on *Let's Go Native* that a musician let me in on the mystery when he finally told me what time it was. With some of the finest talent in the cast, Jeanette MacDonald, Kay Francis, Skeets Gallagher, Eugene Pallette, and with the great Leo McCarey directing and Richard Whiting's wonderful music, the front office at Paramount went out of their way to give us the best orchestra. They brought in 40 musicians who took up more than half of the stage, and also a group of experts called music coordinators to oversee the music through a specially-built soundproof glass cage. The day I was singing, *I've Got A Yen For You,* those experts kept tapping on that glass cage all day and all night. Every time I finished the number, they tapped on the glass wall; and through a speaker they constantly gave direction to "Take it again!" McCarey would scream back at them: "What's wrong this time?" Some of their reasons didn't make good sense to us but, after all, they were the expert musicians. "The saxophones were too loud. We'll have to move them back a little," they'd explain. Well, when the saxophones weren't too loud, the oboes were too quiet. I had been on the set since 8:00 a.m. and must have gone through that song almost a hundred times. At 8 o'clock that night Sam Jaffee, head of the studio at the time, came down to the set and asked, "what's holding you up?" Leo McCarey took one look at me, a worn out thing with parched throat that could hardly stand up, and said, "I'll be damned if I know!" But that did it for him. He yelled over to the glass cage, "All right you guys, now listen! You better get this thing straightened out before we get back, because this boy isn't going to stand here all night waiting for you to get the bugs out of those instruments!" Then he turned to me, "Come on, Oakie, we're going home to get a drink!" We got into his car, and he drove us over to his house. I remember that when we stepped up on the porch, he tripped over a couple of bicycles. "They're my daughters'," he said good-naturedly, as if tripping over bicycles was an

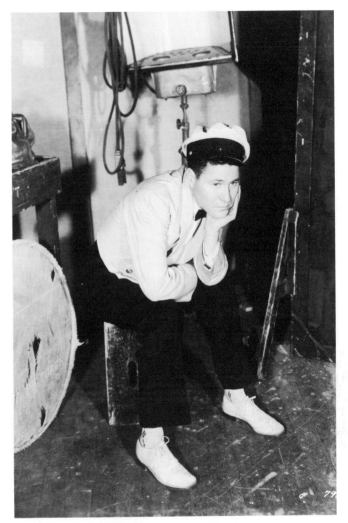

Serious moment while filming *Let's Go Native.*

everyday event. He took me into the living room, and we sat quietly over a drink or two for about an hour. When it seemed to him I was back in voice and could stand up straight again, we got into the car and went right back to the studio. "All right!" McCarey directed into the glass cage, "You be sure you've got those saxes in the right place because I'm not letting Oakie stand up here all night!" "We've got all the bugs out, Mr. McCarey," they called out to him. "We're ready to shoot." I sang *I've Got A Yen For You* just once. McCarey shouted: "Cut! Print it! That's it!" And we all went home before midnight. But it was the night I was singing a number called *Joe Jazz* that I found out what it was that jazzed up those musicians' minds. The number was done in the boat scene, so I was working high up on the deck,

Kay Francis, Jack Oakie and Jeanette MacDonald — *Let's Go Native.*

with those 40 instrumentalists down on the stage right below me. I got along well with the musicians and I always felt that whenever I was played out they were trying to tell me something. Somehow I never quite got the message until I got off the deck that night and went down to the first violinist. We were being held up again, this time waiting for the strings to tune their fiddles. "What time is it?" I asked in tired innocence. I must have hit a proper chord, because he looked at me, then at his watch, and after some quick mental mathematics, explained: "Well, right now Oakie, I'd say it's about ninety-two dollars and seventy cents." "Oh you bastards!" I cried when I realized what he was telling me. "That's what you're all doing! It's the overtime!" When the studios finally stopped that live act, took the musicians off the set, and started to prerecord all music, you should have heard those musicians and glass tappers holler!

OPEN DOOR

I learned early in my motion picture career that an open dressing room door was the framework for kaleidoscopic adventure in Hollywood. As I have never wanted to miss anything, doors to all my dressing rooms were always kept wide open, especially at Paramount. There on dressing room row, I was sandwiched between Clara Bow and W.C. Fields. Clara Bow always had the first room, number 101, W.C. Fields had 103, and for years I had number 102.

When Bow left the lot; I was in line for the honor of number 101, but by that time Sylvia Sydney had a better line than I did and she snagged that first room, so I stayed on in 102. My door was wide open the day that Harold Lloyd came on the lot to make *Milky Way,* and he headed right for it.

"102?" Speedy called through the door to me. (We who knew him well always called Harold Lloyd 'Speedy.') "102 is the wrong number for a comic, Oakie," he said. "Come on down and see a proper number for laughs." I greeted the great performer and joined him in the walk to his dressing room, number 108.

In the vernacular of show business, a "108" is a flopover pratfall. The stunt is just as reliable for a laugh as a pie in the face. "Let's have a 108," the director would say, and the actor would go into a one-and-a-half flopover, and land on his *derriere.* It was backbreaking but sure-fire, and in vaudeville it was considered a standard.

Down at the door of dressing room 108, the publicity department was waiting with a cameraman to welcome the star. They took a picture of Speedy and me at the door and, although I looked up at that number smiling, I also looked up at it respectfully, because not everybody in show business could handle a "108."

Carole Lombard's room was, handily, only two doors down the row from mine. She kept a well-stocked bar, and I could just yell out of my door up to hers whenever I wanted a drink. Carolee, (put the accent on the "o") as we called her, because she had that "e" tacked on the end of her name, was the most gracious hostess on the lot. "Fieldsy," she said to her secretary: Carol Fields (who later married Walter Lang), "you serve Oakie a drink whenever he wants one, no matter when it is, and serve Jack Oakie whatever he asks for." I took advantage of her generosity.

"Carolee!" I'd call out my door, and quick as a

Jack Oakie and Harold Lloyd.

wink she'd send Fieldsy right down with a full glass for me.

One evening after work, George Raft, Gary Cooper, and I joined forces in Lombard's dressing room. We were sitting around enjoying her hospitality and Fieldsy's fine service, when Travis Banton, head clothes-designer at Paramount, came in followed by his helper, Edith Head; they were loaded down, carrying arms full of clothes for a Lombard fitting.

Carole came in right after them and threw us a "Hello, boys." She refused Fieldsy's help to get her out of her wardrobe. "You stay here and fix the boys a drink," she said, and went right through the sitting room into the back room with Travis Banton and Edith Head, and closed the door so that they could work in privacy. Fieldsy continued to fill our glasses as ordered.

Some time later Banton and Head opened the door and came through our sitting room carrying out more "rags" than they had come in with. Without stopping they left us with a couple of tired "goodnights." When Carole came in and joined us, she was wearing a great luxurious full-length mink coat, which she held wrapped tightly around her.

"Don't get up, boys," she said, as she took the drink that Fieldsy fixed for her. "Sorry I can't join

Jack Oakie and Cary Grant.

Carole Lombard and Jack Oakie.

you," she apologized, and stood drinking with us for a moment. "Oh, well," she sighed as she put down her half-finished glass. "I've got to get home to Junior." (She was married to William Powell at the time and, although he was many years her senior, she called him Junior.) "But you stay as long as you like and have a drink on me," she said as she started for the door.

Suddenly she stopped with her back to us, picked up her great mink coat and threw it over her head. "Goodnight you bastards, and have a good time!" she shouted as she "mooned" at us for a fraction of a second. She then quickly dropped the mink and was gone before we realized that she was stark naked. She wasn't wearing a stitch of clothes under that long luxurious mink coat, and the memory of her beautiful behind left us all openmouthed and parched with full glasses in our hands.

One very hot afternoon, when every door was open to invite a breath of air, Tallulah Bankhead and I were sitting in my dressing room enjoying some of Lombard's refreshment, when Eddie Cline, the great comedy director, came in through my open door and joined us. I introduced him to Bankhead, and she began to impress him with stories of grandeur I'd never heard the gal tell before. When Eddie left, Bankhead resumed her beautiful natural voice and asked, "By the way, Oakie, what does that Eddie Cline do?"

"Why, E. Francis Cline is a director," I told her. "He does all of W.C. Field's pictures. He's the best comedy director in the business."

Jack standing in front of the Brown Derby Jewelry store on Vine Street.

Jack Oakie, W. C. Fields and Ben Turpin — *Million Dollar Legs.*

"Oh, my God!" she let out in her deepest tones. "I thought he was with the newspapers! Get him back here — I have to change my whole delivery!"

I had just begun to laugh, enjoying the Bankhead humor, when a screeching cry got us both to my open door at the same time. Carole Lombard was running from door to door screaming, "Come on everybody! Hurry! The black snake is out! Hurry!" Bankhead and I joined Freddie March and old Bill Fields as we all ran after Carole to find out what she was yelling about.

"What snake?" Fields kept asking. "Where's a black snake?"

We made so much noise with Lombard screaming, and all of us running after her, that every window in the writers' building right across the street opened, and leaning way out over the sills, Bill McNutt and Grover Jones, (the forerunners to Ben Hecht and Charles MacArthur for shenanigans on the lot) joined the hollering with: "Where's a black snake?" "Who's got a black snake?" But Carole didn't stop to answer any questions. She kept screaming hysterically: "Follow me! Hurry! The black snake is out!"

"There! There! There!" she continued to scream as she pointed through the open door of George Raft's dressing room. We gathered round his door and looked. "See? There! There! The black snake!" she yelled. We saw George Raft lying on his cot. He was completely naked except for a small handtowel covering his face. The black snake was sure out and Raft sure knew it, but he continued to pose for that still life picture and

never did remove the towel from his face.

A few years later I was working with Betty Grable when she and Raft were the town's twosome. Betty was trying to think of an unusual birthday gift to buy for George.

"Oakie, what the devil do you think I ought to get for that man?" she asked me. Well, the devil must have known that she was going to ask me, because just the day before I had seen a cigarette lighter that must have been designed with Raft in mind. It was a fourteen-karat gold mesh snake, lacquered all in black, with diamond eyes — a gleaming black snake. It was in the window at "Kabotchnick's" (that's what I used to call him), who had the little luxury jewelry shop right next to the Hollywood Brown Derby. "I know just the thing," I told her, and took her to the shop. It was a cute little old thing, but it sure cost a bundle.

"Kabotchnick" looked at the price tag and then at us and then pulled his age-old gag: "Now for you I can let it go for . . ." and he let it go at a very expensive bargain. Grable bought it and I dictated the card. It read, "To the black snake."

Betty was too young to know the significance of the gift and the line. "Oakie, you should have seen his face light up when he took it out!" she told me. It was my guess that Raft wasn't wearing the towel over his face when he received the lighter.

One morning my agent, Morris Small, and I were sitting in my dressing room talking and looking out of my open door, when we noticed one of the most beautiful gals the studio had ever

Groucho Marx, Fay Wray, Jack Oakie, Stuart Erwin with Mitzi Green on his knee, Carole Lombard, Eugene Pallette, Norman Foster and Skeets Gallagher.

Front Row: Mitzi Green, Jackie Searle and Sylvia Sidney; 2nd Row: Dick Arlen, Carole Lombard, Wynne Gibson, Gary Cooper, Rosita Moreno, Norman Foster and Lilyan Tashman; 3rd Row: Stuart Erwin, Eugene Pallette, Clive Brook, Kay Francis, Jack Oakie, Skeets Gallagher and Bill (stage) Boyd.

George Raft and Jack Oakie — *Dancers in the Dark*.

signed come out of the casting office. As she closed the door behind her, she took a handkerchief out of her purse and wiped her eyes. Morris and I could tell she had been crying. She adjusted a large folder she was carrying under her arm, drew herself up, and headed right for my dressing room. She stood outside the door trying to smile.

"Mr. Oakie, would you please autograph your picture for me?" She asked as she opened the folder. There were a dozen or more 8 x 10 glossy pictures of the stars at Paramount with my portrait right on top of the lot. She handed me the picture and burst into tears.

"Here, here, things can't be that bad," I said, as Morris and I helped her up into the dressing room and sat her down in a chair.

"I've got to go home," she sobbed. "The studio is not picking up my option." She had won a "Search for Beauty" contest and had been given a short-term contract with Paramount.

"Well, now, going home can't be all that bad?" I asked, trying to be cheerful.

But Morris, who was always the agent, took a good look at that beautiful girl and asked, "Do you want to stay here in Hollywood?"

"Oh yes! I do!" she said quickly.

"Well, we'll see what can be done about it," Morris said, and went into my back room to use the phone. In no time at all he came back and said,

"Now, little girl, you just sit right here." Then he turned to me and said, "Jack, watch this."

In just a few minutes we saw Fred Datig, the head of the casting department, come dashing out of his door and, without hesitating, he came right straight for my dressing room. He paid no attention to Morris or to me. "Oh good! Here you are!" he said to the beautiful gal. "I've been looking all over the lot for you. Come on now, honey, you come right on back to my office; I want to talk to you."

Morris and I watched the two of them hotfoot it back across the lot. "Now, how did all that come about?" I asked.

Morris was smiling. "It's the oldest trick in the book," he said. "I just called a couple of producers at Universal and RKO and asked them to call Paramount to inquire if the girl was available."

That very beautiful girl stayed in Hollywood long enough to go from movies to television, and become the producer of one of the most popular shows in the history of television. Of course, that good old trick became obsolete when we lost the big studios, but I often wonder if Gail Patrick ever got the picture of what Morris Small did that day. I know she never did get my autograph, because I still have the picture she handed me and left behind.

THE TURKEY WAS A HIT

In show business when a play is a flop we call it a "turkey." Sometimes, however, with the help of an angel a turkey can be saved and become a hit. More than forty-five years ago, during my very early days in Hollywood when I was a brand new contract player at Paramount studios, I once had a turkey on my hands. Luckily, with the help of an angel in Brentwood, it became the hit of the season.

It was on the night before Thanksgiving. Artie Jacobson, Paramount's number one assistant director, and I were standing at the curb, watching the Santa Claus Parade on Hollywood Boulevard. It was the first one they had ever had, and the little thing started at Highland Avenue and came east to Vine Street. The merchants had chipped in for a little old, low buckboard on wheels, with decorated slats sticking up out of the four corners of it, that they called a sled.

Joe E. Brown had agreed to ride in it and play Santa Claus. Four other fellows from the studio walked along with it. One at each corner holding on to the slats and pushing, to be sure the sled would move on down the Boulevard.

In those days Hollywood was just a very quiet little village. All the action was downtown in Los Angeles. The Santa Claus Parade was put on to try to get a piece of that action. It didn't help. Very few people were out there on the boulevard, and very few stopped to see what was going on.

The following year, the merchants got another idea. They chipped in and put blowup pictures of movie stars on the trees up and down Hollywood Boulevard. Mine was put up right in front of the old Hollywood Hotel. Then they tried to charge us for it. They sent their bills to the studios. We didn't pay.

That night, Jake and I stood there at the curb and watched the whole parade, because we knew everybody in it and had fun exchanging jokes as they meandered by. It didn't take very long and, when the sled with Joe E. Brown came up to us, at the end, Brownie was sitting in it so darn low, he had to stretch his neck to look up at us to say his "Ho! Ho! Ho!"

Sam Hardy came up behind me and yelled, "Hey Oakie, look! There goes my suit!" Sam stretched his arm out and pointed an accusing finger over at Duke York. We were so close to each other Sam could wave his finger under Duke's nose. Duke York, who did all of Sam's stand-in work, was holding on to one of the slats pushing the sled.

"Now you take good care of that suit!" Sam warned him. (A stand-in usually wears the star's clothes while the cameraman lights up a scene.) Duke began to brush his suit daintily, to show Sam how careful he was trying to be, while he exaggerated the hard job of pushing the sled. We all laughed so hard we broke up the parade. Brownie's "Ho! Ho! Ho!" was no longer the jolly greeting of Santa Claus. He was "Ha! Ha! Hahing!" and couldn't round those extra large lips of his to say his lines.

Those paraders finally made it down the block to the empty lot on the southwest corner of Hollywood Boulevard and Vine Street, where the official disbanding took place. Today that empty lot is the site of the Broadway Department Store. In those days, it was my short cut home from Henry's Restaurant to my furnished room at Mrs. Powell's little white wooden, two-story boardinghouse on Sunset Boulevard and Morningside Court — 6353 Sunset Boulevard. That was right across the street from the Muller brothers' gas station, which is now the location of the Cinerama Theatre.

Just a few moments after the parade was over, Hollywood Boulevard was once again a quiet deserted street. It was a typical, clammy, foggy Southern California November evening, and Jacobson and I had no place to go. As we stood there at the curb, we were in front of the Iris Theatre. Jake looked up and read the marquee. *Manhattan Cocktails.* Say, Jack," he said, "I worked on that picture with Harry d'Arrast. Let's go in and see what it looks like." H. d'Abbadie d'Arrast was the French director under contract to Paramount. He was married to that beautiful star, Eleanor Boardman.

"OK with me," I said. Besides being glad to get in out of the damp night, I was always interested in what other contract members of the Paramount Studios were doing. I bought the tickets. They cost twenty-five cents a piece. The ticket taker tore the tickets and gave me the stubs, and we no sooner entered the theatre than the house lights went up. Jake and I stood at the back of the aisle as the theatre manager came onto the stage with an usher who was carrying a large fishbowl full of tickets.

Arthur Jacobson and Jack Oakie.

"Happy Thanksgiving!" the manager said. "And now we'll get right to the drawing for the biggest turkey in Hollywood. Everybody look at your ticket stub. We're going to pick the winning number."

A pretty girl who was sitting in the first row went up on the stage. The manager introduced her as a teller in one of the banks. She was chosen to draw the lucky number from the fishbowl. I guess working at the bank gave the girl and the game of chance some validity. As the audience applauded her, she put her hand into the bowl.

"Look at your ticket now," the manager warned, "here comes the winning number." The girl handed him a ticket and he read the number. It had five or six figures, and he read each one very distinctly. There was no response from the audience. He read the number again louder and slower. "Will everybody please look at their tickets," he instructed, but again there was no response. I still had our ticket stubs in my hand so, without thinking, I took direction from the manager; and as I didn't need reading glasses in those days, I just held out my hand and read the numbers.

"Jake, look," I said to Artie *sotto voce*, "we've got the number." I held up the ticket for him to read.

"Yeah," he said, "you're right."

"Here, Jake," I said, "go on up and get the turkey." I tried to hand the ticket to him.

"Oh, no!" he said. "You bought the tickets, the turkey's yours." He shoved me down the aisle as he called out, "Here's the ticket! Here's the number!"

"Ah, here you are!" the manager said when I got up on the stage. He sounded as if I were a prize that he had just won. He compared the numbers, and sure enough I was right, they matched. The usher who had carried on the bowl

of tickets left the stage and returned with the biggest turkey in Hollywood, wrapped in cellophane and ribbons and crinkling with crispness. We all knew each other in those days; even the theatre manager recognized me.

"Jack Oakie," he announced, "has just won the biggest turkey in Hollywood." He handed me the cold heavy package, and I got back up the aisle to Jake through some applause and some pretty fowl jokes.

"Well, what are we going to do with it?" I asked. "You don't expect me to sit through the picture with this on my lap?"

"You're right," Artie said. "Let's go find somebody to cook it for us." We left the theatre. We never even got a seat, and we never ever saw that picture.

When we got out on the street, the "dummy" newsboy, who had been inside the theatre when we won the turkey, came running up to us. "Bah, bah, bah," he made his usual gutteral sounds. He had gone nextdoor to the coffee shop and picked up a knife and fork, and with a napkin tucked into his collar he gestured that he wanted to share in the eating of the turkey. "The Dummy," Joe Hermano, was deaf and dumb. He was a little man less than five feet tall. He used to sell his newspapers in front of Henry's Restaurant, which was on the north side of Hollywood Boulevard, just west of Vine Street. When Henry's closed, he moved across the street and set up his large newsstand right on the Southeast corner of Hollywood and Vine. "The Dummy" was in Hollywood as long as I can remember. He was very popular, and everybody loved him; with his innate sense of humor he got more laughs without sound than we who needed writers to help us talk.

"Very funny!" I said to his joke with the knife and fork, and gestured that we had no way to cook it and he'd have to eat it raw.

"Bah, bah, bah," he said, and returned the eating utensils to the coffee shop. Joe and I were very good friends; he was the best clipping service I ever had. A good many of the old newspaper articles that are in my scrapbooks were given to me by "the Dummy." It was a great personal loss when I learned the tragic news that he was killed a few years ago by hoodlums.

"Well," said Jake, "come on, let's go find somebody to cook it for us. You can't hold on to it all night." He was right. I couldn't put it up with me in my room at Mrs. Powell's, and Jake couldn't keep it in his room on Bronson that we called an apartment just because his Murphy bed could fold into the wall when not in use. (I don't, however, ever remember seeing that bed tucked away. Jake kept it handy at all times for all emergencies.)

Anyway, we had no way to cook it, we had no way to keep it, and I depended on Jake to help transport it. That turkey came into my life before I had a car of my own. When I finally did get my first car it was a shiny black Model A Ford with the newest style in gearshifting. It had a stick coming up out of the floor instead of those three pedals that the standard model had. It cost five hundred fifty dollars, and the day it was delivered to me at the studio the salesman handed me a driver's license.

"I don't know how to drive," I said.

"That's all right. It won't take you long to learn," he said and handed me a gift license giving me the right to drive, just so that he could sell an automobile. I think the salesman was greedy and hoped it would take two or three cars before I learned how to handle one safely. But I wasn't as stubborn as Chaplin. I just petted my car and kept it at the Muller brothers' gas station until I got Ruth Mix, Tom's daughter, to take me out to the wilderness of Van Nuys and teach me exactly how to drive it before I began to put any mileage on it. In the meantime, Frank Muller, who sold me my gasoline, named me his best "one-gallon customer."

So I carried the turkey over to Jake's car, a Wills St. Claire. It was a runabout with a rumble seat, and the paint job was green with red trimming. He had it parked in front of Henry's Restaurant, and it was easy to spot, since it was the only car on the boulevard. We put the turkey into the open rumble seat and, practically in unison, we said, "the Redhead!" Artie was the assistant director of all of Clara Bow's pictures, and she was one of the best friends I had in those very early days. So it was only natural that we should both think of her first when we had a turkey on our hands.

Singing "Sweet Sue" at the tops of our lungs ("Sweet Sue" was the hit number written especially for The Fleet's In), the three of us rode right over to Beverly Hills to 521 Bedford Drive. But Clara Bow wasn't home. We hadn't figured on that, and our silence proved it. Finally Artie said, "Whatta we do now?" I was sharp in those days; it didn't take me long to think of Gene Pallette.

"Pallette! He'll cook it for us!" I said. Eugene Pallette had gone to my mother's school, in Sedalia, Missouri, so when I caught up with him in Hollywood, he felt obliged to sort of look after her son. He was a wonderful friend; that grand character actor with his deep froglike voice was also an amateur chef who loved to put on his high white starched hat and huge apron. His shrimp Newburg was famous at the studio. So we headed

right back to Hollywood and went directly to the La Belle Tour Apartments at 6200 Franklin Avenue. Gene had the penthouse, and I spent many very interesting hours up there with him enjoying that beautiful four-way view. But Eugene Pallette wasn't home.

Well, after that Jake thought of someone, and then I thought of someone, and with the turkey riding high in the open rumble seat, we went back and forth and up and down Hollywood, until it was too late to ring another doorbell. Either nobody was home, or we were turned away with "No thanks! We've got a turkey!" or just "No thanks!"

We finally went up to Jake's apartment. We were tired, and the turkey was warming up. His wilted cellophane didn't crinkle anymore. The three of us flopped down on the Murphy bed. "In the vernacular of show business," Artie said, "we've sure got a turkey on our hands."

"That's show business," I said. "It's a fascinating business. Here's a bird all dressed for the part and he just can't get into the act!"

"Think!" Artie said. "Think! There must be somebody we can call." So I took direction from the assistant director, and started to think. Flash! I suddenly had an electric bulb light up over my head! "Pittsy!" I said. ZaSu Pitts was the best-natured gal in the world. Even calling her at that late hour would not have been considered bad taste.

"You got her telephone number with you?" Jake asked.

"Certainly I've got her number with me!" and I pointed to my head. It's a wonder I didn't burn my hand in the heat of that overhead light! (Joke) I got on the phone. "Pittsy," I said, "I won a turkey in a theatre raffle, and Artie Jacobson and I have no way to cook it or keep it."

She was wonderful. "You boys bring it right out here immediately," she said. "We'll cook it here for you, and you and Artie come to Thanksgiving dinner tomorrow."

Jake and I headed right back out to Brentwood. We drove up the long driveway to her house on that spacious hill on Rockingham Road, and delivered the turkey. Pittsy took it and said, "I've got a good cook, and she'll cook it right along with our turkey. Don't forget now, we'll see you tomorrow; come early."

Thanksgiving Day Jake and I got there early. It was a delicious dinner. We sat at the dining room table and kept right on eating for hours. The two turkeys made a heck of a good entry. They started together and were now finishing in a dead heat. ZaSu had four Great Dane dogs, and they too got in on the feast. They were so big they just stood at

Screenograph

DEAF MUTE 'PAL' JOINS WELCOME FOR JACK OAKIE

By HARRISON CARROLL
(Copyright, 1930, Premier Syndicate)

Several friends of Jack Oakie's witnessed a touching bit of sentiment when they congregated at the railroad station to welcome the comedian back from New York.

Jack Oakie

As Jack swung down the steps a young fellow ran toward him, uttering strange, weird little cries and embraced the actor. The boy was reluctant to let go, and Jack, with moist eyes, explained that he was his pal.

The incident also held a heart throb for everyone else who recognized the boy. He is known as the "Dummy" around Hollywood. "Dummy" is a deaf mute who sells papers in front of a boulevard restaurant where Jack usually has his dinner. He had left his stand in order to be one of the first to welcome his friend home.

Jack has had no time for vacationing since his arrival, for he immediately went into rehearsals for his forthcoming picture, as yet untitled. It's a story of a sailor, and will be directed by Victor Heerman. Lillian Roth will play opposite.

the table and helped themselves from our plates. When we left the dining room and went down the two steps that led into the magnificent living room, the four dogs took over.

I sat in a big easy chair near the steps watching the Great Danes work on the turkey. Pittsy finally decided that dogs should not be allowed to walk on the table. "Oakie," she called to me, "help me take these hounds down to the kennels." We put leashes on the four of them and pulled them through the living room to the front door. ZaSu opened the door, put me out with the dogs, and pointed down the hill. "Jack, you take them down to the kennels and lock the enclosure." Once outside the door, the dogs headed right down the hill and dragged me with them. I finally let go of those leashes, and they went right into the corral to their dinner bowls. I closed and latched the gate.

When I got back to the house, Pittsy and a friend of hers were putting on an act. ZaSu played the piano, and her friend, who had a beautiful voice, sang from behind a screen while Pittsy mouthed the words of the song. They did the act so well that those who had never seen them pull the stunt before thought that ZaSu was actually singing.

I no sooner got back into that easy chair, when the doorbell rang. David O. Selznick and Bernie Fineman, both producer-writers under contract to Paramount Studios at the time, came into the living room. They tiptoed and whispered their hellos, trying not to disturb Pittsy's singing act. I watched them as they neared the two steps that led up into the dining room. Their eyes widened when they saw the food on the uncleared dining room table.

"We're starved," Selznick whispered to me. "Been to a couple of parties before we got here." He beckoned to Fineman to follow him, and they both stumbled up the two steps as they went right for the table. David O. Selznick and Bernard Fineman were hungry! Even the Great Danes had not shown such anxiety when they were at the table.

I had only just begun to make talking pictures and didn't want to be silenced that early in my career. So I saved all my dialogue for the screen and said nothing, as I just sat and watched. Our turkey was a hit!

GRANITE

When Arthur Kober, the great wit, first wrote for "The Oakie College Radio Show," I surprised him by telling him that he had written for me before.

"Why, Oakie, when did I do that?" he asked.

"About ten years ago," I confessed, "I took a word from those folks in the Bronx you write about for *the New Yorker*, who never take anything or anybody for 'granite'. That word, combined with the silent voices of some of the greatest stars in motion pictures, once saved the lives of over one thousand people."

It happened on one of those very cold, damp, dewy, Southern California nights, when newcomers to the West Coast learn that a convertible car isn't all that much fun, because with the top down, the seat which was too hot in the daytime is too cold and wet at night.

Paramount had loaned me out to Radio Pictures (the original name of the RKO Studios) for their musical wonder show, *Hit The Deck,* the screen version of the great Broadway play with the famous and still popular music by Vincent Youmans, and lyrics by Leo Robin and Irving Caesar. The studio advertised that the All-Talking, All-Song Hit, All-Dance Hit had a special added attraction! For the first time on any screen there was one scene photographed in the new invention, color film, called "Technicolor." Once and for all, they said, *Hit The Deck* was going to prove that the screen was the ideal medium for musical comedy!

In those very early days of talking pictures, Radio Pictures Studio was also converting their silent stages into sound stages, and they, too, had construction crews of carpenters and electricians working all day long. So actors had to come to work after the builders went home. We worked all night long and into the morning hours — right up to the time they came back with their hammers and nails.

The entire production of *Hit The Deck* was shot at night and, as the sound equipment couldn't be taken out to the location of a real battleship, they built an exact replica of the U.S.S. *West Virginia,* to make it possible to film in sound. The deck of the battleship, a dock, and a coffee shop made up the huge set. It was constructed away from where the sound stages were being built, and it took up the entire back lot, right up to the stone wall that blocked off the north side of the studio. For realism, the property men burned smoke pots to

simulate a bit of fog, so that the stationary battleship would appear to be sitting in some moving water. Luther Reed, our director, was so dedicated to making this the greatest musical picture that he seemed to lose sight of all other considerations.

That cold dewy night there were about one thousand sailors in the scene, as I sang "Sometimes I'm Happy" to Polly Walker. Polly, a Broadway star, was brought out from New York to star as Loo Loo. She was one of the few gals who got hep to the unglamorous end of movie-making real fast. That was the only picture she ever made, and she was glad to get out of the business alive.

We were working with the orchestra, a choral group, and Victor Baravalle, the music coordinator. In those days of no prerecording, we had to keep doing the song over and over again until we got it right. That night it seemed to be harder than ever to get enough silence on the set. The sound men kept complaining that they were picking up too much noise.

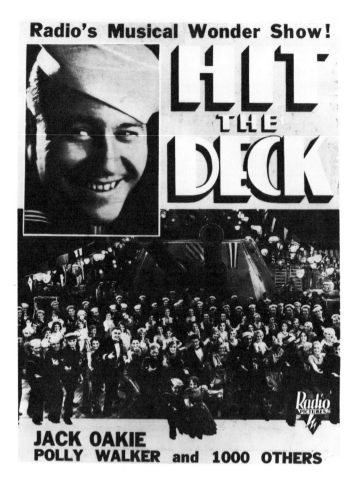

"What's wrong now?" Luther Reed called through his silver megaphone.

"It's the camera," they called back. "It's right on top of Oakie's voice." That early camera's grinding noises were being recorded right along with my singing.

"Well, get some more blankets! Wrap it up!" Luther Reed ordered. The camera was already practically buried in blankets to try to muffle its sounds. By three o'clock in the morning, the musicians were becoming too cold and their instruments too wet to play, and I began having real trouble with that good old Southern California cold night dew. Every time I opened my mouth to sing "Sometimes I'm Happy," I covered Polly's face with my steaming breath. Luther Reed kept trying to move her into positions to avoid my musical smoke screen.

"All right! Let's take it again!" he ordered.

"Mr. Reed, just a minute." One of the property men came up with a pitcher of ice water. "Try having Oakie drink some of this ice water before each *take*" he suggested. "It'll stop the steam." Buckets later when my tongue was too stiff to handle the lyrics, the sound man interrupted.

"What's wrong now?" Luther Reed called

through his cupped hands. His beautiful silver megaphone had become too cold and wet to put to his mouth.

"Can't make out Oakie's words, and the wires are getting cold," he complained.

"Well, do something! Get some blankets! Wrap them up!" Luther Reed was now ordering blankets for cold wires. We stopped for the property men to wrap up the sound equipment, and I took advantage of the wait to find some comfort myself. When I got to the washrooms, there were hundreds waiting their turn.

"My God, what's happening? Is everybody drinking ice water?" I asked one of the property men who was standing in line with me. He shook his head and put his fingers to his lips as if he were trying to keep a secret. "Well, there's sure something in the air tonight," I said, wondering what the mystery was.

He got closer to me and whispered, "Oakie, you're right. There sure is something in the air."

"We ran out of the regular fuel for the smoke pots, and the only stuff we could get was some Nujol over at the all-night drug store." He poked his elbow into my ribs trying to make a joke of it, as he said, "You know, that darn stuff works just as good whether you drink it or just smell it, and this whole darn company's been smelling it for over an hour."

The assistant called, "Let's go! Come on everybody, let's go! Let's take it again!" I got back to the set but, combined with drinking ice water and inhaling Nujol, that cold wet night didn't seem to put me in the right mood for singing a love song.

"All right now, everybody quiet down!" Luther Reed shouted. "And tell those people over there to keep quiet! You up there!" he called to an electrician who was working the sun arc from the top of a fifteen-foot-high parallel. "Tell those people over there to keep quiet!" And he pointed over the stone wall. The electrician looked down from his perch over the wall in the direction that Luther Reed pointed.

"Nobody's making any noise over here, Mr. Reed. No sir. I give you my word, the people over here aren't making a sound." He pointed over the wall and shook his head. "No sir. Not a sound coming from over here!"

Luther Reed looked up at the electrician, looked over at the wall, and couldn't contain his curiosity. "What the devil is he talking about?" he mumbled. The assistant set a stepladder for him, and we all followed his lead and scaled the wall to look. There they were — all those rows of stone and marble, nestling in the stillness of the Hollywood Memorial Park Cemetery. None of us had

Hit the Deck.

remembered that this garden wall separated the studio back lot from that beautiful park. At that time the stars in that park had only been seen and not heard, because the star machine was known as "the silent screen." But the machine had suddenly found its voice, and here we were going through a period of growing pains while the machine learned to use its voice.

That night those growing pains almost killed some of us who were trying so hard to be heard. "See, Mr. Reed, they're not saying a word," the electrician repeated.

"Oh yes they are!" I spoke up through chattering teeth to Luther Reed. "They're saying that actors shouldn't be taken for 'granite'!"

"All right, Oakie," Luther Reed agreed as he said the first warm words that night. "All right. Wrap it up everybody! That's all for tonight!" he ordered.

Arthur Kober said that if I could get just one word of his to do so much for so many, he was glad to be writing for me again.

Fay Cameron with Jack Oakie — *Dancers in the Dark*.

GARBOPHILE

Most publicity stunts used to run off the sun-tanned, oiled hides of West Coast actors just like water from that famous duck's back. But not Greta Garbo's "I vant to be alone." One day a group of us reputed to be movie actors gathered for a drink in Adolphe Menjou's dressing room at Metro-Goldwyn-Mayer when someone noticed Greta Garbo crossing the lot to her car.

"There goes Garbo!" The excited voice had a catch in its throat as we heard, "Hurry! Hurry!" We all leaped to the window to get a glimpse of her. I was leaning over Menjou's shoulder peering out the small inadequate window, when that veteran of sophistication said, "What the devil are we doing? Are we some kind of movie fans? We've worked with the best of them, Gloria Swanson, Norma Shearer, Joan Crawford, Vilma Banky, Clara Bow. Come on boys, back to our drinks!"

He drew himself up and led us back to our glasses and chairs, and we all followed suit by also trying to assume an air of disinterest. But because Garbo did keep to herself and did live her publicity and never was a part of the camaraderie of our little community, it was a much desired coup to see her in person.

One time when I was visiting Claude Binyon at his Toluca Lake home, I looked through the tall hedges that separated his property from George Brent's. I found myself face to face with her beautiful face as she stared right back at me. I did what any intelligent motion picture actor would do: I stood still, opened my mouth and remained silent. It was Garbo who put some action into the scene by pulling down her large hat to cover her face and left me to close the gap.

When I finally could, I ran to tell Claude: "I just saw Garbo! She's right on the other side of the hedge. Come on!" I urged. But Claude played the sophisticate that time. "She's there all the time," he informed me.

"Wow!" I said. (My emotional vocabulary is limited.) But I promised myself that the next time I saw her I would talk to her. Well, the very next time is the one Mary Brian likes to tell about. Mary and I were rowing across the lake in the Mary B, a rowboat I had given her for her birthday. We were on our way to a party at Binyon's house and had to pass George Brent's bank pretty closely in order to moor at Claude's dock. As we came up, there they were, George and Garbo, sitting at the water's

Miriam Hopkins with Jack Oakie — *Dancers in the Dark*.

edge. Although Mary and I were still in the boat, we made an intimate foursome. In the excitement of that unexpected close proximity to Garbo, I forgot I meant to talk to her, and turned instead to Mary and shouted, "Look, Garbo's looking at me, make her stop looking at me, make her stop looking at me!"

George Brent and Greta Garbo left as quickly and as quietly as they could. And Mary Brian still laughs heartily whenever she tells the story of noisy Oakie assuming the Garbo public image. But my promise to talk to Garbo was finally fulfilled when I pulled my car up to a boulevard stop in Beverly Hills. I looked over at the car that had pulled up parallel to mine. It was Adrian, the dress designer, driving Garbo. Sitting on the passenger side, she was just a few feet from me. As we looked at each other I nodded and smiled and, in the fraction of a second the cars paused for that stop sign, we had a long conversation! She said, "Hello."

Later I was in New York preparing to shoot a picture at the Paramount Studios Astoria, Long Island, when the news broke that Garbo was in from Hollywood. The knowledge that Garbo was in the city had New Yorkers looking under brims of ladies' hats hoping to be able to say that they had seen her in person. One evening I was across the street from the Savoy Plaza, when I recognized a press agent I knew from Hollywood. He was at a telescope barking, "See the moon, just twenty-five cents, only a quarter of a dollar to see the moon."

He was surrounded by quite a crowd waiting to look into his telescope. He saw me and knew me, but gave me the old dead fish eye, so I decided to find out why he had such a crowd of impatient customers waiting to look into that scope of his. Knowing his type of work, I couldn't believe it was the moon he was selling: besides, I noticed that his telescopic sights were leveled pretty low for that full shiner which was right straight over our heads at the time.

I tried to get through to him and his telescope. "Get back there and wait your turn!" I was advised. Have you ever been admonished by a crowd of New Yorkers? I waited! It wasn't very long before I too heard the magic word: "Garbo!" Over heads I watched him as he hurried each greedy ogling customer so that I was finally next in line.

"Hi, Oakie," he acknowledged me, now that we were at handshaking distance. "See the moon, just twenty-five cents." And then in a confidential whisper, "Want to see Garbo? For a buck I'll tell you where to look." Without hesitation he moved the telescope so that it pointed to a window at the Savoy Plaza.

"What? No moon?" I asked. I started to hand him the dollar.

"Not for you, Oakie. Please be my guest." When he refused payment I knew he expected something for that dollar; however, I closed one eye and looked. What I saw was the spittin' image of Garbo walking past an open window of the hotel. The image was clothed only in a slip, it stopped to light a cigarette and picked up a comb and leisurely combed its hair. It put down the comb and picked up the still-burning cigarette, and came back to the window for a breath of fresh New York air. I was watching the stilted action of a "B" picture. The image had just so many moves to make and if the press agent hadn't moved his ogling clients fast enough they would have been watching the same show over and over again.

The image was an actress we knew in Hollywood who did look exactly like Garbo. Fay Cameron was a lovely actress who had a part in *Dancers in the Dark,* the Paramount picture with Miriam Hopkins, William Collier Jr., Eugene Pallette, myself and George Raft who was also just making his start then.

"What are you paying her?" I asked *SOTTO VOCE.*

"Fifty bucks a day," he whispered. "And it's like a vacation for her."

Through the studio, he knew of Garbo's traveling schedule and timed this act to coincide with her stay in New York. He brought the actress to New York, rented a telescope, and was receiving a good return on his investment. The dollar he invested in me paid for my silence and, as he shook my hand and pulled me out of the way of the next paying customer, he spoke loud enough for all to hear, "Thank you, Mr. Oakie." And then he passed the word along, "Jack Oakie, folks, he's her number-one fan!"

That's a press agent for you, always letting the public in on your innermost secrets!

Adolphe Menjou, Tony Martin, Jack Oakie and Binnie Barnes — *Thanks for Everything.*

JACKIE-O

"Jackie-O!" he greeted me. I looked up and there he was, Joseph P. Kennedy Jr., the eldest, and I think the handsomest of all the Kennedy boys. He was resplendent in his navy uniform. "May I join you?" he asked, as he stood in the aisle of the plane. I was in the window seat, and the adjoining aisle chair was unoccupied.

"Come on, sit down!" I urged. I was very glad to see my young friend again. He sat down beside me, and we hopped from New York to Florida together. (The flight was called hopping because of the many short stops. There was no direct plane to anywhere in those days.)

"Jackie-O," he loved the sound of that name he had given me, and I loved hearing him say it. "What are you doing here in the East?" he asked. This was 1942, and all the lights on the West Coast were turned off.

"We're so blacked out back there in California," I explained, "they're sending Betty Grable and me down to Miami, where they can light up the marquee for the premiere of *Song Of The Islands.*

That trip was the last time I ever heard Joe call me "Jackie-O." The first time was during the Christmas holidays in St. Moritz, Switzerland, in 1938. The whole Kennedy clan was there, and Joseph Jr. was young enough to enjoy my pictures and just old enough for us to enjoy each other's company. "Jackie-O," he tagged me, and laughed at everything I said. He was the best audience I ever had. His father, who had been my boss at RKO, thought I was good too.

The manager of the Palace Hotel, Hans Badrutt, asked me to play Santa Claus for all the children in the neighborhood. The hotel took great pride in its yearly tradition of having a celebrity play the role for them. They gave me the Santa suit that Charles Laughton had worn the year before, and as I was younger and slimmer in those days they had to pad my stomach with goosedown pillows. The big black belt and buckle held the soft puff in place. When I entered the great ballroom on Christmas Day, there were at least fifty anxious little faces waiting for me. "Ho, ho, ho!" I bellowed, using that very original line for my entrance. There was screeching and clapping as the children watched me put down the huge knapsack filled with gifts for all.

"Ho, ho, ho!" I continued as I sat down in the

Jack Oakie and Lillian Porter — *Song of the Islands.*

big armchair. Joe brought his baby brother, Teddy, over to meet Santa Claus. The six-year-old was so darn curious about my pillowed stomach, I was sure he was going to expose my cover-up. When the investigation had gone just about as far as it could, I lifted him up and set him on my lap. With Teddy on my lap and the rest of the happy, lively audience gathered close around me, I was sure I'd get some pretty good laughs; so I became the comedian.

"Is this St. Moritz, Switzerland?" I asked them, as if I were checking up to be sure I had landed in the right place. Fifty little faces just stared at me with wonder in their eyes. I guessed that they thought Santa Claus, the world traveller, ought to know where he was. "When I came through the lobby just now," I continued, trying for a surefire laugh, "a man stopped me, and told me that he hadn't had a bite in a week. So I bit him." Those hundred wide-open eyes stared at me, wondering what the heck I was talking about. I looked over at Joe; he was laughing. I looked down at Teddy, and he seemed to be chuckling; otherwise there wasn't a snicker in the room.

After a few more gems from the Joe Miller Joke Book, the guide that has guaranteed laughs for almost a hundred years, I decided the high alti-

Victor Mature, Walter Lang and Jack Oakie marching back to set for *Song of the Islands.*

Victor Mature, Betty Grable and Jack Oakie — *Song of the Islands.*

Jack Oakie, Mrs. Rosie Dolly Netcher, (two unidentified guests), Irving Netcher and Joseph P. Kennedy, Jr. — Palace Hotel, St. Moritz, Switzerland, New Years 1938.

tude was against me, and the only way to cut the ice was to give out the presents. I put Teddy down, and opened the knapsack. I was right, my audience came to life again.

"I guess actions speak louder than words," I said to Joe, as he came over to take Teddy by the hand.

"No, no, Jackie-O, you were wonderful," he said. Joe was one of the sweetest, kindest, most considerate young men I had ever met.

"What do you mean, wonderful? I didn't even get a snicker." I was really disappointed.

"It wasn't you," he said, laughing at me. "It's these kids. They don't understand English. They all speak either German or French. But Teddy laughed," he added, hoping it would make me feel better.

That New Year's Eve, I resolved that I would never again use Joe Miller's Joke Book to pull me

through. And that baby who sat on my lap and chuckled must have made the same resolution, because for years now I have listened to Senator Edward Kennedy, and that brilliant young man has never used any of the material I introduced him to that Christmas day over thirty-five years ago.

I brought "Jackie-O" back home with me, and it became one of my most popular titles. It became standard practice to use it up on the call board at the studio. The notice advising the cast that shooting would begin at 9:00 a.m., weather permitting, always had the word "weather" crossed out and "Jackie-O" lettered in over it to read, "9:00 a.m., Jackie-O permitting."

I often think of how surprised Joseph P. Kennedy, Jr. would be to find that the name "Jackie-O" now belongs to a tiny little lady. I'm sure, however, that he would feel as I do, and join me in saying that the lovely little lady enhances the title.

Cary Grant, Edward Arnold, Jack Oakie and Donald Meek — *Toast of New York*.

TALE OF TWO CRACKS

Not all cracks are jokes! Two, brought on by a couple of pretty trembling experiences, shook me up over forty-two years ago. Only one has left a mark that can still be seen, but I remember both very well. The wounds were made only a few days apart in March, 1933.

The first happened on a Paramount Studio set. We were shooting *The Eagle And The Hawk*, directed by Stuart Walker and written by John Monk Saunders, author of *Wings* and an ace pilot himself. Our air story centered around the activities of an English airdrome during the First World War. The air raids and bomb-torn scenes brought on by enemy planes and zeppelins were supposed to be carefully planned by the special effects department. But what we actually lived through was much more dangerous, brought on by the cast working in *International House,* the W.C. Fields and Peggy Hopkins Joyce picture that was shooting on the stage right next to ours.

Every stunt man in the business was working on that next door set. The way they knocked each other about and threw the props and furniture at each other, we didn't expect anybody to come out of that picture alive. They were wrecking the studio! We kept sending over requests for them to keep it down so that we could make our war picture in peace.

That day, Fredric March, Cary Grant, and I were working in a scene in which the property men had set up the walls and ceiling in a trick way, so that on cue we three could drop under the table to safety from the falling debris. But the *International House* wreckers shook our loosely assembled set and brought down our walls and ceiling before any warning could save us. "Duck! Duck!" every member of the crew screamed at us, but we were too late. The three of us were covered with plaster and wood and, although Freddie and I escaped unharmed, Cary Grant's cheek was cracked wide open and bleeding. I was sure things were even worse next door, so I dashed over there as fast as I could, covered with plaster and, looking war-torn, I screamed, "How's my girl?" I was right, *International House* looked more war torn than *The Eagle And The Hawk*.

"Get on back to your dugout!" Fields yelled back at me. "She's all right!" He pointed over to the enclosed portable dressing room that shielded her. After all, her venturesome background didn't

Edward Arnold, Cary Grant and Jack Oakie — *Toast of New York.*

include the danger of ducking from stunt men. I knocked on her door. "How's my girl?" I called in to her.

She came out, looking as beautiful as advertised. "I'm just fine, Jack, thank you." Peggy Hopkins Joyce and I were dating steadily. She was famous for her diamonds and baubles. I was known for making an old sweat shirt stand up in formal company. Our dramatic contrast made good reading in newspapers and moving picture fan magazines.

A magazine interview, which headlined, "Is Jack the Fifth?" read:

> The toast of the Riviera and Broadway didn't talk about her jewels, worth several Kings' ransoms, or her beauty, a topic of comment the world over, or her clothes, which have established a dictatorship in fashion, or her first four husbands: (1) Everett A. Archer; (2) Sherbourne C. Hopkins; (3) Stanley Joyce; or (4) Count Gosta Morner. She talked about her deep interest in Jack Oakie. "Jack is forthright," she said. "He is an even-keel person, always the same. He's the same today as he was yesterday, and as he will be tomorrow."

Cary Grant, Jack Oakie and Edward Arnold — *Toast of New York.*

Jack Oakie, Fredric March and Cary Grant — *The Eagle and the Hawk.*

A. Edward Sutherland, W.C. Fields and Jack Oakie.

In an interview with my mother, Ev, a minister's daughter and a schoolteacher, they asked how she felt about her son's constant companion having been divorced four times. Ev said, "Peggy Hopkins Joyce is no different from the little girls I taught in school. Every one of them dreamed of marrying a millionaire; Peggy just did what they all dreamed about. She married several millionaires."

Peggy Hopkins Joyce is always thought of as an international *femme fatale*. I always think of her as just the girl next door who couldn't even show off for her folks. She brought her father onto our set one day to meet me. She was wearing all her jewelry and a floor-length chinchilla coat, and she tried to be the most sophisticated woman in the world as she gracefully took a cigarette from her platinum and diamond cigarette case. She lit the cigarette and took a couple of puffs. Her father watched the performance closely, and then asked, "Margaret, how the devil can you smoke those things without spittin'?" Even her diamonds seemed to wink at that putdown.

It was March the 10th, and we were working late. At six o'clock we were still shooting a scene supposed to be right outside our diggings (quarters). I was sitting stark naked, bathing in a little tin tub of water. In the scene Freddie March picked up the brush to scrub my back affection-

ately, as Forrester Harvey added some hot water to the tub.

Freddie was going off on leave for a few days, and his lines were, "Well, I'm off to the big city. What would you like most for me to bring back for you?" Being the comedian, I stopped and thought for a moment, and then, resigned to the fact that I could not possibly have my first choice, I said, "My second choice would be some gorgonzola cheese. I'd sure love to have some good old smelly gorgonzola cheese." I closed my eyes, and took a good deep breath as if I could smell the tasty strong dreamy stuff. Suddenly the tin tub began to quiver and leap, and the water shook right out of it.

"Say, who's being funny?" I complained. I was mad! Here it was, six o'clock, and someone had interrupted the shooting of the scene. We'd have to take it over! I opened my eyes and saw the lamps over my head swaying. "Darn that *International House!* Can't anybody keep them quiet?" I was sure those stunt men next door were shaking us up again. "Come on," I called to Forrester Harvey, "get me some more hot water. I'm getting cold." I was sitting in that tub wet, naked, and uncovered.

Just then the flat with the beautiful outdoor scene painted on it started toward me. I looked around and realized everybody was running away, and I was on stage alone.

"It's an earthquake!" That's all I heard! I got up

Edward Arnold and Jack Oakie — *Toast of New York.*

Jack Oakie in a scene from *Toast of New York.*

out of that tub, and grabbed the towel that I was supposed to use as I rose from the tub so that the scene could pass the Hays office. Without worrying about censorship, I didn't wait to wrap it around me.

"Wait for me!" I screamed, and started to run! Barefoot and naked I reached dressing room row.

"Here, Snot. Come on, get in here!" Bill Fields called to me from his room. He put his head out of his door just far enough for me to see his nose.

"Wait'll I get some clothes," I called back to him, and kept running past the two doors that separated our rooms. In seconds I got back to him in my sweat shirt, slacks, and bedroom slippers. I looked around at the group that was well into the second or third bottle of Bill's Four Roses. "Where's Peggy?" I asked.

"Didn't have any champagne here, so she went right on home," Bill said.

The telephones were out of order, but the radio was on. Long Beach had fallen! The whole ocean-side city was a shambles! As soon as I could, I got through to my mother and Peggy. "Are you all right?" we asked each other. We were all fine.

My mother and I were renting 605 North Elm, in Beverly Hills, just before moving into the house I bought for her at 525 North Arden, one street away. She loved 605 because Mrs. Patrick Campbell had once lived there. The very beautiful house withstood the quake very well. "Any damage?" I asked.

"The shake was pretty bad," Ev said. "But we've been looking around, and it seems there's only a crack in the wall upstairs, right above the door of my bedroom. Everything else is all right." We moved only weeks after that disastrous jolt, which ever after has been called the Long Beach Earthquake, so I never did find out whether anything was done about the crack above the bedroom door — not until almost forty years later, when my

Cary Grant and Jack Oakie — *Toast of New York*.

wife and I were invited to a dinner party at that lovely house.

"Is there a crack in the wall upstairs above your bedroom door?" I asked our hostess.

"Oh my goodness!" she couldn't believe the question. "Jack Oakie, do you have X-ray eyes that see through ceilings and walls? Yes, there is a crack above my bedroom door." She admitted. "It has always been there."

"No, it hasn't," I advised her. "It has only been there since March, 10th, 1933."

The other of those two cracks that happened back there in the early part of March, 1933, is the one I still look for in Cary Grant's cheek whenever I see him, but that one has mended so well there is no visible trace of it at all.

PUNDITS

My friend Claude Binyon, who became one of the motion picture industry's best writer-producer-directors, was the young genius who, when he was working on *Variety*, described the 1929 Wall Street crash in his famous headline: "Wall Street Lays An Egg!"

For my seventieth birthday, he wrote me a beautiful letter of reminiscences which included the following:

> Some forty-odd years ago there were dire predictions of your early demise. Said one wise man: "That boy will drink himself to death before he's forty." Said another prophet: "That young man will talk himself to death." Said another seer: "The things that feller says to people, some day real soon he's gonna get his head knocked off." Unfortunately these men have left us, cut down before their time by clean living.

Now, I ask you, why does there always have to be a wise guy? I'm sorry those three are gone, because I'd like to tell them a thing or two about my drinking and talking. When I was young, W.C. Fields gave me some very valuable advice. "Snot," he said, "never quit drinkin'! It's dangerous!" He always called me Snot, and I never quit drinkin'.

Besides, I've always had very important projects to drink to. One of the most important has been the arrival of a group of young men to whom I've been drinking for over forty years.

It started about 1930 with Claude Binyon Jr., and the momentum picked up in 1932 with Richard Arlen Jr., and Bing Crosby's Gary, Skeets Gallagher's Richard Jr., Stuart Erwin Jr., Wesley Ruggles Jr., and Jack Haley Jr. And believe me, taking on a drinking project like that during prohibition wasn't easy. But the boys were lucky. They all arrived at the Cedars of Lebanon Hospital where my friend Gene Delmar was staying for a long run.

When I made Vina Delmar's *Uptown New York*, her husband, Gene, and I became fast drinking partners, and being at Cedars didn't slow us down. The back entrance of Cedars with its emergency sign over the door and its special elevator that went straight on up to the maternity ward, was only a niblick shot from the back gate of Paramount. Grant, my chauffeur, and I were the shuttling system that drove all those expectant fathers to the hospital.

Ricky Arlen and Gary Crosby came so close together they had their christening together, and the dual "dunkin' party" was held at the brand

new home Bing and his wife, Dixie, built at 4326 Forman Avenue at Toluca Lake. He and Dixie had been renting a great big house on Los Feliz from Sue Carol and Nick Stuart, while Dixie's father supervised the building of the Toluca Lake house. When we got inside the hallway on the first visit, we noticed the little balcony built for one just inside the door. "What's that for?" we all asked as we looked up at it hanging there. "That's so Bing can sing to his guests as they arrive," Dixie's father explained. The house was forever after called "Crosby's Folly."

I don't know what it was that kept Gene Delmar in the hospital for so long but, whatever it was, it sure didn't interfere with his drinking. He was still there the day Jack Haley Jr. was born, the youngest of the group. His old man and I were make *Sitting Pretty*. We had just finished the last shot of the day, a scene with Ginger Rogers, when that little red light at the phone started to wink its warning signal that a call was coming through to the set. Haley had been watching that light all day waiting for the call from the hospital. But Flo Mac-Fadden Haley had been in show business all her life, and she wouldn't allow a call to be put through to Jack while the act was going on. He ran for the phone.

"It's from the hospital!" he screamed. "Come on, Oakie, let's go!" Grant drove us down through the trail he had blazed from Paramount to Cedars, and I went right for Gene Delmar's room.

I knocked on the door and put my head in as I opened it. "Hello there, Delmar, I just brought in another father."

In pantomime he pointed to the bureau. "Come on in, Oakie, it's still over there." I opened that long dresser drawer, and there it was fully replenished with bottles of gin and other hard-to-get items. "Who is it this time?" he asked while I fixed our drinks.

"Jack Haley and Flo. They just had a boy," I told him.

"Another boy!" He couldn't believe it. "Oakie," he said, "you're batting a thousand. How many is that now, five or six?" We counted them off and drank to each one.

When I came out of that Emergency door at the back of Cedars that night Grant was waiting to drive me home, and he too must have been counting, as he helped me into the car and asked, "Mr. Oakie, tell me something. I'd like to know if this is a hospital or a speakeasy?"

Right after we made *Sitting Pretty,* Haley went back in vaudeville and did a sketch counting those boys. I caught him at Loews State, and his joke got the biggest laugh in the theatre.

"Oakie was working with me the night my boy Jack was born, he was working with Arlen when his Ricky was born, he was working with Crosby when Gary was born, he was working with Skeets when Richard was born, he was working with Erwin when Stu was born, and he was working with Ruggles when Wes was born. Oakie's next picture is going to be with Polly Moran." The audience howled. If you're old enough to remember Polly Moran and her partner, Marie Dressler, you'll remember what a helluva comedy team those gals were and you'll know how funny Haley's gag was.

My wife and I attended the wedding reception for Jack Haley Jr. and his little bride, Liza, at Ciro's. His old man sat at our table. "Oakie," he asked, "do you remember the day that kid was born?" He pointed over at Junior. "Remember what a tiny little baby he was?" Junior is way over six feet tall and very good-looking; he takes after his mother. He's also very talented and very good-natured.

Over three years ago, when I was sixty-eight, and before he made his very successful picture *That's Entertainment,* Junior gave me a surprise birthday reel. He prepared clips out of about ten of my pictures and arranged them so that we watch my hair become progressively lighter as I become progressively heavier. I go from some pretty fancy dance steps, including pendulum wings, until I'm practically grounded with white hair. It's a wonderful reel, and he made me very happy!

Well, I've been drinking to all those boys for over forty years now. I consider it a wonderful project and worth every drop. Every one of them is successful and darn good at their various jobs and, God willing, I'm going to keep right on drinking to them for another forty years.

As for talking too much, well, talking my head off has been my stock-in-trade. I played the talkie pal on the screen, and my friends must have liked what I said because they had me carry the role right into their private lives. There was only one time that I remember when most unexpectedly I almost had my head knocked off for speaking my mind.

It was after the Alabama-USC game. Johnny Mack Brown, who had been Alabama's great football star, gave a party at the Huntington in Pasadena. I was having the best time of all and wouldn't leave when my mother was ready to go home. "You take the car," I told her. "Let Grant drive you home. I'll get home somehow. Don't worry."

But she did worry. She got Guinn "Big Boy" Williams to promise he'd bring me home. "Don't you worry, Mrs. Offield, I'll bring him home safely," Big promised. Some hours later I got into his little two-seater roadster with the hard top.

"Let's stop off at B.B.B.'s cellar for a drink first," I said. (Bobby Burns Berman's place was on the way home, so I wasn't being unreasonable.)

"No," Big said, "I promised your mother I'd bring you home early because you've got an early call tomorrow." When we got too far west of Cosmo and Selma in Hollywood, where B.B.B.'s was, and that looked hopeless, I decided The Little Club in Beverly Hills just a few blocks away from home would be just as good.

"Let's go to The Little Club," I suggested.

"NO!" Big was adamant. "I promised your mother. We're going straight to your house." When we got to Arden Drive, the street I lived on, he started south from Sunset Boulevard. "What's the number of the house?" he asked.

"I'm not going to tell you. Let's go back to B.B.B.'s." I was going to teach him a lesson. Big drove all the way to Santa Monica Boulevard, then had to go all the way around the block and start over again.

"What's the number of the house?" he asked again before starting down Arden.

"I won't tell you. Let's go to The Little Club instead." I'd get him to listen to me.

He drove slowly down the street trying to recognize the house. "What's the number?"

"I won't tell you!"

"What's the number?"

"I won't tell you!" That kept up until the third time around.

"This is the last time I'm going to ask you, Jack. What is the number of the house?"

"I won't tell you!" With a clenched fist his hammer drop came right down on the top of my head. It felt as if the roof of the car fell in on me. "525 North Arden Drive," I recited as quickly as I could.

Guinn Williams was named "Big Boy" by Will Rogers because of his great strength. A horse once kicked Big — well, that poor animal shouldn't have done that. Big clenched his fist, hauled off, let the horse have it, and the poor beast was knocked out cold. I was sober as I ran up the path to my front door.

There was another time when I was sure I was going to lose my head for talking too much. But that time I was rewarded instead with an experience that had me carrying it a little higher than ever before.

The day I arrived in Paris, the Duke of Windsor was sitting in the lobby of the Meurice Hotel, in an area invisibly roped off. As I checked in, I could see the quizzical look on his face, and could read his mind. "That can't be Whispering Jack Smith," he was saying to himself. He was right; I had brought that darn old habit of talking my head off to Paris with me. I wasn't working, and this trip to Europe was to be a holiday, so I stayed at the quiet Meurice. But the French branch of the RKO Studios found out I was there and planned a premiere showing of The Affairs Of Annabel, the first of a series of pictures I made with Lucille Ball.

The next time I passed the Duke he was with a friend of mine, Berry Wall. This time I could read his lips as he repeated the answer to the question, "Oh, American cinema."

The studio arranged newspaper interviews day and night, and the most important question put to me was, "Mr. Oakie, why are you staying at the Meurice? Why are you not at the Ritz, where Americans usually stay?" My answer was a headline in the English edition of the New York Herald Tribune: "Oakie says, 'If the Meurice is good enough for the Duke of Windsor it's good enough for me!'"

That evening, as the Duke caught my eye (which wasn't hard to do, I was always throwing it in his direction) I was afraid I had gone too far. Although I knew his stomping grounds were across the Channel, I was sure he could pull enough strings in France to order the guillotine and say, "Off with his head!" In the fleeting moment that he held my attention in his command, I expected him to warn me by whipping his forefinger across his throat.

But I was mistaken. Instead, what I had said brought me one of the nicest experiences of my life. He smiled and nodded hello in the most gracious greeting I have ever had. The man was a king, and he made me feel like one, even though he had just quit his job and I was not working. As we say in show business, we were two layoffs, which gave us something in common.

Anyway, what I'm getting at is this: those three fellers that Binyon knew didn't know beans about drinking and talking. If they're considered seers, then I'd rather be the lobster than the wise guy, because the wise guy is the lobster after all.

ASTA

"Oakie, how are you doing?" Walt Disney asked. He came out on the back lot where I was resting between shots. I was making his picture, *Kilroy,* in which I was playing an ex-vaudevillian who had had a dog act and after years of retirement trains a large group of strays from the pound. I was working with about twenty of them, and they had to jump all over me.

"Walt," I confessed, "if this is a contest between me and these dogs, these dogs are sure winning it!"

Disney laughed, "You've worked with a lot of dogs in your time, Jack, so I'm not worried." "You've worked with a lot of dogs in your time," was a heck of a good feed-line for a joke, but Disney wasn't a professional straight man.

"Yes, Walt," I assured him, "I've worked with a lot of dogs!"

In motion pictures, an actor doesn't work with dogs, he works for them. They are born professional thieves, but I've been in love with them all my life, and *Kilroy* was a good picture in which I once again enjoyed having dogs steal my scenes and my heart. In all the years I gladly gave up both, there was only one of those four-legged felons that I ever resented.

He was the greatest rascal of them all, because he not only stole my heart and my scenes, he finally took over and stole my part! Long before show business, there was a member of his tribe that I lived with and loved and lost, and never quite got over his untimely demise.

That first heartbreak happened way back in my early Jefferson School days in Muskogee, Oklahoma. The remembrance of it is best expressed by the dog himself, in a composition I wrote for my English class. My mother must have been very proud that I was learning to read and write because she saved the little piece, which reads as follows:

Asta steals a scene from Oakie.

> I am a black dog. Because I am black as coal, my master called me Tar Baby, when I was a baby. But now he calls me Tarby. One morning I was given to an old mean woman named Mrs. Casey. She was Irish and very harsh to me. I lived nicely until I got big enough to run around and she had to get me a license. She paid the two dollars for one year. One morning she got mad and put me into a sewer and called up the police to come and take me to the dog pound. I thought surely that I would have to go, when a boy came and took me to his home. I have stayed at his house now for two years and I got to sleep in the house. Now I am dying. My master was bothered with rats in his basement so he put some rat poison on some bread and I have got a hold of it and I am dying. But everybody dies, so I am satisfied. I hope other dogs that played with me will fare better.

The fact that Tarby was satisfied because he knew that everybody dies didn't help. I cried myself to sleep for years. Then later, when I first bought our little ranch in Northridge, I bred Afghan hounds. As a breeder, I was advised that the professional thing to do was to pick only the prize of each litter. As I judged the litters myself, every pup was always a prizewinner. At one time there were almost a hundred Afghan hounds overrunning the ranch. I also gained a reputation that turned my home into a dog haven, and a hospital that even included a psychiatric ward for wagless tails.

Like the time John Barrymore died. His Afghan hound, Violet, was brought to me for care. Violet didn't eat well and wouldn't take any exercise. She was failing, and I couldn't sleep for worrying about her. One evening I reported this to John Barrymore's brother, Lionel. "I don't think Violet is going to make it without Jack," I told him. "She must have loved him very much. Remember how she used to put her nose right up into his face?" I reminded him. "Remember how she used to kiss him right on the mouth?"

"Oakie," Lionel recommended. "Get some sleep! Violet didn't put her face up into Jack's because she loved to kiss him. That dog put her nose up to Jack's mouth because she loved the strong smell of whiskey!"

When Violet was taken away from me, I still worried about that beautiful Afghan, and hoped that she would pick up a scent again that would lead to food and exercise. Like millions of others, I too was in love with those handsome "leading men" of the screen — from Rin Tin Tin, the true-blue police dog, to Lassie, the courageous collie, and Buck, the sexy Saint Bernard I worked with in *Call Of The Wild*. I continued to call those four-legged heartbreakers "man's best friend" until one of them stepped out of the handsome leading man class, and began to tamper with my livelihood.

I had just finished working with Buck up north and was back down south, still trying to thaw out, when I went right into *The Big Broadcast*, and started to work with Asta, the wirehaired terrier. (This was before he took the name of Asta.) Perhaps I was still too cold to warm up to what was happening, but I'm sure that's when it started.

In a dinner scene I was playing with Lyda Roberti I didn't trust her, so I threw a piece of meat to Asta to test the food. When he ate it, he rolled over and played dead. No graduate of the American Academy of Dramatic Arts could compete with his death scene. I did my *double take,* but he got the laughs! At the close of the scene when our director, Norman Taurog, shouted "Cut!", Asta jumped up into my chair, looked down at my name printed in large letters on the back of it, and seemed to say, "Oakie, I'm taking over!" Taurog, that famous pipe-smoking director, took the corncob pipe out of his mouth and put it in Asta's for a still picture.

Up until that time I had been very proud to be considered an upstanding member of the C.R.A. (In those days C.R.A. didn't stand for Community Redevelopment Agency; it stood for Comedy Relief Actor.) It was Victor Moore who was the first to accept me as a member of this very elite club. "Oakie, you're a doggone good C.R.A. man," he said. "I'm proud to consider you a member." The compliment had me standing straight up on my two legs.

We C.R.A. men did what we called *reaction comedy*. We always worked on the side of the audience. We were the ones who told them what to laugh at. It was done with *the take,* which I first learned from experts like Harry Langdon, or the *delayed take,* always executed by the greatest expert of them all, Edward Everett Horton. He could have his back to the camera and his full face in the lens. I am credited with expanding *the take* to the *double take,* and then to my *triple with the fade.*

But the C.R.A. is now defunct, having been taken over by the A.K.C. Leading the pack of Siriuses who put us out of business was Asta, that Canine Comic. I should have put some of the real McCoy on that piece of meat I threw him in *The Big Broadcast,* to stop him in his tracks, because from there he went on to blaze his brilliant star in pictures like *The Thin Man* (in which he was playing my part!). There he was, up on the screen, looking around corners, doing *double takes* better than I ever could — after all I didn't have a tail to wag at the audience to milk them.

Yes, I could just hear him as he got up into my chair that day with the corncob pipe in his mouth, "Oakie, I'm taking over, put that in your pipe and smoke it!"

TOO MUCH DIHEDRAL

Luckily I have never had an energy crisis. All of my life I have been blessed with an overabundance of the stuff, and have always used it extravagantly. Fifty years ago I was a phenomenon studied by "energy conservation" experts. Of course the experts interested in me were not trying to control the use of water and power. My experts were front-office experts in the motion picture industry who tried every which way to harness my enthusiasm, both at work and at play, and to control the use of it for box-office returns only.

They called it the Oakie Overflow and many other names from Ebullience to Vim and Vigor, until finally in 1931 my delivery was tagged "Too Much Dihedral," and from every angle the description has continued to suit me just fine.

It happened during the shooting of *Sky Bride*. We were working on location at Waldo Waterman's Metropolitan Airport in Van Nuys; that day not only did my energy fly under new colors, but it also flew at a little boy whose cover-up also overflowed.

Sky Bride was Paramount's big "aviation talkie." Our director was Stephen Roberts, who was always very careful to be sure that Dick Arlen, Virginia Bruce, and I would use the exact words as written by three of motion pictures' greatest scenarists, Joseph L. Mankiewicz, Agnes Brand Leahy, and Grover Jones. Randolph Scott played Commander Hawks, a famous flyer. It was his first picture, and his first and only line was read to Arlen and me, who were also flyers. Looking very handsome in his abundantly medalled uniform, he joined Dick Arlen and me at the plane. He looked up at the wing of the plane, and with authority said the exact words as written, "Too much dihedral!"

"Cut," Stephen Roberts called, happy with the scene. But my reaction to the dialogue prompted Arlen and Scott to decide it wasn't the wing of the plane that had too much dihedral; it was that high flying Oakie, and I've had it ever since.

Randy turned in his suit at the wardrobe department and went home, but Arlen and I still had a long day before us; and Dick was nervous that day because his wife Jobyna was at Cedars of Lebanon Hospital, expecting to give birth to Richard Arlen Jr. any minute.

"Wish I could get off early," he kept mumbling between *takes*. From the way Arlen was acting, I

Jack and his mother, Mrs. Evelyn Offield.

was sure the wrong parent was in the hospital!

Scheduled to work with Dick and me that day was the child star in the picture, Bobby Coogan, and all our scenes were centered around the hangar and the grounded plane. Bobby was still a baby, even too young to read. Some of the publicity stories went out telling folks that I had to teach him his lines; the studio was trying to build him up to be another "Kid," like his famous brother, Jackie. But young as he was, he was pretty precocious, both on and off the screen. He played the part of an annoying little boy, and on the set his rebellious attitude stemmed from his great dislike of acting. He didn't want to be like his brother; he wanted to be a cameraman, and he fought us every scene of the way. Bobby wore little coveralls in the picture, and the wardrobe man, Mickey, had to keep several matching pairs on hand because the baby was still in the pants-wetting stage of life.

Arlen and I had a routine that would advise the director and crew behind the camera when it was time to make a change. "Hey, Oakie! What's

that?" Arlen would ask. "Somebody spill something on that child?"

"No!" I'd pick up my cue. "That's an inside job!"

"Oh?" he'd say, sniffing. "Well, that baby's spoiled!"

"No!" I went on for the laugh line. "He ain't spoiled; they all smell like that!"

We always got a laugh from everybody but the wardrobe man. Mickey's greatest fear was that one day he'd run out of coveralls before the day's shooting was over. And to add to his worries, I discovered that little Bobby scared easily. Just a bit of a "booooooo" would set off the waterworks.

"Oakie, isn't there any way we can get me off early?" Dick kept at me frantically. He really wanted to get to the hospital and be with Jobyna, and the more I listened to him the more I realized that was where he belonged. I watched Mickey lead little Bobby into the hangar, where he had set up a makeshift wardrobe department, and the proverbial electric light bulb lit up over my head! I had an idea!

"Hold on, Dick," I said. "It won't be long now." I walked over to the hangar where Mickey was undressing the baby. "Say, how many of those coveralls you got left for today?" I asked as I watched him make the change.

"This is the last one," Mickey told me sadly. The look on his face foretold the tragedy he was ex-

pecting. So, not to disappoint him, I walked out round to the back of the hangar and with all the dihedral I could muster, I waited. It wasn't very long before Bobby came prancing out dry behind the ears. Just as he got to the corner of the hangar I took full advantage of my opportunity, and with perfect timing for the perfect element of surprise I "booooooooooooood."

Without hesitation I angled my dihedral toward Dick, "All right Arlen, get set. I think we're ready to go home." I was right; that telltale flood of success got us off early.

Almost twenty years later, I was visiting on the Tiffany Stahl lot where Bobby Coogan was still acting and still wearing coveralls. He was playing the oversized character called Humphrey in one of those Joe Palooka pictures. "Jack Oakie!" he called to me excitedly, as he ran over and put his arms around me.

"Bobby! How the devil did you get so big!" I said, hoping his bear hug didn't break any of my ribs. I had to step back to look up at the giant, who was several heads above me and weighed over 300 pounds.

"Jack Oakie," he repeated my name affectionately. "I haven't seen you since *Sky Bride* and that old Metropolitan Airport where you tied diapers on me!" I looked down in remembrance. (The feed-line was too good; I had to use my old gag.) "I bet I wouldn't recognize the old place now."

Maurice Chevalier, Mrs. Offield and Jack Oakie.

124

Bobby was still too young to know how old the joke was — I got my laugh.

Then there was a time when I suddenly realized that having too much dihedral was an angle I could cash in on. It was in the 1920s when Hollywood was a little village, and with my get-up-and-go it was easy to find out where good parties were being given. I never missed a one, always had the most fun, and almost always was the last to leave the festivities. The call sheets for all my pictures always read, "Oakie Permitting," instead of the usual, "Weather Permitting," and so Al Kaufman, the best front-office expert Paramount Studios ever had, took a personal interest in my energy conservation.

No matter how hard I worked all day I could always find a party to go to, and no matter where the party was, Al Kaufman would turn up there too. "Oakie, do yourself a favor, and go home and get a few hours sleep," he said so often I knew the line by heart. "Don't worry," I always advise him, and kept right on going. But one night at Clara Bow's house he finally used a line that got through to me and went right to my heart. After having had some dinner at Henry's, I called the Redhead.

In no time at all I could see Clara Bow's limousine driving up Hollywood Boulevard for me. The chauffeur took me right back to her house at 521 Bedford Drive in Beverly Hills, and sure enough there was a goodly crowd and a fine party in full swing. Al Kaufman was already there, looking as if he were just waiting for me.

His big bulging eyes followed me around all night and finally about two o'clock in the morning, when I felt I was just warming up and still had lots and lots of laughs to get, Al started his traditional plea, "Oakie, go home and get some rest."

"Sure, sure, in a minute," I said, trying to placate the man.

"Jack, you had a big day today and remember you have a big day tomorrow. I mean yesterday and today," he corrected himself. (Being a good front-office expert, I guess the figures between A.M. and P.M. made a difference to him.)

"Don't worry," I said, trying to reassure him, but not making a move to go.

"Oakie," he said more firmly and, showing his knowledge of arithmetic, "Do you realize there'll be 600 extras on that set at nine o'clock! Go home and get some sleep!"

"Don't worry," I repeated and put my arms around the little man. "Bet you a thousand bucks I'll be there at nine o'clock," I said jokingly.

"I'll take it!" Al said quickly before I could stop to think. "The bet's on!"

Now $1,000 was a very small investment for the studio, considering that a delay in shooting a big scene could easily cost up to $100,000. But $1,000 was a lot of money to me, and I couldn't afford to lose it. "Remember now," Al wagged his finger at me, rubbing it in, "It'll cost you $1,000 if you're not on the set at nine o'clock."

"Don't worry," I said once again, offering that dubious advice as he left and I went back to having fun and getting laughs. I don't remember what time I lost my audience that morning, but I was on the set at the studio bright-eyed and alert at nine o'clock sharp.

"Where's Al Kaufman?" I yelled at the top of my lungs as I looked under chairs and tables for him. "Get Al Kaufman down here," I called over to the assistant director. Al came rushing toward me in disbelief. "The gelt?" I asked, "What about the gelt?" and I held out my hand to receive my thou.

He was as good as his word. He held out the check for $1,000 and handed it to me happily. For years, no matter what party I attended — and I kept right on going to all of them — Al Kaufman would show up to place his bet with me, and in the ten years that I was under contract to Paramount Studios I never failed to collect my thou.

I recently took one of those twenty-four-hour urine tests for a doctor who was trying to find out what gave me so much elevation. After hearing his technical explanation about my having excessive adrenaline, I simplified it all for him and said, "You mean I have too much dihedral."

He laughed first and then asked, "What's dihedral?" What he didn't know was that forty-five years ago I had looked it up in the dictionary, and had since asked Ed Lund, the great flyer who had gone around the world with Howard Hughes, and all it meant to me was that I had a lot of energy.

"Just means I get some high-flying laughs," I said.

"Oakie," the doctor said happily, "you've a perpetual spring feeding your fountain of fun."

Well, when you're over seventy that's real nice to hear, but when it comes to fun, I'm only the "offspring." The spring originated with my mother, Ev. There was no time in her life that she ever slowed down. She got her laughs right up to the very last minute, telling jokes to a columnist who could hardly keep up with her rapid repartee. A good example of her great humor happened when we were working together.

Ev had always wanted to be in one of my pictures. And Eddie Sutherland, who directed so many of the movies I made at Paramount, promised he would find the right spot for her. So when we made *Too Much Harmony*, Eddie asked

Jack, Bing and Ev

"Ev" and Jack attend a Hollywood premiere.

Mr. and Mrs. Ochs Adler, Jack Oakie and Mrs. Evelyn Offield.

Jack Oakie, Judith Allen and Bing Crosby.

Jack Oakie, Edward G. Robinson, Clark Gable, Arline Judge and Carl Brisson.

Jack Oakie, Frances Dee and Richard Arlen.

Jack Oakie with Bobby Coogan.

Bobby Coogan and Jack Oakie — *Sky Bride.*

Ev if she would like to play my mother in the picture.

"Yes! Yes!" she said and was the most excited little lady in the world.

On her first day of shooting it was natural to find that Ev had us all gathered around her, and in her magnetic way was holding court. She was sitting in one of the many directors' chairs kept on the set for the cast and the crew. We stars, having proved our shining mettle, had our names embellished on the canvas backs of exactly the same kinds of chairs.

Bing Crosby, Skeets Gallagher, Judith Allen, and I kept our chairs close by her in a protective semicircle, as visitors came from all over the lot to pay their respects. Ev was entertaining everybody with her very gracious stories, and I began to worry about the amount of energy she was expending. When we broke for lunch, I took Eddie aside. "Eddie, please," I implored. "Get to Ev's scenes, she's going to be exhausted!"

"No, Jack," Eddie explained, "she's *too* energetic. I'm waiting for her to get tired enough to look like a quiet, motherly old lady."

When we got back from lunch, Ev looked for a director's chair to sit in again, and was very careful to choose one that was not the property of one of the stars. The chair she chose was faulty and, as she sat down in it, it toppled over backward. Crosby, who was nearest, got to her first and helped her up from the floor. "Are you all right, Mrs. Offield?" he asked Ev, as we all ran to her assistance.

"Bing," she said, as he held on to her, "I noticed that my name wasn't on the chair, and it kind of upset me."

"That does it!" Eddie Sutherland decided. "Let's put the lady to work; she'll never grow old." Well, Ev went right to work and stole the picture from all of us who had those assigned chairs.

After soaring through hours of a very lofty party recently, my wife and I stopped off at the Beverly Hills Brown Derby dining room, before heading over the hill for the northwest corner of the San Fernando Valley, and home. Randolph Scott, looking very handsome and still carrying himself like a uniformed officer, was there with his lovely wife, and they graciously joined us. It'd been a long time since I'd seen Randy.

"Hear you're playing a lot of golf," I said.

"A little," he replied. (He never was one for long sentences.)

"Heard your famous line to the Los Angeles Country Club," I said. (The L.A.C.C. never approved actors for membership. When Randy applied and said he was retired, they questioned

Famous hostess, Elsa Maxwell, Al Kaufman and Jack Oakie.

his vocation. "I'm not an actor," he said, "and I have over fifty pictures to prove it." He was accepted.)

"Guess you baffled them," I said, admiring a good laugh line even when it comes from a leading man instead of a comic.

"Oakie, there's only one line I've ever said that was baffling."

"Too much dihedral!" we said in unison.

"You still have it and you still baffle me," he said with affection. It's nice to have good old friends who find you haven't changed in over forty-five years.

THE SPOOK

I've worked with some of the New York Metropolitan Opera Company's greatest stars, and discovered that the greater the voice, the greater the sense of humor. My discoveries first started in New York when I was still going to De La Salle, the Catholic Military High School at Fifty-eighth Street and Sixth Avenue. (Later this was the site for the Barbizon Plaza.)

We were half a block from the New York Athletic Club, where celebrities worked out to keep fit. Years later it was very exciting for me to be an invited guest at the club, because I remembered that very special member who meant so much to me one afternoon, right down the street in front of my school.

Four of us military students, dressed in our gingerbread winter uniforms, were experimenting with the idea of becoming a quartet. We were between classes, and because we weren't quite sure of ourselves we confined our singing to the street. We tried to keep our voices down, expecting one of the brothers to come out and put a stop to our noise any minute. By about the fourth try of *Sweet Adeline,* it was decided that I was the only one of the four who could do the harmonizing. We started again with "Sweet Adeline, my Adeline . . ." I was now the only one harmonizing to three melodies, when suddenly a bell-like voice rang right through my head! We had become a quintet! The man joined in to help me with the harmony. He was wearing a soft black Fedora hat, and a great black overcoat with a big shawl fur collar. As he leaned over close to me, my cheek rested on his fur collar.

"Boy, what a voice!" I thought, and looked up at him. I recognized my harmonizing partner immediately, leaned right up against that fur collar, and began to bellow as loudly as I could as I tried to follow his lead. We were two harmonies to three melodies who gave *Sweet Adeline* all we had. But all I can remember of our singing that day is that we five finally finished together.

"That's pretty good," he said, his rich voice encouraging us.

"Thank you, Mr. Caruso!" Our quartet said in unison.

"Yes, boys, that was pretty good." We stood there with our mouths open and watched him as he turned and waved to us before getting into his great big black limousine, which had been waiting

Lucille Ball and Jack Oakie — *The Affairs of Annabel.*

for him on the corner. The most famous tenor of our time had just come from the New York Athletic Club, and couldn't resist stopping long enough to help us with our musical efforts.

"Oh boy! Did you hear that?" we asked each other, all talking at once. "Yeah, yeah, yeah, yeah!" We started singing again, "Sweet Adeline, my Adeline." This time we didn't keep our voices down, we had become the most inspired quartet Fifty-eighth Street ever heard. We had just been singing with the great Enrico Caruso!

Gladys Swarthout, one of the most beautiful women in the opera world, an alumna of the New York Metropolitan Opera Company, was under contract to the Paramount Studios. She had a great sense of humor and loved my jokes. Her dressing room was only two doors down from mine on dressing room row, and she loved me to come by in the morning with an Oakie laugh for the day.

One morning during the shooting of *Collegiate,* I got to my dressing room, and the white suit I was to wear in my first scene that day hadn't been brought back from wardrobe. "The Cracker," my stand-in, came in to see if I needed anything. He was one of the most loyal friends I ever had in Hollywood, and I loved him. He was called "the

Jack and Lucy — *The Affairs of Annabel.*

Cracker'' because he came from Georgia, and also because occasionally he had a New England tone that could be likened to the Liberty Bell.

"Cracker, do you know what they've done with my white suit?" I asked.

"What?" he said. "Wardrobe didn't bring down your suit?" He checked through my closet. "You're right! It's not here!" He confirmed the situation, and started to mumble profanities. "Don't worry, Oakie. I'll get it for you." He was mumbling even more when he came back carrying my freshly cleaned suit on its hanger. He was so upset I couldn't understand a thing he was saying.

"Slow down. What are you talking about?" I asked him.

"John Shapiro! John Shapiro! They got orders up in wardrobe to drop everything, and fit John Shapiro!"

"Who's John Shapiro?" I asked. I'd never heard the name mentioned on the lot before.

"That's what I said. 'Who's John Shapiro?' I said. 'He's an actor,' they said. 'So what do you think Oakie is?' I said. 'A Horse?'"

He kept right on mumbling "John Shapiro," until suddenly it dawned on me who he was talking about. The studio was always sending out for great male singers to team with Gladys Swarth-

out in her pictures. I had just read in the morning *Reporter* that they had brought Jan Kiepura, the great romantic tenor, over from Vienna to work with her. I couldn't wait. I ran right over to her dressing room. "Gladys, have I got a laugh for you! You won't believe it!" I told her about the Cracker calling Jan Kiepura John Shapiro. She laughed, and then kept right on laughing and laughing until it seemed to me she couldn't stop. "Jack," she finally said, still laughing, "I can just see the romantic marquee, and she moved her finger through the air as if reading "Gladys Schwartz and Jack Shapiro, in *One Night Of Love.*

This was at a time in the history of the music world when Latin names were considered the most romantic. (My friend Arthur Gordon, a very fine singer, who was married to Nora Bayes, once told me his voice didn't sound good to the impresarios until he changed his name to Arturo Gordoni.)

The title that did hit the marquee was *Give Us This Night.* And not long after that the studio must have run out of good male voices for Gladys, because they put Fred MacMurray and me into *The Champagne Waltz.*

Lily Pons was another opera friend of mine. I named Lily "the Spook," and in answer to an interviewer who asked her if she took offense at

The Affairs of Annabel.

Jack Oakie and Lucille Ball — *Annabel Takes a Tour*.

Jack Oakie and Lily Pons — *That Girl from Paris.*

Lily Pons blocks a sour note from Jack Oakie — *That Girl from Paris.*

Puzzle picture — where's J.O. in this one?

Edward Everett Horton, Jack Oakie and Lily Pons — *Hitting a New High.*

Front row: Lily Pons, Gene Raymond, Herman Bing, Lucille Ball and Jack Oakie; back row: Frank Jenks and Mischa Auer — *That Girl from Paris.*

my calling her that, she picked up a powder puff from her dressing table and covered her face with a film of rice powder. "Booh," she said to the newspaperwoman. "I am ze Spook!" More than anyone else, Lily Pons proved that the greater the voice, the greater the sense of humor. I was introduced to her fun-loving spirit, before I was introduced to her.

In 1936 I was in Saks Fifth Avenue, New York, when Lily sauntered by me, humming. I recognized her immediately. That tiny gal was the top-line canary of the Met, and nobody in the world could hum a tune the way she did. "That's pretty good," I said to her, using Caruso's line.

She smiled and nodded her head, acknowledging that she knew it was good. Then she threw me a couple of real high notes. "That's good too!" I said, continuing to be a judge of music.

"It is VAIREE good," she said, correcting my judgement, and with the most beautiful musical laughter, walked away.

"Did you know who I was that day at Saks?" I asked her six months later when we were making *That Girl From Paris* at RKO.

"Oh, for one leetle meenute you look just like John Charles Thomas," she said. "But when I hear you talk, I know you are Jack Oakie."

She was right about the likeness. I was playing golf at the Riviera Country Club one day when John Charles Thomas saw me. He dropped his

clubs, took my face in his hands, and turned it back and forth examining it from all angles. "Yes!" he said. "Lily is right!" He was not the only one who agreed with her. At a Hollywood Bowl concert, I signed "John Charles Thomas" for some of his fans who called me Mr. Thomas and asked for his autograph. I never like to disappoint anyone.

I made two pictures with "the spook," and that diminutive diva from Paris never behaved like a prima donna. As Kostelanetz told me, "Singing is just second nature for Lily. She never has to clear her throat with hot tea and honey, like other singers. She never worries about being in voice. When you ask Lily to sing, she just opens her mouth and she sings."

In our business, where actors are always asking for something, she never made demands on anyone. One of the only two times that I can remember that she ever did ask anybody to do anything for her, was when she asked me not to blow my cigarette smoke her way. "Jackie, don't blow your smoke in my face. Eet eez no good for my singing," she said.

"Why?" I asked. "It didn't bother Florence Foster Jenkins." I got the biggest laugh from the Spook. (Florence Foster Jenkins was a very rich lady who loved to sing opera. But because of the quality of her renditions she had to hire Carnegie Hall and fill it with her personal friends. She did however make great monetary contributions to the arts.

The other request was made during the recording of Arthur Schwartz's jazz arrangement of "The Blue Danube." Kostelanetz was directing Jimmy Dorsey's swing band for Lily. One of the jazz musicians, called Hill Billy Hillman, loved to read the funny papers while he played his guitar. He spread the comic strips out on the floor in front of him, and read and giggled while he played. Lily watched him lean over and turn the page just as she hit an E over high C. "Just a meenute," she said to Kostelanetz, and stopped the rehearsal. She walked over to the guitarist.

"Heel Beely," she said, "pleeze weel you look at me when I am singing. Pleeze. I am hitting notes almost nobody in the world can hit so pleeze just you look at me while we are working together, yes?"

I was standing with Jimmy Dorsey while Lily was asking Hill Billy to pay attention. "He's been doing that ever since he's been with the band," Jimmy told me. So Heel Beely folded up his funny papers. We all loved and respected her, but most of all we loved her fun. One afternoon I got out of the sound-stage ahead of her. There waiting for her was her limousine with it's license number "L.P. 13". I climbed in and said to the chauffeur: "Drive on." The poor guy didn't know what to do, but decided to get in behind the wheel. Before he could shift, however, Lily came out. She tried to open the rear door and couldn't because I was holding it on the inside. "Please go away little girl." I said. "Scat." She jumped on the running board and said: "I'll take you to lunch." "I'm not going to lunch." I told her. "Drive on my good man." The chauffeur started the car, but couldn't go because Lily held on. "Little girl." I said. "You can't stay out there in the cold," and reached out and hauled her in through the window, head first. She was screaming with laughter.

One of her most unexpected shenanigans was the way she would spook Kostelanetz. Lily discovered his weakness, and when least expected she would touch off his ticklish nerve as she walked behind him when he was conducting the orchestra. She was so tiny no one would see her until she sent the great conductor up into the air. His batan would fly fifty feet across the room as he would leap almost as high. "I know eet eez indaycent," she would confess to me. By the time I made the second picture with her, *Hitting A New High,* Kosty was learning to conduct with his eyes in the back of his head.

Lily called me the other day from Palm Springs. "Jackie, theese eez Lily," she said in her beautiful coloratura French tones.

"I don't believe it," I teased her.

"Yes, eet eez Lily," she insisted.

"All right," I said, "if you're Lily Pons, prove it. Sing me a couple of choruses of the "Bell Song" from *Lakme."*

Without hesitation the spook went right into hitting those high notes, and thrilled me with her haunting fun-loving spirit. Once again Lily Pons proved that the greater the voice the greater the sense of humor.

Jack Serenades Lily

Vinton Haworth, Eduardo Ciannelli, Jack Oakie, Lily Pons and Edward Everett Horton —
Hitting a New High.

Fritz Feld and Jack Oakie in a scene from *The Affairs of Annabel*.

Jack Oakie, Alice White and Pepito (a famous Spanish clown) in *Annabel Takes a Tour*.

Jack Oakie and Gladys Swarthout — *Champagne Waltz.*

Eric Blore, Jack Oakie and Edward Everett Horton — *Hitting a New High.*

Sonja Henie and Jack Oakie — *Iceland.*

ICELAND

Before *Sun Valley Serenade* was distributed, Twentieth Century-Fox, unsure of what they had, sold their ice-making machine. Although Sonja Henie was the star, they doubted that an ice skating picture would have audience appeal, and were grateful for the chance to recoup some of their investment. Herbert Yates of Republic Studios bought it eagerly for his skating star, Vera Hruba Ralston. It was the only one in Hollywood and a bargain at three-quarters of a million dollars. But when Sonja's picture hit the theatres, it was such a great hit the studio got another story for her immediately. They also got Johnny Payne and me, called the movie *Iceland,* and advertised it as bigger and better than *Sun Valley Serenade!*

Bruce "Lucky" Humberstone directed, William Le Baron produced, and the original screenplay was written by Robert Ellis and Helen Logan. We had Sammy Kaye and his orchestra, and songs by Mack Gordon and Harry Warren. Johnny Payne and I were Uncle Sam's fighting marines. We'd been on the picture a couple of weeks and those military uniforms were too warm to work in and not warm enough for that cold stage when just sitting and waiting.

I was sitting with "Lucky" Humberstone, feeling chilled, when he got the news that dropped his body temperature too. "What's the matter, Lucky?" I asked him. "Can't you get this air conditioning unit leveled off? We're all going to get pnuemonia."

"That's not what's bothering me. Sonja skates tomorrow," he told me.

"So Sonja skates tomorrow. Nothing to worry about there. She sure knows how to do that!"

"Oakie, she can't skate without ice. Don't you understand? We don't have any ice! The studio sold the ice machine to Republic, and Yates won't even rent it back to us." He looked so awful I wondered why they called him "Lucky."

"My, oh my, oh my," I sympathized. "Listen, Lucky, if somebody doesn't turn down that air conditioning, tell Sonja she can skate on me. I'm turning into a block of ice."

One of the electricians came over. "Mr. Humberstone."

"Yeah?" Lucky didn't even look up.

"We've got the air conditioner under control." He stood there.

"Good!" I offered my thanks when Lucky didn't speak.

"Mr. Humberstone," he started again.

"Yeah?" Lucky repeated himself.

"About the ice-making machine." He hesitated.

"Yeah?" This time Lucky's ears pricked up.

"Well, you don't need it," he mumbled.

"We don't need it?" Lucky looked at the man, wondering why he now had to put up with stupid electricians.

"No, sir. We can make ice with the air conditioner." He delivered the line with the expertise of a Ned Sparks, one of the great stone-faced underplayers of all time. There was ice on schedule for the next day's shooting, and gratefully the studio took their cue from the electrician's delivery and underplayed his reward.

Some of our most beautiful actresses use some pretty spicey language on our motion picture sets. But that little ice skater, Sonja Henie, never did. Although her strong drive for professional perfection could have invoked it many times. That drive for perfection is what made her an Olympic champion. But it was her fun-loving nature and good sense of humor that sealed our lifetime friendship.

For years we had a running gag. "Oakie, how are you?" she'd love to ask, just so that I could answer, "O slo." And that little Norwegian would howl.

Sonja had just married Dan Topping (owner of the New York Yankees) when we were making *Winter Time.* All the fashionable shops in Beverly Hills had orders for engraving, embroidering, and embossing her new initials on everything she could get them on. Handerchiefs, scarfs, linens — everything was being monogrammed, Sonja Henie Topping. One afternoon on the set, Sonja and her mother (who was her constant advisor and confidante) and I were sitting in our low canvas-back, director's chairs, waiting for the crew to set up for the next *take.* Sonja was holding her handbag on her lap. It was the largest alligator handbag I had ever seen. It too was emblazoned with the three huge gold letters of her initials.

"Sonja, you need a caddy to carry that around for you," I said.

"Oh, no," she laughed, and held it up proudly, so that I could appraise the three fourteen-carat gold letters. Ben Silvey, Darryl Zanuck's hardworking, money-saving man, came up to us. He had Bill Ihnen, the set designer, with him.

"Miss Henie," he said, as he stood there

141

Jack Oakie, Sonja Henie and Cornel Wilde — *Wintertime.*

towering over her, "we got a little money problem." Big old Ben got right to the point with the charm of a Shylock. "Bill Ihnen here tells me that if we can use the archway that we got up on stage two, we won't have to build another one on this stage for the finale. So if you don't mind, would you please skate through that archway again for the finale?"

Sonja favored perfection, not economy. She didn't say a word. She sat there thinking. Actors are easily taken off guard, and I could see she was trying to be careful before making a decision.

Miss Henie," Ben asked again, when she didn't speak, "would you please skate under that archway we got on stage two?" She turned to her mother, and the ladies exchanged their thoughts in Norwegian. We three men listened, but didn't understand a word they said. Sonja didn't look up at Ben, she just shook her head. We all understood that. It meant "NO!"

Ben Silvey looked to me for help. "Mr. Oakie . . . ," he started, but my pantomime explained that it was the little lady who used the skates. "Miss Henie," he pleaded, "we'd just be duplicating

what we already got, see?" Sonja and her mother went into another discourse in Norwegian. This time they spoke a little louder and used gestures to underscore their words. Again, Sonja just shook her head, "NO!"

Ben reached for silent, Bill, and drew him into the picture. "Look, Bill here assures me the archway will work perfect, Miss Henie. We're just trying to save a little time, see?" Once again, Sonja and her mother discussed the situation in Norwegian. "Please, Miss Henie?" Ben asked with a lachrymose plea. "We wouldn't ask if we weren't sure that it'd be perfect, see?"

Sonja looked up at him, at last. "Now, just a minute, Mr. Silvey," she said. "Let me ask you something. Will there be room enough for the two other skaters to go through the archway with me?" There was a twinkle in Ben's eyes. I could see he felt the tables had turned! Now she was asking him a question! He turned to Bill Ihnen, who was as Irish as Paddy's Pig, and started a tirade at him in Yiddish.

"Zol zine mit glick! Zi mier gezundt! Zol zine mit mozel!" he quoted Yiddish proverbs and

sayings, and even threw in some swear words, and Bill didn't understand a word. Ben was imitating the Norwegian act that Sonja and her mother had just pulled on him. He got off a good one and we all enjoyed the joke. He then quickly took advantage of Sonja's laughter and interpreted it as her acceptance of the archway. "Thank you, Miss Henie," he said. "Everything's going to be all right." And he started off just as quickly.

Sonja's mother got up and went along with him and Bill, to check up on that archway on stage two. Sonja and I were alone for only a moment before I saw her professionalism take over again. "Oh, Jack!" she said. "If they let me look bad just so that they can save a little money, I'll be so mad!" She was holding that huge alligator bag so that it sat up on her lap, and she seemed to press her chin onto the top of it as she clenched her teeth in anger. "I mean it, Jack! I'll be so mad!"

"Sonja, honey, if you get mad enough," I said, pointing to her bag and those three mammoth gold letters which read S.H.T., "just dot that I!" All orders for initialing were cancelled!

Grisha and Jack.

GRISHA

I remember a time when a little sentence was delivered so perfectly, that it took the rise out of a Russian who was bred for detente long before we began to sell wheat to the U.S.S.R.

Gregory Ratoff and I had been friends for many years before he directed me in *Something To Shout About* at Columbia Studios. Grisha, was a very talented actor who was also a director-producer. But acting, directing, or producing, he was first and always an actor and one of the greatest scene stealers both on the stage and on the screen.

I saw him do the play *20th Century* on the stage of the old El Capitan. At that time, the theatre was on Hollywood Boulevard, near Highland Avenue. It was later rebuilt into the Paramount for motion pictures.

Eugenie Leontovich, his wife, starred with him, but he was so dynamic, half the time the audience forgot that the beautiful and very talented actress was up there on the stage with him. "Grisha," I said, when we met backstage after the opening night performance, "you're stealing the whole play from your wife." Ratoff had a habit of neighing in reaction to everything. He whinnied at me happily and said: "Hoikey, you are right. I am doing to my wife on the stage what I do to her at home in bed." (He was very proud of his conquests in both arenas.)

I was the victim of his scene stealing art many times. In *Once In A Lifetime,* and in *King Of Burlesque,* none of us had any defense at all when that man was performing, and he never stopped acting whether awake or asleep.

He once put on a very detailed performance of a Russian relaxing for me alone, as I sat across the room in the quiet of his home one evening, with only Eugenie coming in occasionally to serve us both some vodka and serve him some of his favorite whole salt fish.

"Hoikey," he said as he lifted his glass, "with vodka you can never get drunk."

I disproved that theory before the end of the evening.

Eugenie put some gypsy music on the victrola and put her fingers across her lips to warn me not to talk. Ratoff closed his eyes and went into his act. He sipped a bit of vodka, then picked up a whole fish with his fingers and ate on it and sipped alternately. When the bones were clean he held

Jack Oakie, Jack Haley and Gregory Ratoff — *The Sky's the Limit.*

the skeleton of the fish by the tail and dropped the whole thing head first into his mouth, after lots of slurping and sucking as he pulled the carcass through his teeth, the climax came when he pulled the whole thing out of his mouth and proud of his accomplishment held it up for me to see. There it all was, tail, bones, and head all in tact.

I sat and watched Ratoff perform until the wee hours of the morning. Besides being fascinated, I was also sipping vodka and couldn't get up. On *Something To Shout About,* his screen credits were only for producer-director, all his acting was on the set and gratuitous. One day Ratoff had his friend, the great composer and pianist, Sergei Rachmaninoff come on the lot to visit. Although Grisha acted out some pretty entertaining scenes for him, it was his compatriot who took the final bow.

First a young man tried to introduce himself to Ratoff who pretended to be too busy to listen to him.

"Mr. Ratoff, I'm from *Look Magazine.*" He kept repeating.

"Look! Spook! Nook! Fook!" Ratoff screeched at him trying to dismiss him. I was sitting with Rachmaninoff as Grisha walked towards us. Suddenly he stopped and did a double-take as if he had just realized what he heard. "Oh! Look!" He said to me, "Hoikey, he's from Look!" "We would

Jiggs, the famous Hollywood chimp, squares off with Jack —
Something To Shout About.

him off. He looked over at us and shrugged to show Rachmaninoff how important and busy he was. The tall artist remained immovable in the low director's chair and gave Ratoff a silent Ned Sparks fish-eye.

Then the studio photographer came over and asked me to come out into the alley to take some stills with Jiggs, the monkey who was in one of the vaudeville acts Ratoff had in the picture. Grisha invited Rachmaninoff to join us all in the alley. I sat on a bench with Jiggs and just for fun I began to throw some of my Mussolini faces at him. I jutted out my jaw and raised my hand in the "Great Dictator" salute, and Jiggs imitated me immediately. The ape was so funny the photographer had a field day. He took pictures of me acting with Jiggs until he ran out of film. Rachmaninoff seemed to be enjoying the picture session very much, so Ratoff began to take some bows.

"Wal," he said proudly to his friend, "haf we got something here!"

Because the great musician had been so quiet all day, when he finally nodded his head as if he agreed with Ratoff, and then pointed in my direction, we all stopped to listen and hang on his every word.

"Tell me something Grisha," he said in his deep musical voice, "how much are they paying the monkey?"

That little sentence deflated Ratoff and gave us all something to shout about.

like to do an interview with you Mr. Ratoff." The young man explained. "Hall right, young man. For Look, hokay." Ratoff agreed to have the interview. "But come back tomorrow," he said putting

Hazel Scott at the piano accompanying a stellar sextet: Jack Oakie, Lily Norwood, Don Ameche, Claire Trevor, William Gaxton and Janet Blair — *Something To Shout About.*

146

ERNEST V. HEYN
Executive Editor

HELEN GILMORE
Associate Editor

PHOTOPLAY
combined with
movie
MIRROR

SEPTEMBER, 1941
VOL. 19, NO. 4

OAKIE — On the Spot

He's so honest, it'll make

you blush. Some lively double-

talk about — and by — the

beloved "old Oakie bucket"

THINGS WE LIKE ABOUT JACK

BY SARA HAMILTON

THOSE clothes: The breath-taking nerve behind the man who dares wear them. His mugging. His "beeg mouf" good humor.

Those things we like about Jack Oakie.

Crazy as it seems, we go for his burgundy slack suits (red, neighbor), his red suede shoes (the glorious ham in him) and bright yellow scarf that sets the whole thing off like a cock-eyed sunset going down for the count of nine.

We like his outsized exhibitionism that livens up a town like the glow on W. C. Fields' nose. His never-ending flow of gab, a rich ripe humor that couldn't be shut off with Hitler's secret weapon, whatever that is.

His everlasting cry of "Well, this is show business for you," is as familiar to Hollywood as the call of the bull moose in mating season. We even get lonely for it when Oakie's not around.

We confess to a healthy respect for Oakie's ability as an actor and firmly believe, as do others, he knows more about the technique of motion-picture acting than most any other veteran in the business today. And as a scene-stealer, well, there's no one in the business can touch the old Oakie bucket.

He has no more dignity than a low-brow goat and on him it looks good. It tickles us pink, the way he shocks Hollywood with his easy familiarity with visiting dignitaries from the outside world who never forget him.

Bosses, executives, big shots are all one and the same bag of peanuts to Oakie. He's as easy, as loud and raucous with his boss, Darryl Zanuck, as he is with the motorcycle cop out in the Valley.

You can't impress Oakie, the Mayor of old West Van Nuys, and people have simply stopped trying. They know only too well what will happen to portions of their anatomy.

Recently Lieutenant Colonel Zanuck brought onto the set of "The Great American Broadcast" his commanding officer, General J. O. Mauborgne, Chief Signal Officer of the U. S. Army. Oakie, always the first to greet all visitors, had no more idea that this man was an army big shot and Mr. *(Continued on page* 91)

Oakie—on the Spot
Things We Like about Jack

(*Continued from page 48*)

Zanuck's General than fly. It wouldn't have made any difference anyhow, for all Jack caught was the word General which he instantly abbreviated to "Gen." Good old "Gen."

Posing together for pictures, Jack threw the General into hysterics by confiding, "No use for you to try to look good. They'll only caption this picture, 'Jack Oakie and Friend'."

His honesty is bigger than the man himself, in pounds and square inches. He actually had the hemstitched audacity to try to steal scenes from Charlie Chaplin, the man who brought him back in "The Great Dictator." And he's so gosh-darned honest he sits up and tells you about it.

CHARLIE first suspected something was going on when he asked for a playback of some dialogue just spoken by him and Jack. The conversation sprang forth from the machine while Charlie listened attentively. Finally, turning to Oakie, Charlie said, "What are you doing to me? Something's going on."

"Oh sure," Oakie grinned back. "I'm stealing your lines. You see, I begin my dialogue before you quite finish yours. That throws the attention to me."

From then on it was a race to see who could pick up the other's lines first.

Yes, we're dumbfounded at that honesty of his that has him saying, "Listen, honey, comedians are a peculiar tribe. They speak of each other as clever performers, but they don't like each other, never have, never will—and don't let anyone ever try to tell you differently."

Now you beat that one for freshness and deep-rooted honesty and we'll move out of town.

His patience! It's a revelation, really. He'll go over and over a scene with newcomers, anxious to help unless (and you newcomers note this) they feel they know enough to put one over on Oakie. And then heaven help them.

Recently a starlet giggled coyly, "You can't steal a scene from me, Jack Oakie. I've got the camera right in front of me."

Jack said nothing. When the scene was over the newcomer taunted, "Well, I had you that time."

"You sure did, honey, only—"

"Only what?" Her voice held a note of suspicion.

"Well, honey, I knew this was going to be a close-up and you see the close-up camera was right over here on my side all the time."

Without a word she walked away. Babies should never try putting one over on Papa Oakie.

His patience in little things that usually upset a man, any man, is wonderful to behold.

We met at the Derby for lunch. For one thing, the table wasn't steady and tipped every time Jack touched it.

The waiter was nonplussed. "Now, my good man," began Oakie in a voice quiet as a bombardment over London, "I have a suggestion. A small suggestion. Let us say we take this piece of melba toast. Thus. Now, let us take the toast and place it thusly under this leg of the table. Presto, it works."

The table sobered up like a stew after ten bromides.

Then came annoyance number two. The Danish pastry he had ordered fixed just so (it was Jack's breakfast) turned out to be something else again. There were no complaints. He ate it. But about an hour later he quietly went through all the directions again and this time got it right. He ate that, too.

His generosity in the thing actors least like to give—their time—is another of the many reasons we like Oakie. He will and has sat for four hours with a writer in order to give a good story. And he never forgets to express his gratitude for a line, a word in a written paragraph.

His intelligence is an admiration-getter. He studies the psychology of every director under whom he works. He knows the type that encourages, the type that drives with mental whips as it were, the ones who withhold all comment until the shooting's over and then shower the deserving ones with praise.

He can analyze a scene and tell exactly what it needs, why it hasn't jelled, why it's off balance.

We like Oakie, too, for the lump that so obviously chokes his throat, that shuts off a stream of loud rowdiness as if a key had suddenly turned, the peculiar dewiness in the eyes set in that mugging pan when the name of his mother, the mother who adored him, is mentioned.

"It would have broken her heart to have known I was off the screen so long," he says. "I'm glad she never knew."

His bewildered hurt, the almost little-boy disappointment in not winning the Academy Award he so wanted and his friends hoped he'd win, endeared him to everyone.

"Beeg mouf" Oakie. Gay, spirited, childish-hearted, talented beyond our consideration, he'll remain forever a name not to be forgotten in Hollywood. A personality. A character. An actor.

For that we admire him.

Okay, Oakie.

On the set for *Something To Shout About* Hazel Scott, Jack Oakie, Janet Blair and company.

Loretta Young drops in on the *Something To Shout About* set to a hearty welcome from William Gaxton, Jack Oakie, Don Ameche and Gregory Ratoff.

SHEETS

My friend Dick McInnes told me a story last night, which brought back some theatrical remembrances that are tied up in sheets. I met Dick about ten years ago when he was a writer, director, and producer of a television show. That show is no longer aired. Dick has talent and served his apprenticeship a long time ago, but as so many others, he has had a couple of tough show business years. Not that he hasn't made ends meet, it's that they've only just about touched; there's been no overlapping for a long time. But somehow, in show business talent survives because there's so much nourishment in hope.

Dick's story reminded me of the many roles that sheets have played in theatrical careers. There is so much that goes on between them, and under them, and on them, that we sometimes forget that there is something about them that is beyond our understanding. My, oh my, some of the things I remember when I think of sheets!

There was the time we all almost lost our jobs, when I was in the chorus of *Innocent Eyes,* the Shubert musical. The star was Mistinguett, the French chanteuse. We were playing the old Winter Garden, and her dressing room was not large enough to hold all her wardrobe. So her clothes were hung on an open rack and placed outside her door. She complained to the wardrobe mistress that all her beautiful costumes were getting soiled, since they were hanging out there in the open on the dusty stage. Mistinguett had very little knowledge of the English language. She refused to address the audience as Ladies and Gentlemen because she had seen those words lettered above the doors that lead into the men's and women's toilets in our country. So when the little old wardrobe mistress suggested that she "take a sheet" (to cover the clothes), the French star became so indignant she sent for Zeke Colvin, our stage manager, and demanded that the little Irishwoman be thrown out of the Wintergarden. She refused to go on and threatened to close the show. With words and gestures and by bringing in extra-large sizes of white percale to cover the clothes, Zeke finally explained and saved the show.

Sheets continued to play an important part in my life during the run of *Innocent Eyes.* Although at the time I was wearing my twenty-five-dollar alley-rabbit coat (called raccoon), I was freezing to death as I stood outside in the falling snow on Forty-fourth Street near Broadway in New York City.

My neck hurt from looking up at that second-story window above the Blue Ribbon Saloon, as I kept stomping my feet to keep warm while waiting and praying for the signal that meant I could come up and get between the sheets of the bed. I was sharing the one-room furnished flat with Bill Burdee, who was also in the show, and I had to wait for him to let me know when he and his girl friend were no longer using the room.

I often think that the sheets used in that room had to be made of asbestos. But although they were hot, they were at least dryer than the sheets I shared with Harry White, the Russian dancer who had a specialty number in the show. Harry took some leaps and crazy knee drops, and in order to keep his dancing legs and sore knees fit, he took nightly treatments which meant sleeping with hot salt bags wrapped around his knees. He also used a vibrator. The bed always shook, though I found that part of it relaxing. It was when the hot salt bags broke that the discomfort set in between those sheets. To this very day, my friend Harry White still claims that he and his broken salt bags were the forerunners of the popular water bed.

Anyway, all this came to mind when Dick told me of his extravagant sheet ploy at Bullock's January White Sale, and (only the good Lord knows how) it became a sleeper and brought his pad into the winner's circle.

Dick received an unexpected gift of money for Xmas. Now this was a Xmas when all the necessities of practical living were right down front-center, staring up at his self-conscious performance. He knew the role that the little roll was supposed to play, but somehow he couldn't cast it in that direction. At Bullock's department store, he stood at the counter looking down at the expensive silk sheets, which the salesgirl spread open before him in soft folds. Although the price tag read "50% off," it would still take the entire windfall to buy the set of two sheets and two pillow slips.

He gently rested his hand on the creamy white silk. Nothing moved so richly under his hand ever before. He was afraid to finger the material because a hangnail might pull at the beautifully woven delicate threads. He just let his hand lay lightly on the smooth silky luxury and closed his eyes as he pictured his bed made up in silk sheets and silk pillow cases. He told me he stood there and allowed himself the exquisite sensation of believing that while lying between those silk sheets the phone would ring, he would reach over to his night stand, and still luxuriating between the folds of silk, he would answer the call he had been waiting for for months, and accept the job that would turn out to be better than he even dared dream it would be.

"No, no!" he said to himself. "I'd better pay the phone bill instead of thinking about lying between silky satin smoothness." "No! no!" he said aloud as he turned from the counter abruptly and took the escalator down to the street floor. He went down two steps at a time as he tried to hurry away from temptation. He finally jumped off the moving steps taking the last three in one leap, and without hesitation he ran right around the structure and got back on the up side of those power driven stairs, and took those two at a time to quicken the mechanical ascent.

The salesclerk was still there, the sensuous, costly (although half-price), elegance was still spread in beckoning folds. "Wrap them up!" he shouted, "before I change my mind!" That night he slid into bed between those new sheets. "Dear God," he prayed, "nobody can feel this good and not be called on to do a good job of work." He slipped away into a deep restful sleep that mended and healed all the wounds and bruises he had reaped during the plowing of those last tough years.

At nine o'clock the following morning, the phone rang. He reached for the receiver and answered the call from between those silk sheets. Dick is again writing and producing, and directing a regular show for television. Do you think this true story will raise the volume of business at Bullock's January White Sale?

Remember, there are things about a sheet that a bare explanation cannot cover.

Oakie swaggers along *Tin Pan Alley.*

CAR BARNS

"Oakie, do you remember your first date, and some of the things it led to?" I was recently asked.

"I most certainly do!" I said without hesitation. Her name was Louise Patterson, she was the prettiest girl in Muskogee, Oklahoma, and I was secretly in love with her right up to our first date. It was on November 12, 1908, when she came to the masquerade party that was given for my fifth birthday. I wore a real baseball suit, and I was sure she was going to find me irresistible. She came as "Mrs. Wiggs of the cabbage patch." She was so beautiful, it didn't matter that she won the prize for the best costume, which was the biggest red India-rubber ball I had ever seen. What did matter was that she spent the whole afternoon bouncing the ball with Mace Harrison! My best friend!

Well, I guess that threw me, and led to my determination to prove that I could play ball better than anyone in all of the Oklahoma Indian Territory. No matter what size or shape, I've been one of the happiest ball players ever since.

When we went up to live in New York City (to attest to my resolve), I made the number-one basketball team at De La Salle. Down under the Queensborough Bridge, on the rockiest diamond imaginable, I played baseball with the Hudson River Dock Rats, and believe me that good old hard and solid early training stood me in good stead when I played baseball for Paramount. When the studio bought Ring Lardner's famous baseball play, *Elmer The Great* and gave me the part of Elmer Kane they sent Mike Donlin, the star outfielder for the New York Giants over to RKO where I was working on *Street Girl*. They wanted him to teach me how to throw a ball. When Mike realized I knew how to throw a ball he asked me not to tell the studio. "Oakie, don't tell Paramount you're this good. They're paying me $500 a week and I'd like to pick up the money." So every day at lunch time we played catch for about five minutes. And as Elmer the Great, the audiences could tell I wasn't faking it! I could throw a ball.

Then they felt that I could carry one too, so they had me tackle the game of football. I played in *Collegiate, College Humor, College Rhythm,* and *Touchdown,* and then when Paramount Pictures ran out of titles, Twentieth Century-Fox picked up the ball, and had me carrying it again in *Rise And Shine.* I was thirty-seven and played a freshman; Linda Darnell was seventeen and played a senior.

We sang and danced in the Mark Hellinger Production directed by Allan Dwan, to music and lyrics by Ralph Rainger and Leo Robin, with dances by Hermes Pan.

I still love to play ball, but now I don't run; I just enjoy walking after that small hard white one, and I've been lucky. In golf tournaments I've won salad bowls, plates, and cups — it's been a picnic.

"Come on, Oakie," my interrogators complained. "We didn't mean a date that close to the turn of the century." Once again I was being reminded that I'm over seventy. "Update that date a little," they suggested.

"All right," I said, "there is a date that of all dates always comes to mind first, because that was the date that led me to Hollywood and the movies."

"That sounds more like it."

Well, I was a late teenager and she was an early one, and it happened when I was in the chorus of *Innocent Eyes.* We were still breaking in the show out of town before coming into New York's Winter Garden Theatre. The big number we were working on was a ballad called "Organdy Days." The romantic music was written by Sigmund Romberg and Jean Schwartz, and the dance arrangements were by choreographer Seymour Felix. The girls were dressed in billowy organdy gowns, and the boys wore white tie and tails. Our star, Mistinguett also did a specialty in the number. It was a formal number and I always felt elegant dancing in it.

While playing the Detroit Shubert Opera House three of the girls left the show, and Zeke Colvin, our stage manager, had to find replacements for them. "Oakie, come on up town with me tonight after the show, I want to catch *The Ernie Young Revue,*" Zeke said. "You have a good eye for the ladies, you can help me pick three girls for the replacements."

So we saw *The Ernie Young Revue,* and I pointed out three girls who were dancing in it that night. Zeke thought that one of the girls I had picked was a little too plump, and her eyes a little too big. "Look at those eyes!" he said. "They're so big they look like they're going to pop right out of her head!"

But I thought she was the most beautiful girl I'd seen since Mrs. Wiggs of the cabbage patch. All three girls got jobs in our show, but because the

Shuberts had a rule that the boys and girls working in their shows were forbidden to fraternize, I never did get to meet them.

It was on the train going into New York that I finally took the liberty of approaching the girl with the great big eyes. I was nervous, expecting that there probably was another Mace Harrison around somewhere, but it wasn't like that at all. She was so easy to talk to. It seemed we both had been dreaming about the same things all our lives. We both wanted to be great dancers.

"I want to be the most famous ballroom dancer in the world," she said. "Someday I'm going to dance with Maurice. I don't know how, but I dream about it all the time. Can you imagine the thrill of being his dancing partner?"

"Well," I said, "someday I'm going to be a big musical comedy star. I want to sing and dance and have a style all my own. You know, like Harry Richman. He sure has style!"

After we opened at the Winter Garden in New York, in order to keep dreaming we had to break the Shubert rule. The old car barns, where the trolley cars were housed, and repaired, and turned around, were right back of the Wintergarden from Fiftieth Street to Fifty-first Street, and Seventh Avenue to Sixth Avenue, and easy to get to for our secret meetings. We'd sit and talk and dream and try out new dance steps. We were told the Shuberts made their rule to keep us on our toes, but breaking it never interfered with our dancing one iota. Our dreams kept us so light-hearted we had more elevation than any other dancer on the stage.

Years later the car barns were torn down, and the Hotel Manger and the Roxy Theatre were put up right on the spots where we had had our secret special meetings. When the New York run came to a close, I was asked to go on the road with the show. The Shuberts gave me a raise and a specialty number, so I said I'd go. But she said, "No, I'm going to join *The Passing Show,* and she left for Atlantic City.

Just before we left New York to open in Providence, she called me from Atlantic City. "Meet me at Pennsylvania Station," she said. "I've got to talk to you."

"I'm going to be tested for the movies!" she said, as we came up out of the station to Thirty-fourth Street.

"Who says so?" I asked. She was so excited she didn't seem to make good sense.

"MGM Harry Rapf from MGM."

"Are you sure?" I couldn't believe she was taking the offer seriously. "Remember you have those great big pop eyes. What if you don't photograph, you'll be giving up a good job," I tried to warn her.

"I'm going to make the test." She had decided she was going to take the chance.

"You sure you know what you're doing?" I asked again. I didn't want her heart to be broken. She knew what she was doing, so we wished each other good luck and said goodbye. I went on tour with *Innocent Eyes,* and she went on to test for the movies. It was January 1925.

After *Innocent Eyes,* I went into *Artists and Models,* and then I went into vaudeville with Lulu McConnell. I began to see her in movies, and while on tour I'd watch for her pictures. She became more and more beautiful on the screen and showed more and more skill in her talented performances. Once in a fan magazine interview she talked about me as her steady boyfriend.

It was two-and-a-half years later, June 1927, that I followed her out to Hollywood. I made movies at Paramount and she was at MGM, and there was no car barn between us for years. Finally, one night I attended a gala premiere. It was a formal affair and I wore white tie and tails. As I entered the lobby of the theatre a voice over the back of my shoulder whispered, "I haven't seen you look like that since 'Organdy Days'."

I turned around singing, "When hearts are young in Organdy Days." There she was, the date that led me to Hollywood, now known the world over as Joan Crawford.

"Jack, don't you wish that we could get into a chorus today?" she asked. We laughed — enough years had passed for us to know that we had left those dancing dreams behind us at the old car barns, which were also no longer there.

Sid Grauman encourages Jack Oakie "signing in" at Sid's famous Chinese Theatre.

154

AN UNSETTLING EXPERIENCE

My friendship with Sid Grauman was warm and richly rewarding, but being with Sid was always a risky and unsettling experience. Late one afternoon during World War II, however, the rewards were well worth the gamble.

Having saved some of my ration of gasoline stamps, I drove out to my little ranch in Northridge in the San Fernando Valley. It was the time when without food or fuel, the valley was left mostly to the wildlife, and I always found it a luxury to be able to get out there to do some much needed work. I was down at the bottom of the orchard watering a row of newly planted baby orange trees, when the call came through. "Mr. Oakie!" the housekeeper called down to me from the head of the orchard. (I have about two acres of citrus planted on a slope that levels off into a field where the barns are. The new trees were to help prevent ground movement in that low area and hopefully stave off a washout during the rainy season.) "Mr. Oakie!" she screamed again. "They're still on the phone! They say it's an emergency!"

I was making *That's The Spirit* at the Universal Studios and had only just got out to the ranch after a pretty heavy day's shooting schedule. I sure wasn't up to any night time retakes.

"Tell the studio you can't find me," I called back. I had my heart set on getting those trees watered before it got dark.

"It's not the studio!" She shouted back at me. "The man said to tell you to hurry because the cement is getting hard!"

"The cement is getting hard?" I said to myself, feeling like a blockhead. "All right!" I called up to her. "Tell them I'll be right there!" Reluctantly I turned off the hoses and went up to the house to answer the phone. It was Sid Grauman. He had promised to put my handprints and footprints in the forecourt of his Chinese Theatre, (now Mann's Chinese Theater), and I didn't believe him. "No, Sid," I said, knowing full well his capacity for practical jokes. Sid was a master showman. All of his friends unwittingly became acting members of his impromptu comedies. "No, Sid, I'm not driving all the way into Hollywood for a laugh!"

I remembered a very special night when Sid used to have vaudeville acts at the Chinese Theatre. (In those days, during the early 1930's, not only did he book a regular full vaudeville bill, but he also used to get all us local moving picture per-

sonalities to play what he called the "Midnight Show," and we did it for him just for fun. Abe Lyman would bring his band into the lobby and entertain, before we all went into the theatre to put on an improvised show before the last movie.)

That night I was sitting right down front center, anxious to watch that great performer, Jimmy

Jack and his wife, Vickie, with Sid Grauman.

Savo. Jimmy was using "River Stay Way From My Door," for his finale. All his gestures were carefully rehearsed, and when he got to the climax of the song he stopped and waved frantically at the floor as if to hold back a great deluge from a raging river. What I didn't know as I sat there looking up at Savo, was that night after night Sid Grauman had watched him stop at the very same spot on the floor and sing directly to it "River Stay Way From My Door."

The temptation for a joke was too great for Sid. So one night after the theatre was closed, he got a carpenter to drill a hole in the floor of the stage exactly where Savo stopped to fight the river. He then had a hose and nozzle attached to the hole from under the stage.

I was only an arms length away, looking up into his face, when Jimmy got to that well-rehearsed location and started to push against the imaginary onslaught of the river. "River Stay Way From My Door" he sang with a loud voice and broad gestures, just as little Sid turned on the hose full-force. We in the first row were also inundated.

"Oakie, it's not a joke!" Sid insisted over the phone. "I'm serious! You've got to come in! And Jack, please hurry. The cement man has the mixture all ready to go and it's getting too dry to pour."

"No, Sid." (I still didn't believe him.) "I'm watering some baby orange trees and plan to stay out here at the ranch tonight."

"All right! I'll tell you what we'll do," he said in his deep, soft, most gentle con man's voice. "We'll make your cement green so that the people will always know that you have a green thumb and love trees."

It was awfully hard to say no to Sid even though I was sure I was the foil in another of his practical jokes. So I took a chance and drove into Hollywood. When I got to the theatre, I could hardly believe it! Sid was truly preparing to put my hand prints and foot prints into a block in the walk of his Chinese Theatre! There was a goodly crowd roped off in the forecourt, and the cement man was waiting for me, wetting down the green colored mortar that was already poured and smoothed in the block that was to be mine.

"You see, folks!" Sid shouted to the crowd. "I told you he'd be here!" He grabbed my arm and led me right down to the edge of that fast-drying cement that every motion picture actor hoped he could step into somewhere down the line in his career. I kneeled down reverently and was handed a special pencillike all-metal pointer.

I wrote, "Dear Sid: My little tootsies don't stumble over 'em."

I no sooner got up than Sid said, "Let's go on over to the Brown Derby and get something to eat." Little Sid was always hungry but ate very sparingly. It seemed to me that he just looked at food but never ate it. He would always order two or three entrees — chicken, lamb chops, steak and all the fixin's — and then just look.

"Sid, what are you doing?" I'd ask him. I was always shocked to see all that food set before the five foot, ninty pound little man.

"Well," he always explained, "if I don't like the chicken or the chops, then I have the steak for a backstop." He always wanted a backstop when he was hungry and didn't eat. The only thing I ever saw him eat was ice cream. Sid lived at the Ambassador Hotel, and in all the many years I drove him home we always stopped in at the coffee shop for ice cream. He ate barrels of it before going up-

Jack and Vickie with Sophie Tucker.

Although I knew Sid would just order and look at the food, I was hungry, and so we got into my car and started east for Vine Street and the Brown Derby. As we crawled along Hollywood Boulevard at that twenty-five miles an-hour speed limit we were put down to after Pearl Harbor, Sid began to laugh. "I knew it!" I said, still suspicious that the ceremony at the Chinese Theatre was another one of his jokes. "You're having the whole thing erased!"

"No! No! Jack. I promise you, your hand and foot prints are in the Chinese Theatre forecourt cement forever." He said. He started to laugh again as he pointed ahead to his Grauman's Egyptian Theatre. "I'm laughing because I realize how lucky I am right now not to be stuck with a Grauman's Japanese Theatre."

The doorman at the Egyptian was dressed in a long bright red coat and hat, with lots and lots of gold braid draped across his breast. "Sid," I said. "You sure know how to dress up your theatres." I told him how thrilled I was in 1927 when I first arrived in town. The very first movie I ever saw in Hollywood was at the Grauman's Chinese Theatre.

Douglas Fairbanks and Lupe Velez were playing in *The Goucho,* and the most exciting part of the program was seeing the lifelike wax figure of Fairbanks dressed as the Goucho, in all the glory of the authentic wardrobe, standing in the lobby. "You know I got the idea for those life-size wax figures quite by accident," he said, and then told me a very picturesque story of a practical joke he once pulled on Charlie Chaplin.

It seems Sid met a furrier who had come out from the East to hold a fashion show in Los Angeles. He brought a couple of life-size wax mannequins with him to model the fur coats. "One of the dolls was a beautiful brunette and the other a gorgeous blonde. Never saw two better looking quail in my life," Sid said.

As he watched the furrier drape his furs over the two figures, Sid got the idea that he would like to test the lifelike appearance of the gals under more personal wraps. He begged the furrier to let him borrow the mannequins for a night, and so for a very agreeable fee the wax figures were delivered to his room at the Alexandria Hotel. But instead of sending the dolls with all their parts assembled, the furrier had taken them apart and boxed them for safety. "I didn't bother with the arms and legs," Sid said. "I just put the two torsos in my bed and set the heads on the necks as best I could."

He then called Chaplin. Charlie was living at the Los Angeles Athletic Club at the time. "Charlie," he said, "I have two of the most beautiful girls here in my room and they're both anxious to meet

stairs to bed. The only other time I ever saw him eat — with no backstop — was the evening at Ciro's when we went to catch Sophie Tucker's show. She had a sensational new comedy team working with her called Martin and Lewis. That night Sid ordered a can of sardines. "Serve them in the can!" he stressed as the waiter looked at him quizzically. The little things were brought in the can with the lid folded back, and it was Sid's joy to see that they hadn't been disturbed from their tight fitting. He ate them right out of the tin, relishing them with lemon and onions — no backstop.

you." Although Sid had gotten Charlie out of bed, Charlie anxiously said, "I'll be right over."

With the wax heads resting on the pillows and the covers pulled up to hold them in place, Sid carefully got into the bed between them and then dimmed the lights. It wasn't long before Chaplin knocked on the door, and Sid called from the bed in a whisper, "Come in, the door's open." Charlie came in, and taking his cue from Sid's whisper and the very dimly lit room, he closed the door quietly and tiptoed over to the bed. There they were — three heads showing partially over the covers. "Charlie," Sid whispered from between the beautiful blonde and brunette, "they're very shy, they don't talk very much."

So Charlie, being the comedian, decided he wouldn't talk either and began to make his advances in pantomime. He was wearing a long overcoat, and instead of just taking it off he went into a strut and began disrobing like a stripteaser. He paraded back and forth as he took one arm out of a sleeve, then hugged the coat to him as he went into a pirouette.

"You know Charlie's a great dancer," Sid said, as if I needed reminding. "Well, he went into a ballet number, twisting and turning till he got down to his long-sleeved long-legged underwear. Then he leaped like a Nijinsky and came flying through the air and landed on the bed."

It seems the bounce decapitated the ladies and both heads went rolling on the floor. "The look on Charlie's face told me he was ready to send my head rolling with the other two," Sid said. "So I hid under the covers. Do you know that Charlie didn't talk to me for six months!"

Well, that's how Sid began to use lifelike wax figures for the theatre. He was the forerunner of the wax museums. He was also the very first to find a way to use arc lights to herald the opening nights of motion pictures. Grauman went in to see Otto Olsen, an electrician who had a little electrical shop right down the street from the Hollywood Brown Derby.

"Say, I'd like to get more light up around the theatre to tell the people we've got a show going on here," Sid said. Olsen began to talk about more conventional bulbs, but Sid said no, that wasn't what he had in mind. "How about a searchlight?" Sid asked. "Isn't there some way we could throw some searchlights up into the sky? That would bring people into the theatre!" Even Sid was surprised when Olsen liked the idea and said, "Yes, I'm pretty sure I can handle that."

So arc lights began to be used in front of Grauman theatres, and today even meat markets are opened with the beckoning lights that Sid invented. Not only are his many theatrical innovations used over and over, but so is his very original wit.

In 1945 after a very beautiful service at the Wilshire Boulevard Temple, I was standing in line waiting to say my last goodbye to a good friend director-producer, Mark Sandrich. Little Sid was standing right in front of me. As we waited our turn to pay our respects, the fellow in front of Sid turned to him and quietly remarked that it was hard to believe that Sandrich was gone because he looked so good. "Well, he should!" Sid said, explaining the phenomenon. "He spent the last two weeks in Palm Springs!"

When tape recorders first hit the market, Vickie and I got one, and anybody who even came near our house had to speak into it. Sid had dinner with us one night and Vickie got out the tape recorder. Grauman gave one of the most heart-rending talks. He praised my work, our home, and the delicious dinner we had just had. Then he paused a moment, and with that devilish Grauman tone in his voice he said, "Just a minute, folks. Vickie and Jack just left the room to greet some guests that have just arrived. While they're out, I want to tell you the truth about this place. The trip out here is too long, and when you get here they have a dog that lifts his leg on yours — and the dinner! Why the chops were so tough you couldn't cut the gravy. If you're driving out this way and get to the Oakie Ranch, don't stop, keep right on going!"

Then he signed off with, "This is Sid Grauman, the little showman" — his trademark.

WORKING FOR A QUITTING CLAUSE

The first time I'd ever heard about it was when Claudette Colbert pulled the stunt. I was working on *Sea Legs* and also on *Paramount On Parade,* and when I wasn't in front of the motion picture camera, I was posing for still pictures for the publicity department.

The pictures I made were called the "bread-and-butter" pictures of the studio. They cost nothing and made millions, and supported the prestige productions that cost millions and made nothing. Paramount had me working twenty-four hours a day, seven days a week, and when there was a lull they loaned me out to other studios.

It was a day when I was running between cameras, and I happened to pass the Claudette Colbert set when they were breaking for the day. I couldn't believe it! It was only six o'clock at night! "Where's everybody going?" I asked one of the grips.

"Home," he said simply, as if that was a word I was accustomed to hear at that time of night.

"Home!" I screamed. "It's only six o'clock!"

"I know," he said. He kept his voice down, and the son-of-a-gun put on an act of superiority that would have won him an Academy Award.

"Come off it!" I said, trying to get him back down to my station in life. "How do you all get to go home at six o'clock?"

"Well," he became confidential, and told me the secret that haunted me for years. "Claudette Colbert has a six o'clock quitting clause in her contract!"

About a year or so later I was loaned out to Universal for *Once In A Lifetime.* I was innocence abroad when I decided to try out the six o'clock quitting clause. For two weeks I walked off the set exactly when the hands formed a perfectly straight perpendicular line right down the center of the clock's face. It never occurred to me that Universal's front office would get in touch with Paramount's front office, and not knowing how closely those legal minds in motion pictures were enmeshed, I was enjoying the luxury of going home only twelve hours after I left it.

It was very early on the Monday of my third week on the picture, just before I was to step into the set for my first scene of the day, when I was stopped in my tracks by an errand boy. I never saw the lad before that day and have never seen him since, but I shall always remember the look of

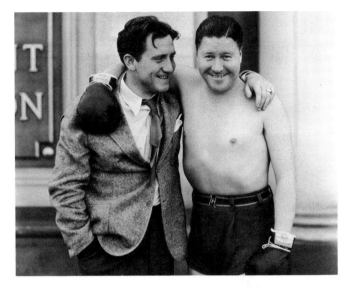

Spencer Tracy and Jack Oakie — *Looking for Trouble.*

satisfaction on his face as he handed me an open memo from the Universal front office. He must have enjoyed what he read — I certainly didn't. "Mr. Oakie, you do not have a six o'clock quitting clause in your contract, and we are fining you 1000 dollars for the time you have taken in breaking early the past two weeks."

Russell Mack, our director, was standing right there, so I handed the note to him. "Oh, no! he said. "How stupid can they get? Handing you a thing like this just before you go into a scene. What the devil do they think you are — a machine! Leave this with me, Jack. I'll take care of it."

"By the way, Jack, did you have the six o'clock clause in your contract?" he asked.

"No," I said, and shrugged with a deep sigh to show him how disappointed I was. "But I tried."

"Oh, you Oakie." Russell Mack was one of the sweetest guys in the world. Anyway he kind of understood me. "Go on, wait in your dressing room, I'll take care of it."

"OK." And thinking about that 1000-dollar fine, I said, "You know, I just don't feel like being funny right now."

Luckily they cancelled the letter and the fine, with an apology saying they were sorry I didn't have a six o'clock quitting clause in my contract. Not half as sorry as I was! Now that perpendicular line that read six on the clock was lying flat on its

Jack Oakie, Arline Judge, Constance Cummings and Spencer Tracy — *Looking for Trouble.*

Jack Oakie, Warner Baxter, Alice Faye, Shaw and Lee (at the piano) — *King of Burlesque.*

face. More than ever before I was hoping that someday it would stand up for me.

About a year later I was loaned out to Twentieth Century. Zanuck hadn't yet merged with Fox, and we were shooting at the Samuel Goldwyn Studios. I was teamed with Spencer Tracy in *Looking for Trouble,* and the talk was that with his underplaying and my jumping around we were a perfect twosome. Not looking for trouble, I steered clear of my quitting clause ploy, but it was at the Goldwyn Studios that I saw one of the most regal positions a six ever had on the face of a clock!

George Arliss was working on the next stage to ours, so while waiting for our crew to set up for the next scene, I sneaked over to watch the great actor perform. The cameras were rolling, and that magnificent English voice was booming through the stage. I tiptoed over to get a close look and there he was; the man looked ten feet tall in his red satin robes. Jenner, his valet, stood beside me. "Who's he playing?" I asked.

"Cardinal," Jenner whispered in a one-word answer.

"Great team!" I said. "I always bet on the 'Cards'."

I don't think Jenner had ever heard of St. Louis or baseball, anyway he wasn't listening to my jokes, because he suddenly stepped right into the set while Arliss was still talking, and with his back to the camera, announced loudly enough for the

entire company to hear, "It's six o'clock sir!" Without hesitating he removed Richelieu's satin robe, and helped Arliss into a dressing gown as he led him out of the set.

"Just a minute!" the assistant director yelled. "Let's finish this one shot!"

"Mr. Arliss does not work after six o'clock," Jenner said. The man, who had seemed ten feet tall just a moment ago on the set, paused as he came toward me. "I hear you are a good team," he said graciously, complimenting Spence and myself. I looked down at the giant who didn't even reach my chin. "Thanks," I said, "but I've always been for the 'Cards' myself. I put my money on the Cardinals everytime." The artist laughed, as I watched his six o'clock exit. George Arliss had a double play going for him! The Cardinal was a Giant!

The last time I'd ever seen that quitting clause give anybody a lift was on *King of Burlesque.* Warner Baxter had it in his contract. "Oakie, I've got to quit at six o'clock," he told me. "After six my face begins to fall." It's a funny thing, but he was absolutely right. At one minute after six every muscle in that handsome man's face began to droop.

Anyway, right after that the Screen Actors Guild came in and took all the fun out of trying for that quitting clause. Six o'clock stood up for everybody. It became the law!

SOME SOUND THOUGHTS

On September 23, 1976, I was listening to the Ford-Carter debate being televised from the stage of the old Walnut Street Theatre in Philadelphia, when suddenly I realized I was watching a silent picture. For me, suspense and drama had entered the program. "Trouble with sound," I said to myself. "They sure both come together!" For that half hour of silence, my thoughts on sound took me back almost half a century, and it seemed to me nothing had changed; they were still doing the same things, only different people were doing them.

But fifty years ago, on a set very much like the highly publicized television one (well, it too had just a couple of wooden chairs and tables), the sound men got over their trouble with a Hollywood trick. The innovation was used so often it became a legend. The first time I ever saw it used was on my own first talking picture, Paramount Studio's very first picture with sound, the 100-percent, all-talking comedy-melodrama was titled *The Dummy*. We in the picture thought it was aptly called *The Dummy*, because that's the way we all felt about starting to talk for moving pictures. None of us knew what we were doing. Not even Ruth Chatterton, or Fredric March, or John Cromwell, who were brought in from Broadway because of their great theatrical talking talent. Besides those three great stars, Paramount also signed up the veteran stage director, Robert Milton, to direct the talking actors in their talking picture.

It was the very first day of shooting, and Fred Kohler (one of the great villains of silent pictures), ZaSu Pitts, and I were in the very first scene. The set was soundless. We had been tiptoeing and whispering all morning, constantly being warned that the sensitive sound equipment could hear a pin drop outside the stage. It was pretty tough on those of us who had made silent pictures. We were so accustomed to hearing the shuffle of feet and furniture, jolly jokes, and laughter, all the while the camera was cranking away shooting a scene.

Virgil Miller, the great cameraman on my first picture *Finders Keepers* was the most sociable conversationalist, while cranking away, photographing beautiful Laura La Plante. When Wesley Ruggles, who was directing, called "Cut," Virgil Miller, who would still be discussing a dinner party, would just swing the crank in triple time, bring it to an abrupt stop, and notch the film. (To notch the film was to tear a wedge off with your fingers, so that the cutter would know where the scene ended and another began.)

J. Roy Hunt, our cameraman on *The Dummy*, was considered an ace who had invented a great many things to improve the camera. He had been behind a lens a long time and knew what he was doing. He was also a very wealthy man. His background and money gave him the security the rest of us lacked, on that first day on that first talkie.

Roy was lining up that first shot, with ZaSu and myself sitting on a couple of wooden chairs and Fred Kohler standing there waiting to say the very first words to be recorded for a talking picture at Paramount. "Don't worry about me," he kept reassuring Robert Milton. "I've been on the stage before. I know how to throw my voice out there."

"Good, good!" Bob Milton whispered, showing his confidence in the performer. "Good, good!" Pittsy and I were ready, Fred Kohler was ready, but Bob Milton still didn't call, "Camera! Action!"

I should stop here to explain something that was never publicized for folks outside of motion pictures: the introduction of sound to pictures was not very friendly. In those very early days there was conflict in every arena of the industry, and of all the contestants, the real heavyweights were the cameramen and the sound men. Roy Pomeroy, the head of the sound department, put a young man on our picture to handle the knobs that controlled our voices. He was called the mixer.

Roy Hunt looked through his camera for a final check of the lights, ZaSu and I held our breaths while Fred was preparing to throw his voice, when suddenly there was a scream that pierced that silent sound stage and put us all into trembling shock.

"Get that thing out of there!" Roy Hunt screeched, his face still in the box. The only sound on the stage was that of chattering teeth. "Come on, get that thing out of his face!" he screamed again. The microphone was swinging off the end of a stick so close to Fred Kohler's face it just missed knocking his teeth out. There was still no answer from the mixer. "Come on now, get that damn thing out of there or I'll get it out for you!" Roy was turning purple with rage. He started into the set to tear the mike down, when the mixer somehow got there before him.

"That mike stays right where it is!" he said squarely into Roy's face.

"Well, I'm not photographing that hunk of hardware!" Roy shouted right back at him, trying to reach over his shoulder at the thing he was shielding. "Get it out of there!"

"Can't! I've got to hear what they say whether you photograph it or not!"

"Oh, yeah!" Roy had never taken such lip from anybody. "You get that thing out of there or you'll never hear anything again!"

"Well, it stays right there or you're never going to be able to see anything again!"

That did it! "We'll see about that! You come on outside and let's settle this right now!" Roy started off the stage and the mixer joined him.

When they came back from the alley, the mike was taken down from overhead and things were laid underfoot, and the legend made its first appearance. A great big bowl of flowers was brought in and planted right in the center of the wooden table, and the microphone was propped up behind it so that it was hidden from the camera side. Pittsy and I got ready to hold our breath again, but Roy Hunt was still up on his high horse.

"Mr. Milton!" he called over to Bob. "Would you like to check this before we go?"

"Oh, yes, yes," Robert Milton said. (I don't think he had ever looked through a camera before.) He stepped over and looked into Roy Hunt's hand grinder. He kept looking and nodding his head with approval. When he stepped back he shook his fist at Roy enthusiastically. "Good, good! Just what I want! Good! Very Good!" Robert Milton sprang away from the camera jauntily. He seemed a very happy man.

Roy Hunt looked over at me, shrugged his shoulders, and beckoned to me with his little finger. I joined him at the camera. "Oakie, take a look," he whispered. I looked into the box. All was black; the lens was closed. I went back into the set, sat down next to Pittsy, and held my breath harder than ever. I certainly wasn't going to make a sound. Finally, Robert Milton called, "Camera! Action!"

And at last Fred Kohler spoke those first lines, "What-did-you-think-I-was-going-to-do?-Stay-in-Chicago-forever?" The recitation was clear and precise. It could have easily carried to the second balcony, but none of us knew if it should be considered good or bad. Robert Milton kept taking it over and over again, and we all kept going back and forth to an adjoining stage to hear it played back. We all finally played it safe and agreed

unanimously that the bowl of flowers was working just fine.

The Dummy was a box office hit, and all the columnists and reviewers explained just how this new form of movie-making was accomplished. One wrote: "Robert Milton brought a new experience to screen actors. While making the film the cast was called upon for thorough rehearsals before the first camera crank was turned! He even rehearsed during stage waits while lights and sound equipment were being adjusted."

Another wrote: "The sound synchronization and registration throughout was very good. The mechanical difficulties which have confronted the Talker producers are being overcome."

After the first planting of that bowl, the flower market in Hollywood boomed. There was a bowl of flowers on every set in the industry. The flower growers could hardly keep up with the demand. Despite the fact that the industry had picked up this new scent for sound, making talkies was still no bed of roses. There were a couple of times when the bowl of flowers just wouldn't work.

Like in Chinatown Nights, when Wally Beery and I had to walk up the aisle of the theatre saying our lines. "There's a bird on the wire!" the sound man called to our director, "Wild" Bill Wellman. That was his way of complaining about some static.

"Well, go on out and shoot him!" Wild Bill yelled back at him.

We tried the scene several times. "Can't hear them," the sound man shouted.

"You can hear a pin drop!" Wellman screamed. "Why the hell can't you hear them?"

There was no way they could set up a bowl of flowers in the aisle as we were walking, so Wild Bill picked up a pillow, put the mike on it, and walked backwards on tiptoe holding the thing practically under our noses as Beery and I walked and talked into it. That of course was long before anyone thought of inventing the perambulator.

Another aisle problem was on the train in Once In A Lifetime. I always see that lampshade swinging in our faces as Aline MacMahon speaks to the conductor, and I wonder what Southern Pacific thought when they saw lamps hanging from the ceiling's of their moving trains.

Well, when I watched that half hour of television silence, I still believed "a picture is worth a 1,000 words," and I kept waiting for a sound man to come in and set up a bowl of flowers, after which I was sure President Ford and Carter would come on again and I would hear them say in unison, "What-did-you-think-I-was-going-to-do.-Stay-in-Chicago-forever?"

It is only a little over a year since President Carter's silent television exposure, and in his short era from silence to sound he has learned that there is suspense in silence and trouble with sound. His use of long silences and three words is a Bing Crosby delivery I saw started over forty-five years ago backstage at the New York Paramount Theatre.

I was standing in the wings with Dixie the night Bing stumbled into that three word delivery. Bing was singing the number, "I Surrender Dear," to Harriet Hoctor's toe ballet routine. The stage was set up for her like a steeplechase racetrack, with hurdles for her to leap over, and the property men hid Bing's microphones on the posts of the hurdles. Bing started at the first hurdle and sang into the mike, "We played a game," then in silence walked to the next hurdle and hit his marks in front of the mike before singing the next three words, "of stay away." Again he walked silently on to the third hurdle and mike before going into, "But it cost more"; silence again until he got to the fourth hurdle and sang into the mike, "than I can pay," Bing went from hurdle to hurdle and back again singing three word phrases until he got to the finish, "I surrender dear."

More and more, President Carter is using my pal's phrasing with more silence than sound, and in his three-word delivery he seems to be saying, "Without you — I can't — make my way," and more and more I feel he expects us to reply, over hurdles, "We surrender, dear."

Jack Oakie, Shirley Temple and Charlotte Greenwood in a scene from *Young People*.

SHOES

Having been a dancer, I learned to love and respect shoes. In all my adult life I have never thrown a pair away. My shoe collection goes back almost sixty years, as does the collection of steps danced in them. I am now pushing seventy-four and find the pull of gravity getting graver and graver. Getting shoes and steps up off the floor is no longer the buoyant elevation it used to be. For some years now I have settled down to just shuffling my way through Hollywood gala dinner dances.

The other night, once again with my usual flat-footed resolve, I was dressing for a black tie affair and reached for a pair of suitable patent leathers which were on the convenient third shelf of my shoe closet. For no reason at all they seemed to get stuck. While trying to wrest them from the ledge, I was forced to look way up above eye level to the storage area of the very top shelf. A pair of shoes covered in cozy beige-colored flannel shoe socks demanded my attention, and fast! They were moving forward and were ready to topple.

"Hold on there! Just a minute!" I called out. Reaching up, I steadied them by holding on to the toe tips with my finger tips. Then I kicked the handy footstool over close enough to stand on and get up there before those shoes could make any more headway. Somehow the pair just wouldn't get back in their place. No matter how hard I tried I couldn't find a way to close the door on them. I finally gave them their way and cradled the obstinate pair in my arms and brought them down. I sat down on the stool and set the shoes on my lap.

"So you want to come out," I said to them. (Some people talk to plants, I talk to shoes.) I stared at the protective flannel covers wondering which shoes they were, and I decided I could guess without looking in on them. I could feel the metal taps on the toes and heels that meant they were sure a professional dancing pair. I began to finger them through the soft cloth. "Oh, God!" I couldn't help crying out. I could feel ridges all through the leather. "They're all dried up and cracked," I said. "These must be a pair of some very, very, old, old ones." "I'll bet you're over fifty years old," I said, patting them affectionately, and feeling again the skins which were so definitely dried up and wrinkled with age.

Now more than ever I wanted to identify them

through the covers to prove to them that they hadn't been forgotten. Then going back over half a century it suddenly came to me. "You're the I. Miller's that I wore in the chorus of *Sharlee,*" I said, and started a soliloquy that finally made me late for the affair.

Sharlee was a new musical, presented by John Cort, but these shoes weren't new even then. By that time they had been on the boards several times and had even received program credit. The listings used to read, "Costumes by Eaves," "shoes by I. Miller," and as we used to say in the chorus, "Faces by God." The try-out opened out of town on my birthday, November 12, 1923. We played the first half of a split week in Scranton, Pennsylvania, finished the week in Wilkes-Barre, Pennsylvania, and then came right into New York and opened at Daly's Sixty-third Street Theatre in a rainstorm.

The stars were Eddie Nelson (not to be mistaken for Nelson Eddy), Juliette Day, Sidney Grant, and Frances Arms (lovingly called Frankie). That rainy opening night I ran through the back alley to the stage door in these shoes, squishing and squashing all the way because they were rain-sodden. There were holes in both soles.

But I wasn't the only one with wet cold feet at Daly's Sixty-third Street Theatre. Out there in that alley, rain soaked, was Abe Lastfogel, anxiously waiting for his girl, Frances Arms. That night, while I took steps to fold some newspaper pages into my shoes, he took steps that made Frankie Mrs. Lastfogel for over fifty years. He also took some steps that led him to the head of the William Morris Agency.

Dancing on newspaper print didn't slow me down one iota. One of the notices read, "There was a satisfactory amount of pep displayed by the chorus; in fact the chorus is one of the speediest of which Broadway may boast among all it's speediest shows."

With all that speed, I guess we weren't fast enough; *Sharlee* only ran two weeks.

After the Wednesday matinee of the closing week, Ralph Reader, another member of that speedy chorus, and I were on our way to get something to eat before the evening performance. As we came out of the backstage alley onto Broadway, we saw a crowd milling around at the Century Theatre down at Sixty-first Street. Even

Chorus scene from *Innocent Eyes* (Jack Oakie is third from the left) at the Winter Garden Theatre, New York.

two blocks away we could tell they were all dancers. "Come on, Oakie," Ralph said. "Looks like something's going on over at the Century. Let's go on down there."

"O.K.," I agreed. I knew Ralph knew more about show business than I. When later he returned home to England, he became one of London's important theatrical producers. He was also honored for the work he did for the "Girl Guides and Boy Scouts. His steps led him to the initials, Ralph Reader, C.B.E. In 1938 when I visited London, he was in a show with Stanley Lupino, called *Light Up The Fleet*, a great hit. He invited me to the theatre, and at the opening of the second act the chorus came out carrying signs that read, "Welcome to England, Jack Oakie." Which was quite a thrill for me! Needless to say, ours has been a lifelong friendship.

We walked over to the Century, a Shubert house. *The Student Prince* was playing the theatre, but the action was going on upstairs in the building at the Century Roof. We crowded into the elevator with the others and went on up. Sure enough, Jack Mason, the dance director, was interviewing dancers for the cast of a new Shubert show called *Innocent Eyes*. The star was Mistinguett. This was going to be an important show.

Just as Ralph and I got in line with our fingers crossed, Jack Mason pointed in our direction. We couldn't believe it, he was pointing right at us.

"Hey, you two." We both stepped forward, and to steady our feet we broke into a speaking duet. "We're up the street at Daly's Sixty-third in *Shar-lee*. When we saw the look of hesitation come over Jack Mason's face, we continued in unison, "But we're closing this Saturday." The quick explanation that we would be free to take the job worked. "Good, good," he said. "You're both in."

Jack Mason had seen our show and knew what we could do. "Report here for rehearsal, ten o'clock Monday morning," he said. We had taken steps in the right direction, and hungry but happy we danced all the way back to Sixty-third Street.

That Saturday, after the last matinee of *Sharlee*, I stood in line again on the stage of Daly's Sixty-third Street Theatre. This time I was waiting my turn to pick up that little 2½ x 4 ecru pay envelope. The business manager was in his traditional place down-stage center, at a little folding table under a single work light bulb. I signed his slip and he handed me my salary. The envelope was just bulging! There were no deductions in those days and that fat little envelope was full of cash! This time I knew exactly what my very next step would be, and I took it. When I reported to the Century Roof that Monday for rehearsal, these I. Miller's had the best leather soles money could buy!

With heavy heart I took them out of the flannel covers expecting to cry over the cracked, dried up, wrinkled leather. Oh, no! I couldn't believe it!

Scene from *Young People*.

Scene from *Young People*.

Charlotte, Shirley and Jack — *Young People*.

Jack and Shirley in a scene from *Young People*.

Jack and Shirley Temple Black

They were not the I. Miller's! "Why, you're my alligators!" I said to the rich brown skins with their beautiful natural ridges, which I had mistaken for cracks. They weren't the least bit dry. They were soft and supple without a single sign to show that I hadn't worn them for over thirty-five years. I bought them in New York at Saks Fifth Avenue, when I was back there to attend the premiere of *The Great Dictator* at the Astor Theatre.

I didn't wear them until I got back home and reported to Twentieth Century-Fox for *Young People,* with Shirley Temple and Charlotte Greenwood. I had the taps put on the toes and heels and went right into rehearsal for the dance numbers, directed by Nick Castle and his assistant, Geneva Sawyer. I never took them off. These alligators danced all through that picture. One of the great numbers was "On Fifth Avenue," which was written especially for us, music by Harry Warren and lyrics by Mack Gordon.

"Fifth Avenue" was one of the biggest hit numbers of all time. I began to hum it and sing the lyrics as I slipped into those active shoes. I remembered all the lyrics and would give them to you here, but I think that printing them in this story might incur a big ASCAP royalty.

I went right into the Nick Castle steps, and remembered that Shirley Temple was eleven years old at the time we did them in these shoes. Today Shirley Temple Black is the United States Chief of Protocol at the White House, having served as United States Representative to the United Nations General Assembly and also as our Ambassador to Ghana.

When I sat down to take them off — after all, alligators and a tuxedo weren't in the social swim of things — they just wouldn't come off. Then I remembered some pretty good friends who never waded in that fast-moving whirlpool called the Social Swim of Things. My good friend, Senator Francis I.I. Brown of Hawaii, wore white tie and tails without shoes. Of course that was over forty-five years ago, when he and Winona Love were visiting and I went down to the Ambassador Hotel to call for them. There he was all ready to go — white tie and tails and bare feet.

I also remembered the gaiety of the dinner dance hosted by Howard Hughes in the Ambassador Cocoanut Grove. He even got special Chef Henri Bassetti to supervise our dinner. But he danced with my date, Jean Harlow, and some of the other ladies, Grace Moore, Susan Fleming, and Ginger Rogers, wearing his famous sneakers. Of course that too was over forty-five years ago.

I also remembered that the famous crooner known the world over as Bing Crosby once wore a brown-and-white left shoe with a black-and-white right one when he should have been wearing dress shoes. Of course, again that too was over forty-five years ago, but it cinched it for me, I was shod for the evening.

With crocodile tears of happiness that seemed to lighten my step, I wore the alligator shoes, taps and all, with my tuxedo, and danced and danced all night.

BENCHLEY

It seems to me it was only yesterday that Bob Benchley and I were a couple of very young fellers living at the Grosvenor Apartments in Beverly Hills. Then I read *Jaws,* written by Peter Benchley, Bob's grandson. Grandson! I know that Bob would have been very proud of Peter, because *Jaws* is gripping. It held on to me until I read through the very last page. What kept getting away from me was that darn age-old question, "Where does the time go?"

Over forty years ago, when Bob was at MGM and I was at Twentieth Century-Fox, we had apartments in that grey stone building at 173 South Rodeo Street. We used to have what we called "special meetings," and some of them right out in the hallway. When I attended the New York premiere of *The Great Dictator,* Bob and I had a "special meeting" in 21 after the show.

His first line to me was, "Oakie, how's our little grey home in the West?" His question put a lasting title on that good old meeting ground of ours. Now whenever I pass "our little grey home in the West," I think of Bob Benchley, one of the greatest writers and humorists of our day. I remember his quick dry wit, and I can still hear those sharp barbs he'd throw through that grinning giggle of his.

We were friends long before the little grey home in the West period, and one of the most unforgettable examples of the man's talent and humor was what he did with a script and situation one night at Tony's, over forty-five years ago, in 1929. At dinner that night, Bob rewrote the last scene of my first starring picture, and then added an exclamation mark to the end of that eventful evening, with his rebuttal to a lesson in pronunciation.

A. Edward Sutherland had just finished directing me in *The Social Lion.* The picture was still in the process of being edited, but Paramount Studios was so happy with the way it was shaping up that they rewarded us both. They raised my billing. For the first time in my career, the studio put my name over the title of the picture. "Jack Oakie, in *The Social Lion.* I was a star! And then they sent both of us back to New York to shoot our next one, *The Sap From Syracuse,* at the Paramount Studios in Astoria, Long Island.

In those days it was a great bonus to be sent to New York to make a picture. We out on the West

Robert Benchley and Jack

Coast were considered country cousins; we did feel as if we were coming out of the backwoods, and always looked forward anxiously to a trip East. To make things even more festive, Eddie got married to Ethel Kenyon, and the three of us took that honeymoon train, the Santa Fe Chief, to Chicago.

In Chicago, Ernie Byfield met us at the station with a big limosine, and shot us right up to his Sherman house. As we walked into the lobby, we met Joe Frisco, who was headlining the vaudeville show down the street at the Palace. I had been on the bill with him many times when I was in vaudeville with Lulu McConnell.

Displayed in the lobby was a life-size picture of Abe Lyman, to advertise that he and his orchestra were playing in "The College Inn" in the hotel. The cleaning women had just polished the forty or more brass cuspidors and stacked the shining things under Lyman's picture. "D-D-Don't tell me that guy won all those cups!" Frisco quipped, as he pointed to the picture of Lyman and the cuspidors. Since I had been on the West Coast making pictures for two years, it was a real homecoming to see Frisco and hear his stuttering humor again. Ernie Byfield gave us a beautiful suite, where we bathed, and then treated us royally on the penthouse Sherman roof, which looked like a Roman garden.

About three o'clock we were chauffeured back

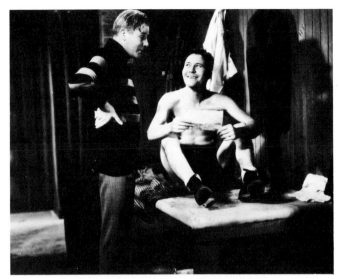

Skeets Gallagher and Jack Oakie — *The Social Lion.*

Photo by Cecil Beaton

to the station to board the New York Central 20th Century, and in the luxury of that overnight speed, we came into the big city. By this time, I think Ethel Kenyon was thinking that a twosome was the proper number for a honeymoon, so on our very first evening in New York, Eddie and I went off alone to meet Bob Benchley at Tony's for dinner. Tony's was just a tiny speakeasy, but it was *the* meeting place. The drinks were dependable (usually gin), and the food was really good. Tony's wife did all the cooking herself.

The murals were caricatures of his patrons, and mine was painted right up there alongside Benchley's. Bob and I didn't notice the likeness in those days, but a little later on in our careers, we shared the experience of being mistaken for each other in public places all over the world. Tony's attracted mostly writers. The little room was a hotbed where ideas were nurtured. Influenced by the impact of Tony's environment, Eddie got right down to the business of telling Bob the story of *The Social Lion.*

"Oakie plays a prizefighter, and Skeets Gallagher plays his manager," Eddie explained. "Now, get this!" (Eddie felt we had one of the best running gags that had ever been on the screen.) "All through the picture, Oakie's shoelaces became untied. Especially in the ring! Every time he's about to win a match, his opponent tells him that his shoelaces are untied, he looks down to tie

them, and he gets knocked out. He's a good fighter, but he never wins a match."

That famous Novocain look on Benchley's face didn't change as he interrupted, "Wait a minute. I've got an idea."

"No, no. Listen to this tag," Sutherland went on. "At the finish, Jack is on his way to New York for the big match, he kisses Mary Brian goodbye at the railroad station, and gets on the train. Now! As he waves goodbye to Mary, we pan down to his shoes; he's standing on the lower step of the car, his laces are untied, the train pulls out, and we've got the shoe laces trailing along the station!" The audience knows what the finish is, we don't have to tell them! See?"

"Eddie, how would you like to let Oakie win the big fight?" Bob asked quietly.

"Bob, I don't see how we can," Eddie said. "We've got this shoelace gag running all through the picture. No, no, we can't let him win."

"Eddie, there's a new invention called 'zippers.' Have you seen them yet?" he asked.

"No," we both answered.

"What are they?" Eddie asked, not quite following Bob's train of thought.

"Well, they're like a strip of gears that mesh. They're putting them on men's pants in place of buttons. You can just zip up your pants in a second. No buttons! If you can get the studio to put them on Oakie's boxing shoes to take the place of the shoelaces for the big fight .... See what I mean? What do you think?"

"My God, Bob!" Eddie got the idea. "What a tag, and we don't have to change a thing! We just add a scene!" Eddie got on the phone right there and then. He called the West Coast and gave instructions for them to take a close-up of Skeets Gallagher.

171

Skeets Gallagher, Jack Oakie and Mary Brian — *The Social Lion.*

Jack chauffers Mary Brian and Virginia Bruce in *The Social Lion.*

"The Skeeter," was to be watching me from the ringside with a smile. The next day the wardrobe department was put to work on the zippers, and I did my added scene at the studios there in Astoria, Long Island.

When the picture was released, it had the Bob Benchley ending, which went like this: During the big fight, my opponent tells me that my shoelaces are untied. This time I don't look down; instead I smile, and let him have it with my right, and knock him out. The camera pans to a close-up of my shoes; there they are, neatly zippered up with bright shining zippers. The camera cuts to the Skeeter at ringside, a smiling happy fight manager. The referee brings me to the center of the ring with my hand raised! At last I am a winner!

That same night, after the excitement of rewriting the tag of *The Social Lion,* we all relaxed. Tony treated us to some of that back room gin and joined the celebration. Smith Reynolds and Alexis Thompson came to our table for a drink; they had both just returned from European trips and started to compare notes. "Did Libby like Switzerland?"

Lex Thompson asked Smith Reynolds, who was married to Libby Holman. "Did she enjoy the 'sheing?"

"Loved it!" Reynolds said. "Libby sat right there at the Palace Hotel and watched the 'she-ers' come in."

"Did you see Bruno when you were there? He holds the 'she' records in Switzerland," Lex informed us.

"She?" Benchley asked with a twinkle in his eye. "She-er? She-ing? What's all this conjugation about?"

"Why, Bob," Smith Reynolds explained, "in Europe the sk is pronounced sh, we don't say ski, we say she."

"Oh?" said Bob, like a child who had just been taught a lesson.

"Oh!" And then he suddenly turned to me, and put the knowledge to the test.

"By the way, Oakie," he asked, "Didn't you used to do some 'skit' in vaudeville?"

Tony's was a very small place. Everybody there that night learned I had been in vaudeville!

COUNTING

"Sale Of The *Kansas City Star*" headlined the article in my morning *Los Angeles Times*. I felt the familiar twinge that comes to a senior citizen when reading the name of an old friend in the obituary column. Now that I'm pushing seventy-four I try to avoid twinges whenever I can, but I couldn't let a headline go by that seemed to be counting out a newspaper that had been so much a part of my life for so long.

So I read the article. "Scores of employees became wealthy when the paper was sold for 125 million dollars to the Capitol Cities Corp., Inc., a New York broadcasting and publishing conglomerate. The sale of the paper caused many mixed feelings among the employees. 'I never saw so many unhappy rich people,' one said."

"I guess that old adage, money isn't everything, still counts," I said to myself, remembering some very warm and mixed feelings of my own regarding that solid Midwestern newspaper. But as I've heard many times, whether you're rich or poor it's nice to have money, so I was very glad to read that, through the proceeds of the sale, some of the folks working on that good old prestigious *Kansas City Star* were now described as "instant overnight millionaires."

"My, oh my, oh my," I figured to myself. "With all that much money, there sure must be a lot of counting going on." And I recalled that I too had counted money many times through the proceeds of the sale of the *Kansas City Star*.

Almost sixty-five years ago, when my father died, I was sent up from Muskogee, Oklahoma, to live with my grandmother in Kansas City, Missouri. Grandmother entered me in Woodland School, and the very first day after attending classes I became associated with the *Kansas City Star*.

Every afternoon I picked up my bundle of papers at the corner of Eighth and Woodland, and with that great stack of *Kansas City Star*'s tucked under my arm, I ran for the trolley car and boarded it just as it came around the corner from Independence Avenue at the top of the hill. Being very agile in those days, I hopped on the car while it was still in motion and went through the aisle selling my papers as the car went down the hill. At the bottom of the hill I jumped off quickly before it stopped, ran across the street, and hopped on the next car going up again. I sold the *Kansas City*

Star going up and down the hill. All the motormen knew me and most of my customers got to be regulars. The *Star* cost two cents, but more often than not the folks would give me a nickel and tell me to keep the change for a tip.

Every night after dinner I spread the coins out on the floor of grandmother's living room and looked forward to the ritual of counting the pennies, the nickles, the dimes, and the quarters. Then I stacked the coins, arranged the stacks, and then rearranged them, making each stack accountable for its own and separate future score.

I did a lot of counting through the proceeds of the sale of the *Kansas City Star*. For example, I finally counted enough to buy roller skates. Boy, after that when grandmother gave me the dime and sent me all the way to Nafzigger's bakery for the three loaves of bread, I whizzed down over the curbs all the way, and coming back, even though I could hardly see over those three great

The Photo-Story of JACK OAKIE'S LIFE

HE STARTED OUT AS A WISE-CRACKING CHORUS BOY WHO WAS WILLING TO TAKE A CHANCE—AND HE ENDED UP—FAMOUS!

JACK OAKIE was born in Sedalia, Missouri, the son of Mr. and Mrs. James Madison Offield. His real name is Lewis Offield. He attended grammar school in Sedalia, high school in Kansas City. His mother taught in the public schools of Muscovy and Sedalia after her father died, later opened her own school of expression. Her pupils were all girls, and their feminine influence. She felt too much pills were all girls. Jack had no dates. He lived with his grandmother there, was a good student, very popular, but had no dates. Liked all girls, treated them all as sisters. Upon his graduation, went to De LaSalle Military Institute, a school for boys in New York. Attended there for the regular four-year course, then went to Wall Street for his first job. He was on the Stock Exchange—but he was only a call-boy and messenger, drew $25 a week. Did little work, caused little trouble among the other employees, held the job three years. Then Lulu McConnell, heard of the amateur funster while casting for the Junior League Follies, contacted him, gave him a part. He began as a lowly chorus boy. Then the partnership lasted until 1927. During that time Oakie was very successful on the stage, became a headliner, and when Lindbergh flew the Atlantic, became a headliner, and when Lindbergh flew the Atlantic, that "if Lindbergh took a chance and

made it—so can I." Immediately left for Hollywood. Upon reaching it. Has been very active in films ever since. Altogether, he's been in 85 pictures. Jack's favorite actress is Joan Crawford—whom he met in 1932 when he was making a picture with her. His favorite actor is Spencer Tracy. Jack is married. Director Sidney Lanfield first introduced him to Venita Varden, whom he married soon after, gave her a beautiful home for their apartment. They're far from the city, have only one neighbor, seldom return to the city at night. They rarely attend night clubs. Jack doesn't care for most sporting events, always has the same seats. When he's working, they play bridge in the evening, go to bed by midnight. Jack gets up at six-thirty, never has breakfast in bed. Usually he has orange juice, sausage, eggs, toast and coffee in the morning. Jack likes setting, but he isn't sentimental about it. He and his wife live pretty much by themselves, are called "those mad Oakies" by friends. Jack is a natural clown, is very much the same in real life as he is on the screen. His wife also has a sense of humor. Once he received from a fan, made her taken an electric train for Christmas—and he really enjoys it! But they're happy, settling down in their own fashion. Jack stands five feet, eleven inches, weighs 175, has blue eyes, brown hair.

Mr. and Mrs. James Madison Offield, whom you see above, gave birth to a son in Sedalia, Missouri, on November 12, 1903, and named him Lewis. But the name didn't stick. You probably never even heard of Lewis Offield, and yet you know him well. He's the famous comic — Jack Oakie

And here you see little Lewis Offield, age eight months, facing a camera for the first time. He looked quite serious in those early days—but it wasn't long afterwards that he turned to comedy

There is no doubt his marks in discipline were justified. Lewis was a regular Huck Finn, as this clipping from the Sedalia paper points out. Yet his worst offense was removing "Mo" from "Modern School Reader

Lewis was a good student, had no trouble with any particular subject. His best reports were in history, his worst, of course, in deportment. Here's a bit of his work, with teacher's notations in pencil

Lewis acquired his elementary education in Sedalia, Missouri, then went to Kansas City to live with his grandmother, attend high school. He was very popular there, but he had no dates

It seems the boys in the Stock Exchange thought Lewis was from Oklahoma, who decided it—but Lewis wouldn't conform to "Oakie" nickname—and replaced his real name. At any rate, Lewis from Missouri became Jack Oakie, reached the top. From chorus boy he worked up, and in 1923 he saw his name in theater lights—for the first time. Was he proud!

Mrs. Offield had a school of expression—but Jack had his own way of saying things, stuck to it. But she may have had some influence

He worked at the Stock Exchange three years—as call-boy, messenger, at $25 a week. Then he joined the Junior League Follies, teamed up with Lulu McConnell. That lasted until 1927

Drawing inspiration from Lindbergh, who "took a chance and made it," Oakie decided he'd do likewise. With a single letter of introduction he went to Hollywood in 1927 —and took the town by storm! By 1933, he had lived comfortably in Beverly Hills

When this picture was taken, Jack had been in pictures for two years, but he still was playing bit parts. As often as not, he wasn't even billed. But though his parts were small, he had many of them. He and his mother lived comfortably in Beverly Hills

From high school, Lewis went to De LaSalle Military Institute in New York. He was then fifteen years old, a member of the first-string basketball team and the star. Even four years of military school discipline couldn't throttle the irrepressible Lewis. But he didn't know at that time his comedy was going to make him very famous

Even though he wasn't a feature player, Jack was well known to movie-goers in 1929. In that year, while on a stage tour, he returned to Brooklyn, where he'd first headlined. Rubinoff was on the same bill, so Jack posed with the fiddle—for a gag

Jack Oakie doesn't confine his clowning to the entertainment world. A natural comedian, he's always out for a laugh—and usually he gets it. But here's one time when it seems he wasn't successful. This picture of Oakie and his mother was taken in 1929

My Precious Boy:
I am as proud of you as the greatest actress... I never say all the little nice things... me, I am sending the little clipper! I want you to... memorize or the little schemer... I must send the jubilee — I... Salvatore... neighbor...

My Grandmother — Mrs. Harriett Jump

loaves as I embraced the huge sack with both arms, I still skated up over those curbs in leaps. My elevation was good because I had the best *Kansas City Star* skates in the world.

I always counted enough for that big five cent chocolate Hershey bar at Eli's confectionery store. Sometimes I counted enough to sit at the counter for an ice-cream soda. Of course when grandmother treated we always sat on those wire chairs at one of the little round soda tables, and I always had a chocolate-nut sundae.

But the times I counted the most was when I went out selling the extras. Extras cost five cents. I'd get twice as many of them, get on the trolley car, and go way out into the suburbs, and keep selling the paper until late into the night. "Extra! Extra! Extra!" I'd call going up and down dark quiet streets. I could see the houses begin to light up as people turned up their gas jets or came to the door with a kerosene lamp to see what the extra was all about.

I'll always remember the night in 1916 when Woodrow Wilson was elected president. There were no radios in those days and everybody counted on the dependability of the *Kansas City Star*. I made a bundle on that extra!

But with the *Kansas City Star* I also remember a great deal of other counting, besides the counting I did through the proceeds from the sale of the paper. I still count an article of news from

Colorado Springs, Colorado, as one of my most frightening experiences.

One evening, while lying on my stomach on the floor of grandmother's living room with the *Kansas City Star* spread out in front of me, I saw my mother's name pop right up out of the page at me. I began to read aloud, "The automobile carrying Mrs. J.M. Offield of Muskogee plunged over the embankment at the gorge in Ute Pass."

"Grandmother!" I jumped up and took the paper to her. "Isn't this about Ev?" I asked. Grandmother read the article quickly, snatched her shawl, and I followed her as we dashed down to Eli's confectionery store to use the neighborhood telephone. I stood close by her and listened as she finally reached mother at the hospital and talked to her. Ev was very lucky; the two other people in the car were killed. For the rest of mother's life, however, she carried a heavy steel plate in her left forearm. I always remember seeing her little trick of cradling her left arm and pocketbook in her right arm in a way that relieved the weight of it.

Not too many years after I left Kansas City, the *Star* did something that really counted in helping a young beginner in Hollywood. It was in those very early days of Talkies, when a lot of us fellers who had been making silent pictures were afraid of being counted out, but the studios were greatly influenced by such powerful papers as the *Kansas City Star*. In those days, printer's ink was the

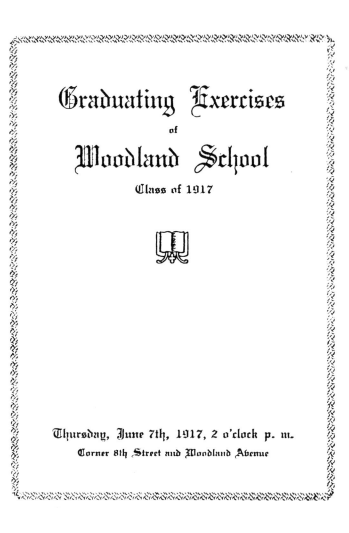

mother's milk of movies. And it was only nourishing at body temperature — not too hot, not too cold.

In 1929, when I opened in *Fast Company,* the *Kansas City Star* came up with some lines about me that were so palatable that when Paramount Studios ate them up, they helped me grow. The picture opened at the Royal Theatre, 1022 Main Street, Kansas City, Missouri.

Although I played Elmer, Evelyn Brent was the beautiful actress whose star billing was contracted above mine. But not so in the *Kansas City Star*'s stories. The paper paid no mind to the studio's billing. "Jack Oakie In *Fast Company*" the article was headlined, placing my name above the title.

> Ring Lardner's famous story *Elmer The Great* with Evelyn Brent and Skeets Gallagher. This Jack Oakie lad who plays Elmer is the easiest and most natural comedian to hit a screen in years. He doesn't resort to makeup, falls, chases, or trick clothes to get laughs. *Fast Company* is a fast-cracking comedy with Jack Oakie establishing himself as an actor as well as a personality.

That article from Kansas City sure counted in Hollywood. Paramount began putting my name

up above the title and kept it there for almost ten years, and then I took that prestige with me to RKO. Grandmother lived long enough to see me act in theatrical musical productions, in vaudeville, and in the movies. When she died the *Kansas City Star* treated her royally. The following excerpt is from the story about her interesting background.

> Mrs. Harriett Murray Jump died in Kansas City, Missouri, on Monday, June 30th, 1930. Daughter of the late Rev. James and Mary Long Atkinson Murray, she was born on July 10th, 1846. On March 7th, 1867 she was married to Rev. Albert Jump. Her joyousness, her marvelous memory and gift of education made all with whom she came in contact see the funny things in life and laugh with her.

And just about a week before we lost her,

> Mrs. Harriett Jump, Jack Oakie's grandmother, at Research Hospital, Kansas City, Missouri, although 85 years old and ill, sat up in bed and enthusiastically discussed her film comedy grandson. "He's a great boy, Jack," she said. "He's a wisecracker and I think he gets it from our side of the family.

On all counts this much respect meant a great deal to my mother and me and all our family. In 1960, another *Kansas City Star* headline that

PUBLIC SCHOOLS
of Kansas City, Mo.
CERTIFICATE OF SCHOLARSHIP

This Certifies that

Lewis Offield

having satisfactorily completed the Prescribed course of Study in the Elementary Schools, is entitled to admission to the High Schools of Kansas City

BY ORDER OF THE **BOARD OF DIRECTORS** OF THE
SCHOOL DISTRICT OF KANSAS CITY. MISSOURI.

Hal M Cook President.   *J. J. Cammack* Superintendent.

Ida L Barley Principal

Secretary   *Woodland* SCHOOL.

June 8 1917

counted so much to me was when my wife, Vickie, and I arrived at the Union Station in Kansas City.

The Oakies are going to Sedalia, Missouri, where Oakie's birthplace, 522 West Seventh Street, is to be marked during the city's centennial celebration program. Oakie was quick to ask if the Woodland School is still standing at 1820 East Eighth Street. "I was graduated from there," Oakie said, "and want to go by to pay my respects before we go home." "You know," Mrs. Oakie noted, "President Eisenhower is being honored in his home town on the same day that Jack Oakie is being honored by his home town. If Mamie is holding her head high, I'll bet I'm holding mine just a little bit higher.

Having had so many wonderful personal experiences with the *Kansas City Star,* I can well understand the mixed feelings of the folks now with the paper, who are counting their money and counting their memories, and my heart goes out to them all on both counts.

NED WASHINGTON

Thursday, last, something was bothering me! I knew that I had already fed my unicorn, had gone through my four hours of transcendental meditation, had gotten through my four thousand push-ups, had written four hit songs which I do every day, yet, something was bothering me! Ah, a flicker, a flicker then, a small light, then, a flash! I had it. It was getting near Jack Oakie's Seventieth Birthday! The eternal boy was going to be seventy. A seventy-year-old Huckleberry Finn! Oh, no! Now, that's something to conjure with. Will Rogers is supposed to have said "I never met a man I didn't like." I don't believe it. In fact, I don't believe he ever said it. It is too much of a generalization. Being of a suspicious nature, I don't even feel sure that Will Rogers liked Will Rogers. I have met a lot of men I didn't like; some I couldn't stand the sight of, and some I abhor. But I have met a number of men I LIKE-LIKE-LIKE. Jack Oakie, I LIKE-LIKE-LIKE!

> At the biblical four-score and ten
> We've had some remarkable men
> There was Einstein, Marconi
> And a drunk named Mahoney
> From an Illinois town they called Skokie
> NOW THERE'S OAKIE!

Jack Oakie was put here for a very special reason. There was no element of the accidental involved in his BEING. I have always felt that the Maker, knowing that this was to be a vale of tears assigned certain individuals to administer to the needs of his children. He knew that one thing they were going to need badly was "laughs." He touched Jack Oakie on the forehead and told him to go forth and to do and say things that would make people feel lighthearted. Jack never let HIM down. I've gone with Jack from his Rah-Rah collegiate days at Paramount Studio to the present day. Parenthetically, someone once said "Paramount hasn't won a football game since Jack left." End of Parenthesis. Little did people realize the scope of his talent until he essayed to portray Benito Mussolini in "The Great Dictator", an unforgettable performance that remains as one of the highlights in the annals of motion pictures.

> For years now we've stood in great awe
> Of Da Vinci and George Bernard Shaw
> But I'm open to wagers, like all golden-agers
> In time they grew feeble and pokey
> BUT NOT OAKIE!

Recently, I had a strange experience. I had occasion to take a train ride through Missouri. As we approached Independence, Missouri, one of the train-men felt it fitting and proper and rightfully so, to point out that this was the birthplace and the home of former President Harry S. Truman, a man of quite some esteem. Shamefully, I confess, I was not excited. Later, we came to a little town called Sedalia. Immediately, lights started to flash in my mind. This was the birthplace of Jack Oakie! In a half-trance I could see Jack bare footed and grinning on each street we passed. I could see him "conning" the other kids out of their marbles, throwing rocks at passing freight cars as all kids did in those days and speaking again of marbles I had to practically drag myself back to reality before I lost some of mine.

> On the bench we have Barney Baruch
> And a songwriter friend who's a "kook"
> In Japan, they'd say "Ah So!"
> You passed up Picasso
> But they all seem quite corny and hokey
> GIVE ME OAKIE!

Mr. First Nighter! Mr. Red Shoes! Mr. Happy! Mr. Yuk-Yuk! Jack, you never needed a fright-wig, a turkey bladder, a pratfall. Nor did you ever have to have your pants fall down to make people laugh. You did it with the sheer strength of your personality, your whimsey, your brilliantly comedic mind that functioned without the aid of any gimmicks or "shticks." You are an "original," a Rembrandt, a Dali, one of a kind! Few people of talent ever attain their full potential. You are one of that very select few. A world is in your debt for all the humor and happiness you brought us who sit and wait for someone like you to lift us out of it all. You have been bountifully blest with a wonderful wife, your lovely Vicki, and I am quite sure that her presence helps you keep that perpetual smile on your face. My wish for you now is that you live One Hundred and Twenty years and three days! Why the three days? So you won't die suddenly at One Hundred and Twenty!

> I like things quite calm and serene
> Excitement to me's Fulton Sheen
> But if I had my "druthers"
> Forget all the others
> Tho' he's salty and fiery and smoky
> I'LL TAKE OAKIE!

Ned Washington
Nov. 12, 1973

HAROLD ADAMSON

Dear Jack,

Forty years ago I arrived in Hollywood. On my first night, I had dinner with a real movie star — Jack Oakie — and our mutual agent, Morris Small. I remember — it was Sardi's Restaurant on Hollywood Blvd. With your elephant memory, you could probably tell me what I had for dinner — I forget. Since that memorable night, you've always been one of my closest friends.

I remember some of the wonderful, crazy Jack Oakie moments when no one knew exactly what you'd do next — like the time on the Joe Palooka set — when you took the baton away from the orchestra leader and gave Lupe Velez the beat. All those old memories and all the new memories — I treasure.

I've spent many birthdays with you and I hope to spend many more. One of your birthdays that stands out in my memory is the night Sedalia was written to you from me — a tribute to you and the town that gave birth to Jack Oakie — that wonderful clown.

Today you are seventy, but to me you will always be 29 like the day I met you. As I have said before in song —

"You're still a Freshman at heart
Tho you've never won any college degrees
You're Summa Cum Laude at Grauman's Chinese
And when you hear laughter that wonderful sound
You know that Jack Oakie's around."

Happy Birthday, Jack —

Love,
Harold

FAME AT LAST

When I was a young actor, just starting in the motion picture business, Lionel Barrymore once told me, "If you live long enough to make the full circle, you start out with obscurity, go the round, and end up with obscurity." Well, I have gone the round, the full 360 degrees. But just because I live in Northridge, I have been able to disprove Lionel Barrymore's spherical sightings.

Not only is the location of my habitat the cause of this phenomenon, but my love of fish is a contributing factor. I love fish. But just because that succulent dish smells fishy while being cooked, I never get to eat it in the peace and quiet of our home.

When we bought our little ranch, very few people lived out our way. The mailman, who whiled away his time at our house, told me that of the forty or so names and addresses that comprised the town, there were days when not even one of them had a letter for him to deliver.

Northridge was known as the horse capital of the world, and some of the most famous thoroughbreds were born and bred on the hundred acres that made up our backyard. The Northridge Farm, owned and operated by the J.H. Ryans, played host to many of the most colorful performers on the race-tracks of the world.

Our house is on the top of a hill, and in those days the metes and bounds of our acres were separated from the horse pastures at the bottom of the slope only by a white corral fence. Among the many very famous thoroughbreds, Roundtable, Stranglehold, and Mafosta held court out there in the fields for us to watch. There were also the Makeup Man group, owned by Gordon Phillips, and I'm A Bad Boy, owned by Lou Costello of the Abbott and Costello team. I'm A Bad Boy lived up to his name one day and nipped me when I tried to find out from the horses' mouth just how he intended to run that afternoon at Hollywood Park.

Down at the broodmare barn it was always most interesting to watch those stars at work. Their individual behavior in this most delicate of performances sure proved that they all had personalities of their very own.

Jack Cartier, known as Animal Jack, was one of the finest trainers in the business. He always kept a chair handy for me especially when Call Bell was on. "Sit down, Oakie," he advised. "Call Bell will

wear you out with his love making, he's the romantic type, he just takes his time."

Call Bell was a slowpoke; he loved to keep the mare on tenter-hooks waiting for his attentions. He would take his time, look her over, and then walk away. He'd lead the groom around to the other side of the barn where he would then whinny a love call. In a little while, in a walk as slow as a racehorse could manage, he'd return to visit with the mare again. Once more he'd meander away for a spell, and then come back again to get further acquainted with the patient mare.

I sat and waited and watched that horse handle the trainer and the grooms. They had to play right into his hands because he had sired a lot of great babies and besides there was a lot of money involved in letting him call the shots. They let him walk them back and forth until he was good and ready, and sometimes it took more than an hour of old-fashioned horseplay before he finally "went to the post."

My good friend Jimmy Durante, one of the greatest horse players of all time, had a pretty good winner named the Schnozz in his honor. We had the christening up on the lawn in my back yard, and when they brought the horse up from the farm Jimmy posed with him.

"Place your bets," Jim announced, "There's gonna be some measurements taken here." Bets were placed and measurements taken, and Durante insisted that he won by a nose. "Schnozz," he said to the horse as he petted his nose, "you blew it!"

The motion picture *The Story of Seabiscuit* was shot on location at the farm. Shirley Temple was the star. She had her twenty-first birthday during the making of the picture and so David Butler, the director, gave her a party at my barn. I worked with Shirley in *Young People* and celebrated her eleventh birthday during the making of that picture. Then when she was eighteen, I joined the birthday party over at RKO where they burned down the schoolhouse (a miniature on the cake), to show how grown-up she had become. But down at the barn I watched closely to be sure she blew those candles out fast, I didn't want the barn burned down. I was with Shirley Temple Black recently at Twentieth Century-Fox at an affair to honor her outstanding work as an outstanding citizen. The girl who blew out candles in my barn has become a very bright figure for our country.

Of all the great horses that I knew at the farm there was one that was closest to my heart because I actually played midwife to him. But the only return I got for all my trouble was one good laugh. In my type of work, however, any investment that pays off in laughter is considered a good bet.

It all started one day when my wife, Vickie, and I were having some lunch out on the veranda. I looked down the hill to the field. From our house we had a complete view of the farm and all the barns and pastures — one of the most beautiful of all pictures we have ever known in our lives. I could see a horse lying down in the alfalfa field.

"Isn't that the mare we've been watching?" I asked. I got up to be sure, and I could see her heaving. We then heard her neighing, which sounded pretty urgent, and we could see that there wasn't anybody around to help her. We ran down the hill and climbed over the fence to see what we could do, but when we got to her it was all over; the little dark wet thing was out there at her side.

"Get Animal Jack," I said, and so Vickie ran to the barns to get help. I stayed to comfort mother and child. I put my sweater over the foal and waited for the experts. Animal Jack and Vickie came back in the jeep. We bundled the colt in a blanket he had brought, then Animal Jack sat on the back of the jeep and I lifted the baby up and gave it to him to hold in his lap. We drove very slowly back to the barn with the mare following her new born.

"Oakie, please don't tell Veloz that the colt was born in the field," Animal Jack begged me.

CLAUDE BINYON
November 12, 1973

Dear Jack:

Congratulations on this, your 70th birthday — and before I drown myself in a sea of nostalgia let me add that I am joined in this greeting by your ol' poker-playin buddy, Shorty.

Now — how do I remember thee? Let me count the ways:

I recall that some forty-odd years ago there were dire predictions of your early demise. Said one wise man: "That boy will drink himself to death before he's forty."

Said another prophet: "That young man will talk himself to death."

Said another seer: "The things that feller says to people, some day real soon he's gonna get his head knocked off."

Unfortunately all these men have left us, cut down before their time by clean living.

You may have imbibed a little now and then, but I must say you were always considerate of others. I remember, for instance, what was supposed to be the last day's shooting on "College Humor" — a scene outside a dairy. The shot was lined up, and we sat in the hot sun awaiting your arrival. After several hours of waiting, during which we all exchanged little pleasantries, there finally was a phone call from you.

"Hi," you said, "guess where I am" — and promptly hung up. I've always remembered that — how even in your most troubled hours you thought only of us.

And who can forget those wonderful poker games in the thirties? The stakes were small but the excitement was great, and the pictures rattled on the walls. Do you remember the night when someone brought a guest to the game, and when Bud Ralston wrote his regular report on that night's game he made this entry: "$11.75 — lost to a Stranger"?

Remember our great fishing expedition to Big Bear, when you planted yourself in the lodge's Rumpus Room when Shorty and I had to leave to keep a date with the Arlens on their boat? When Shorty and I got to the beach, we saw in newspapers that you had been detained in the San Bernardino pokey for eccentric driving.

I think the only sad experience we had with a picture was "Shoot The Works." Dorothy Dell, your promising young leading lady, was killed in a car accident right after we finished shooting. And Lew Cody, a great character, died before the picture was released. I still remember the weird feeling I had when I later listened to Dorothy's voice singing "With My Eyes Wide Open I'm Dreaming."

One of my most cherished memories is of your mother, Evelyn Offield, bless her. She was intelligent, patient, tactful, but strong-willed when she knew she was right. And when she brought us a kitten one day as a gift I knew it would turn out to be a very fine cat. It did just that. I have never before or since seen a house cat actually scoop live fish out of Toluca Lake — and it topped this achievement by scaling our six foot brick wall holding a large, live rabbit in its mouth to feed to its kittens.

Jack, I have rambled, but I have written these thoughts of the moment just as they came to me, and perhaps they will stir some old memories.

In conclusion may Shorty and I say that we think you have picked a fine bride in Vicki, and we're sure you two kids will be very happy in the many years ahead.

Love, Claude

A pair of Jacks — Oakie and Dempsey.

A pair of jokes — Jack Oakie and Jimmy Durante.

"Aw, quit worrying," the vet assured him as he supervised the work while eating an apple. "That field is cleaner than the barn." He took a big bite through to the core.

"Oh, so this is Veloz and Yolanda's baby?" I asked, taking the vet's advice and trying to relax. It made good sense that such a beautiful graceful animal should belong to the famous graceful dance team, who also had a chain of dancing schools all over the country. Their famous trademark read, "Walk in and dance out." Well, I never did tell Frank Veloz that I helped born his colt in the field, but I did watch that shiny black yearling grow and run and romp through the pastures.

Frank named him Black Dancer, a perfect name for a horse who was sure to learn all the right steps. When he was scheduled to break his maiden, at Santa Anita, I was there bright-eyed and alert, early and ready for that first race. I had seen his workouts and clocked him many times down at the six-furlong tack at the farm. He sure was a racing fool. In the Turf Club, Frank Veloz was sitting just a table away from me. He behaved like a choreographer who just knew his pupil was going to make the big time. I could see his dancing feet under the table. He was so light-hearted, he couldn't keep his heels on the ground, and he kept going into some occasional toe work. Frank looked over and smiled, "Hello, Jack. Going with the Dancer?" he asked happily.

"Sure thing," I confided with a knowing wink. We showed each other that we both knew a good bet and were enjoying the knowledge.

When Frank got up to place his bet on that winning horse, I joined him. He went to his window and I stood in line at mine. I put my two dollars down and said with authority, "Black Dancer to win!" The ticket seller knew the right number, took my two crisp dollars, and pushed the button. The ticket danced right into my hand, and I did a lighthearted dance right back to my

seat at the finish line. Frank was back at his table tapping his toes with joy. The horses were led out, and that giant of a big black shiny horse that I once held in my arms paraded by us with his ears up and tail high — good signs in a horse ready to run. I joined Frank in some toe taps under my table. We just couldn't keep our feet still.

At last it came, that call we were waiting for from the famous announcer, Joe Hernandez, "They're off and running!" And so they were. All the horses broke but Black Dancer. He hovered around the starting gate seeming to wonder whether to make his start to the left or to the right. The race was over when he finally took off, and as he passed us at the finish line I recognized the steps he was doing — a nice, gentle, slow minuet. I watched him dance gracefully off the track and looked over at Veloz, whose heels were flat on the ground now with lead in his shoes.

"Say, Frank," I called over, "that Dancer sure needs more lessons!" The teacher of dance steps all over the world broke into a horse laugh. I got my two dollars worth.

I had another experience with a horse dancing that decided me to confine all my dance steps to my own feet. My Tennessee Walker, Ginger, and I used to spend many hours up in the Santa Susana hills just north of our ranch. The only creatures Ginger and I had to be wary of were the coyotes and snakes; otherwise the hills were ours alone.

One morning as we rode up Devonshire Street to Reseda Boulevard, Ginger slipped and did a four-legged split that Charlotte Greenwood would have envied. There he lay right in the middle of the intersection. There was nowhere close enough for me to walk for help, and in those days no moving traffic ever passed that way for weeks on end. For more than two hours I waited and urged with words of encouragement until Ginger finally made it on his own. I walked him home that day and decided to send him down to the farm to retire from our daring escapades. He did have a long and happy life but under a new name. The stable hands called him Oakie and used him to draw the manure cart.

In those days horses were not the only things we grew on our ranch; we also had an orchard. It was called a family orchard, because we didn't grow or pick for commercial use. We were young and ambitious and planted both citrus and deciduous. We had orange trees, lemon, grapefruit, lime, fig, plum, peach, apricot, and nectarine. Watering was a full-time chore because we did it all by hand, and one of our best watering helpers was Jack Dempsey. The Champ owned apartment houses in Santa Monica, so whenever he was in town he loved to come out to see us in the country and water the trees. The Champ and I dug the wells and pulled those heavy hoses from tree to tree and after a good hard day's work in the orchard we'd dive right into the pool for a swim together.

The last time I talked to the Champ on the phone from New York he asked me if I was still watering our trees and taking those great swims. Well, I no longer dig wells or pull hoses or have water to work with. The trees are still here but they have to make do with our sparse rain, and I no longer take those quick dives. I now enter the pool cautiously from the shallow end and descend slowly step by step.

Besides the orchards and horse farms, Northridge was famous for turkey farms. The Huntsinger Turkey Farm, one of the largest breeders in the country, was just south of our farm, and the combined sounds of the gobblers and the horses made the only night music in the world that can ever again put us so restfully to sleep.

Northridge was the place, way out in the country, where we planned to live when we retired. In the meantime, while still working hard at making movies, we lived in town and drove out to the ranch on weekends.

To come in from town, before widened streets and freeways, you had to come west on Ventura Boulevard, then north on Reseda Boulevard, and when you got to Devonshire Street, our street, Reseda became a dead end, blocked off by the hills. Devonshire Street, although designated State Highway 118, was just a narrow road with an archway formed by tall eucalyptus and cork oak trees.

When the city fathers cut a path through the hills taking Reseda Boulevard north for one mile, we called it the New Road and loved to explore that mile of unpaved adventure to Rinaldi Street. The Department of Water and Power, who installed the road for their use, built a large concrete slab that covered some underground equip-ment. There at the foot of the mountains and at that slab Vickie and I used to rest, look up at the stars and also behave like two very normal young people who had all the privacy under the sky in the whole wide world.

Today as we try to drive through the traffic at the corner of Reseda and Devonshire, where Ginger lay sprawled for a couple of hours, and which has now become the busiest intersection in the valley and one of the most dangerous, with shopping centers on all four corners, we often think of Ginger's split and of our very private adventures, and wonder how in the world so much movement can come running over so much peace and quiet in so short a time.

But during those very quiet days we used to take walks through the fields and hills to rehearse the songs and dance steps for the musical movies I was making. I remember I learned all the lyrics to "You'd Be So Nice To Come Home To," Cole Porter's great hit from *Something To Shout About*, by singing it at the top of my lungs. Once the Hound of the Baskervilles heard me and from somewhere far off in the distance he became a critic with his whining howl.

We were so isolated in those days that most of our groceries had to be brought in from Hollywood and Beverly Hills. For an ice cream, we used to have to bicycle five miles to Topanga Canyon and Devonshire Street, to the old two-story corner brick complex called the Chrysler Building. It housed the only drugstore and ice cream fountain in all of the far northwest valley.

On those bicycle trips we could take off our sweaters, hang them on a branch of a grapefruit tree in an orchard along Devonshire Street, and two or three hours later come by and pick them up on the way home. If vehicles had been monitored at that time, I think the aggregate would have been two or three a month.

The little old lady who owned the building and ran the drugstore also had the only telephone in that vast area. Her store was a haven for the actors working on location up at the Iverson Ranch in those rocky hills where almost every Western picture in our business was made. They came down out of those hot dry mountains dressed like cowboys and Indians and stampeded her telephone. Actors have to keep in touch with their agents especially when they're out on location.

"Movie actors!" she'd complain. "All you movie actors ever do is use my telephone! You keep using my phone so much you keep breaking it!" It was true. Her phone was out of order a good deal of the time. But all phone service was a newly installed device in that area of trees and rocks and

Jules C. Stein presenting Jack Oakie with a proclamation of "Lifetime Citizen of Universal Studios."

Jack Oakie and Laura LaPlante examine scroll as Jules C. Stein beams his pleasure.

hills. I don't think the wires had had time to become acclimated.

In the early 1940s we experienced a tide of interest in the valley that began to swell our population. Janet Gaynor and her husband, Adrian, the distinguished dress designer at MGM, and their young son, Robin moved next door. Although their house was about five acres away, we shared the same hilltop. They too loved the peace and quiet of Northridge. But Robin had no neighborhood friends, and all his pals had to be bused in from town. Mostly he just played with Pepper, his dalmatian, and Dusty, the little Chihuahua, and Bimbo, the foreman's no-breed dog down on the farm. But his best friend was our Christmas Boy, half shepherd, half collie. Robin had his own little house and staff, across the driveway from his parents' big house, and many's the evening we'd have to whistle for Christmas Boy and then soon hear the screen door of Robin's house open and slam shut as our dog came home in a lope. When the second World War was upon us, the tide ebbed and people stopped coming our way. The lid that was put on all traveling also clamped down on our trips to the ranch, and the area was left mostly to the wildlife.

Robin and his folks went right back to the city. The day the Adrians moved, Robin came over to say goodbye to Christmas Boy, his sleeping companion. Robin was very happy about going into town to live. "Now I'll have lots of friends to play with," he said.

But a few years later when mobility became freer again and people began to move out to the

valley, we too moved into our ranch. We noticed that most of the boys who had passed through this way during the war came back to California to live, just as they told me they would during the Hollywood Canteen days when I was washing dishes to help.

The farms and groves began to disappear, so did the hills and mountains, and houses took their place.

When the thoroughbreds were gone, the farm was temporarily leased for Arabian horses. Liz Whitney (Mrs. Cloyce Tippett) called from her Llangollen Farms in Upperville, Virginia and asked me if she could use my barn for her great horse, Mr. Gus, which she was planning to ship to California.

But even the Arabians were on their way out, because the farm was going up for the subdivision of houses, so we never did have the pleasure of boarding Liz's Mr. Gus.

With the loss of the horses there is now no other use for the barn than to store my great big heavy theatrical trunks, which had for so many years traveled the country with me in vaudeville, and which are also no longer in use.

But during the early days of the great growth of the valley, Vickie found a little grocery store not too far from the ranch. She was delighted to learn that the proprietor would even deliver her grocery orders. "The man said it would be a privilege to oblige!" Vickie told me happily. I was in the midst of my ablutions one day, when a giant of a man carrying several cartons entered my bathroom.

"Hey! Jack! Here's the stuff your wife ordered," he said, as he presented me with the grocery order personally. Somehow, he had come straight

183

through the house, up the stairs, through my bed-room, and into my bathroom. "Glad to do it any-time. Say how about an autograph?" he asked as he still tried to hand me the cartons, although he could see my hands were not free to do anything about receiving them. Vickie arrived before I could think of a way to meet the unusual situa-tion.

"Will you please bring those things back down into the kitchen!" she demanded.

"Sure thing." He was very agreeable. "I just wanted to see him in person," he explained. His explanation didn't help. That little incident put an end to our neighborhood patronage.

Although stores and restaurants grew up around us, Vickie always feared that their close proximity to home might lead to their blazing a trail to my bathroom

Finally, the house where Janet Gaynor and Adrian and Robin had lived was torn down. The acres on their side of our hill were graded to street level. The ground looked like a high round loaf that had been cut in two. But a great retaining wall was built to cover and hold the raw earth and keep it from falling away. Right down there, about twenty feet below our yard, a Chevrolet agency moved onto the property and began to sell its cars. The neighborhood had changed!

Until very recently, Vickie has never allowed

herself to take advantage of the conveniences af-forded us by these progressive turns of events. It was I who saw the sign first! "Every Wednesday, fish fry, all you can eat." It was emblazoned on a mammoth electric sign in front of the nearby Howard Johnson's Restaurant. My own name up on the marquee of a theatre never gave me as much pleasure. I must have read that sign four or five Wednesdays before I ventured to suggest, "Let's try that fish fry. It must be good, or all those people wouldn't keep going back for it."

"I'd love to," Vickie said. But she was still reluctant to patronize the neighborhood.

But I insisted. "My hair is white now. Nobody will even notice us."

"What about your pictures on the late, late, late show?" she argued.

"I'm wearing a different color hair now," I reminded her. Well, my love for fish and Vickie's love for me got us to Howard Johnson's fish fry. When we entered the dining room there wasn't a table available.

"Let's go," was Vickie's quick decision. But the delicious smell of fish had me taking deep breaths, and my digestive juices were out of control.

"Let's sit at the counter," I suggested through very sibilant esses — after all my mouth was watering.

"Do you think you'll be comfortable?" (my wife is a worrier.)

"I'll be comfortable as long as I can have some of this fish fry," I said and went right to the corner stool. A bright-eyed and starchy waitress took our order and in no time at all I was squeezing lemon juice over the most wonderful brown crisp flounder. Vickie was happy too, because the fish was all Howard Johnson promised it would be. I was commending him on his integrity in advertising, when suddenly a little girl reached up and put an autograph book under my arm and onto my plate.

"Mr. Oakie, can I have your autograph?" she asked. She'd picked up a goodly smear of my tartar sauce and I wondered how adding ink could improve it.

"Young lady," I asked, "who sent you over here to ask for my autograph? Your grandmother?"

"Oh, no!" The child was indignant. "I came over by myself. Anyway my grandmother isn't

here. She lives in New Jersey." I was wiping the child's book and looking for a place to put my name, hoping that the ball point pen she gave me would not only write under water but also under fish.

Vickie took on the guise of an enquiring reporter. "How old are you?" she asked.

"I'm nine years old," the little girl admitted freely.

"My goodness!" Vickie was surprised. I guess she'd forgotten that anybody could be that young. "How come you know Mr. Oakie?" she asked, feeling sure the nine-year-old had never seen me in pictures.

"Oh, everybody knows Jack Oakie!" the child answered proudly, as if she had passed the quiz with flying colors! "He's the man who lives up on the hill, back of the Chevrolet agency!"

"You see?" I turned to my wife. "Fame at last!"

Of course that little girl has one of the best autographs I ever signed.

JACK OAKIE'S FILMS

Finders Keepers (silent), 1927, Universal, Wesley Ruggles, director. Cast: Laura La Plante, John Harron, Eddie Phillips, Andy Devine, Edmund Breeze

Sin Town (silent), 1927, Pathe, Gordon Cooper, director. Cast: Eleanor Faire, Hugh Allen, Bob Perry

Road House (silent), 1927, Fox, Richard Rosson, director. Cast: Lionel Barrymore, Maria Alba, Warren Burke, Joe Brown, Julia Swayne Gordon, Tempe Pigott, Eddie Clayton

The Fleet's In (silent), 1928, Paramount, Malcolm St. Clair, director. Cast: Clara Bow, James Hall, Bodil Rosing, Eddie Dunn, Jean Laverty, Dan Wolheim, Richard Carley, Joseph Girard

Someone To Love (silent), 1928, Paramount, F. Richard Jones, director. Cast: Charles (Buddy) Rogers, Mary Brian, William Austin, James Kirkwood, Mary Alden, Frank Reicher

The Dummy (first talkie), 1928, Paramount, Robert Milton, director. Cast Fredric March, Ruth Chatterton, John Cromwell, Fred Kohler, Vondell Darr, Mickey Bennett, ZaSu Pitts, Richard Tucker, Eugene Pallette

The Wild Party, 1929, Paramount, Dorothy Arzner, director. Cast: Clara Bow, Fredric March, Shirley O'Hara, Marceline Day, Joyce Compton, Adrienne Dore, Virginia Thomas, Jean Lorraine, Kay Bryant, Alice Adair, Renee Whitney, Amo Ingram, Marguerite Cramer, Phillips R. Holmes, Ben Hendricks Jr., Jack Luden, Jack Raymond

The Man I Love, 1929, Paramount, William Wellman, director. Cast: Richard Arlen, Mary Brian, Baclanova, Harry Green, Pat O'Malley, Leslie Fenton, Charles Sullivan, William Vincent

Close Harmony, 1929, Paramount, John Cromwell, director. Cast: Charles (Buddy) Rogers, Nancy Carroll, Harry Green, Richard (Skeets) Gallagher, Matty Roubert, Ricca Allen, Wade Boteler, Baby Mack, Oscar Smith, Greta Grandstedt, Gus Partos, The Aber Sisters

Chinatown Nights, 1929, Paramount, William Wellman, director. Cast: Wallace Beery, Florence Vidor, Warner Oland, Jack McHugh, Tetsu Komai, Frank Chew, Mrs. Wing, Peter Morrison, Freeman Wood

Street Girl, 1929, (first picture made by new RKO), Wesley Ruggles, director. Cast: Betty Compson, John Harron, Ned Sparks, Eddie Kane, Joseph Cawthorn, Ivan Lebedeff, Guy Buccola, Doris Eaton and her chorus

Sweetie, 1929, Paramount, Frank Tuttle, director. Cast: Nancy Carroll, Helen Kane, Stanley Smith, William Austin, Stuart Erwin, Wallace MacDonald, Joe Depew, Charles Sellon, Aileen Manning

Hard To Get, 1929, First National, William Beaudine, director. Cast: Dorothy MacKaill, Louise Fazenda, James Finlayson, Charles Delaney, Mickey Beaudine, Edmunde Burns, Clarissa Selwynne

Fast Company, 1929, Paramount, A. Edward Sutherland, director. Cast: Evelyn Brent, Skeets Gallagher, Gwen Lee, Sam Hardy, Chester Conklin, Eugenie Besserer, Bert Rome, Arthur Housman

Hit The Deck, 1929, RKO, Luther Reed, director. Cast: Polly Walker, Wallace MacDonald, Ethel Clayton, Marguerite Padula, June Clyde, Franker Woods, Roger Gray, Harry Sweet, Dell Henderson

Let's Go Native, 1929, Paramount, Leo McCarey, director. Cast: Jeanette MacDonald, James Hall, Kay Francis, Richard (Skeets) Gallagher, William Austin, David Newell, Charles Sellon, Eugene Pallette

The Social Lion, 1930, Paramount, A. Edward Sutherland, director. Cast: Mary Brian, Skeets Gallagher, Olive Borden, Charles Sellon, Cyril Ring, E.H. Calvert

The Sap From Syracuse, 1930, Paramount, A. Edward Sutherland, director. Cast: Ginger Rogers, Granville Bates, George Barbier, Sidney Riggs, Betty Starbuck, Veree Teasdale, Malcolm Dunn, Bernard Jukes, Walter Fenner, Jack Daley

Paramount On Parade, 1930, Paramount, A. Edward Sutherland, director. Cast: Maurice Chevalier, Helen Kane, Ruth Chatterton, Clara Bow, Leon Errol, Mitzi Green, Nancy Carroll, George Bancroft, Clive Brook, Zelma O'Neal, Nino Martini, William Powell, Buddy Rogers, Fredric March, Skeets Gallagher, Gary Cooper, Harry Green, Richard Arlen, Jean Arthur, Fay Wray, Mary Brian, Evelyn Brent, Virginia Bruce, Lillian Roth, Stuart Erwin, Kay Francis, Dennis King, Warner Oland, Jackie Searle, Stanley Smith

Sea Legs, 1930, Paramount, Victor Heerman, director. Cast: Lillian Roth, Eugene Pallette, Harry Green, Albert Conti, James Gibson, Henry Roquemore, William Bechtel, Richard Cummings, Jack Byron

Uptown New York, 1931, Tiffany Stahl, Victor Schertzinger, director. Cast: Shirley Grey, Leon Wycoff (Ames), George Cooper, Henry Armette, Raymond Hatton, Alexander Carr, Lee Moran

Sky Bride, 1931, Paramount, Stephen Roberts, director. Cast: Richard Arlen, Virginia Bruce, Bobby Coogan, Tom Douglas, Louise Closser Hale, Harold Goodwin, Charles Starrett, Randolph Scott, Hooper Atchley, Syd Saylor, Frank Rice, Harry Stafford

The Gangbuster, 1931, Paramount, A. Edward Sutherland, director. Cast: Jean Arthur, William (stage) Boyd, Wynne Gibson, Tom Kennedy, William Morris, Albert Conti, Francis McDonald, Pat Harmon

June Moon, 1931, Paramount, A. Edward Sutherland, director. Cast: Frances Dee, Sam Hardy, June MacCloy, Ernest Wood, Wynne Gibson, Harry Akst, Frank Darien, Ethel Sutherland, Harold Waldridge, Jean Bary

Dude Ranch, 1931, Paramount, Frank Tuttle, director. Cast: June Collyer, Stuart Erwin, Mitzi Green, Eugene

Pallette, Charles Sellon, Cecil Weston, George Webb, Guy Oliver, James Crane

Touchdown, 1931, Paramount, Norman Z. McLeod, director. Cast: Richard Arlen, Peggy Shannon, Regis Toomey, Charles Starrett, George Barbier, J. Farrell MacDonald, George Irving, Charles D. Brown, (the All-American Football players), Morley Drury, Jesse Hibbs, Russ Saunders, Nate Barranger, and the great Jim Thorpe, and Mrs. Norman MacLeod

If I Had A Million, 1932, Paramount, Ernst Lubitsch, director. Cast: Gary Cooper, Roscoe Karns, Joyce Compton, Lucien Littlefield, May Robson, George Raft, Wynne Gibson, Charles Laughton, Frances Dee, Charles Ruggles, Mary Boland, Alison Skipworth, W.C. Fields, Gene Raymond

Dancers In The Dark, 1932, Paramount, David Burton, director. Cast: Miriam Hopkins, George Raft, Lyda Roberti, Fay Cameron, William Collier Jr., Eugene Pallette, Maurice Black, DeWitt Jennings, Paul Fix, George Bickel, Frances Moffett

Sailor Be Good, 1932, RKO, James Cruze, director. Cast: Vivienne Osborn, Gertrude Michael, George E. Stone, Max Hoffman Jr., Lincoln Stedman, Hutley Gordon, Gertrude Sutton, Charles Coleman, Louise MacIntosh, Crawford Kent, Carlos Alvarado

Once In A Lifetime, 1932, Universal, Russell Mack, director. Cast: Aline MacMahon, Sidney Fox, Russell Hopton, ZaSu Pitts, Margaret Lindsay, Gregory Ratoff, Louise Fazenda, Onslow Stevens, Robert McWade, Jobyna Howland, Claudia Morgan, Gregory Gaye, Mona Maris, Carol Trevis, Deacon McDaniel, Eddie Kane, Frank LaRue, Johnnie Morris

Madison Square Garden, 1932, Paramount, Harry Joe Brown, director. Cast: Marion Nixon, Warren Hymer, Thomas Meighan, William Collier Sr., William (stage) Boyd, ZaSu Pitts, Lew Cody, George Rosener, (and the famous champions) Jack Johnson, Tom Sharkey, Tommy Ryan, Mike Donlin, Billy Papke, Stanislaus Zbyszko, (and the famous sports writers) Damon Runyon, Jack Lait, Grantland Rice, Ed. W. Smith, Westbrook Pegler, Paul Gallico

Million Dollar Legs, 1932, Paramount, Edward Francis Cline, director. Cast: W.C. Fields, Andy Clyde, Lyda Roberti, Susan Fleming, Ben Turpin, George Barbier, Hugh Herbert, Dickie Moore, Billy Gilbert, Vernon Dent, Teddy Hart, Hank Mann, John Sinclair, Sam Adams, Irving Bacon, Ben Taggart, Chick Collins, Sid Saylor

The Eagle And The Hawk, 1933, Paramount, Stuart Walker, director. Cast: Fredric March, Cary Grant, Carole Lombard, Sir Guy Standing, Forrester Harvey, Russell Scott, Leland Hodgson, Kenneth Howell, Douglas Scott, Craufurd Kent, Adrienne D'Ambricourt, Yorke Sherwood, Virginia Hammond, Jacques Jou-Jerville

Alice In Wonderland, 1933, Paramount, Norman Z. McLeod, director. Cast: Charlotte Henry, Richard Arlen, Roscoe Ates, William Austin, Billy Barty, Billy Bevan, Gary Cooper, Leon Errol, Louise Fazenda, W.C. Fields, Skeets Gallagher, Cary Grant, Roscoe Karns,

Ethel Griffies, Sterling Holloway, Edward Everett Horton, Mae Marsh, Polly Moran, Edna May Oliver, May Robson, Charles Ruggles, Jackie Searle, Ned Sparks, Ford Sterling

College Humor, 1933, Paramount, Wesley Ruggles, director. Cast: Bing Crosby, Richard Arlen, Mary Carlisle, Mary Kornman, George Burns and Gracie Allen, Lona Andre, Joe Sauers, James Burke, Jimmy Conlin, James Donlin, Lumsden Hare, Churchill Ross, Robert Quirk, Jack Kennedy, Howard Jones (the famous USC coach), Eddie Nugent, Grady Sutton, Toby Wing and The Ox Road Coeds

From Hell To Heaven, 1933, Paramount, Erle Kenton, director. Cast: Carole Lombard, Sidney Blackmer, David Manners, Adrienne Ames, Verna Hillis, James C. Eagles, Shirley Grey, Bradley Page, Walter Walker, Berton Churchill, Donald Kerr, Nydia Westman, Cecil Cunningham, Thomas Jackson, Allen Wood, Rita LaRoy, Clarence Muse, Dell Henderson

Sitting Pretty, 1933, Paramount, Harry Joe Brown, director. Cast: Ginger Rogers, Jack Haley, Thelma Todd, Lew Cody, Gregory Ratoff, Mack Gordon, Harry Revel, Jerry Tucker, Hale Hamilton, Walter Walker, The Pickens Sisters

Too Much Harmony, 1933, Paramount, A. Edward Sutherland, director. Cast: Bing Crosby, Skeets Gallagher, Judith Allen, Harry Green, Ned Sparks, Lilyan Tashman, Kitty Kelly, Grace Bradley, Anna Demetrio, Mrs. Evelyn Offield Oakie, (Jack's mother), Shirley Grey, Billy Bevan, Red Corcoran, Sammy Cohen, Henry Armetta, Del Henderson, Cyril Ring, Lona Andre, Verna Hillie

College Rhythm, 1934, Paramount, Norman Taurog, director. Cast: Joe Penner, Lanny Ross, Mary Brian, Lyda Roberti, George Barbier, Helen Mack, Franklin Pangborn, Dean Jagger, Mary Wallace, Joseph Sauers, Julian Madison, Robert McWade, Harold Minjir, Bradley Metcalfe

Shoot The Works, 1934, Paramount, Wesley Ruggles, director. Cast: Dorothy Dell, Alison Skipworth, Arline Judge, Lew Cody, Roscoe Karns, William Frawley, Paul Cavanagh, Frank Prince, Monte Vandergrift, Jill Dennett, Lee Kohlmer, Tony Morlo, Ben Taggart, Charles MacAvoy, Ben Bernie and his band

Murder At The Vanities, 1934, Paramount, Mitchell Leisen, director. Cast: Carl Brisson, Victor McLaglen, Kitty Carlisle, Dorothy Stickney, Gertrude Michael, Jesse Ralph, Gail Patrick, Charles B. Middleton, Donald Meek, Lona Andre, Colin Tapley, Toby Wing

Looking For Trouble, 1934, Twentieth Century, William Wellman, director. Cast: Spencer Tracy, Constance Cummings, Arline Judge, Joseph Sauers, Morgan Conway, Judith Wood, Paul Harvey, Franklyn Ardell

Call Of The Wild, 1935, Twentieth Century, William Wellman, director. Cast: Clark Gable, Loretta Young, Frank Conroy, Reginald Owen, Sidney Toler, Katherine deMille, Lalo Encinas, Charles Stevens, James Burke, Duke Green, Marie Wells, John T. Murray, Mia Marvin, Bob Perry, Arthur Housman, Harry Wood, Sid Grauman, Philip G. Sleeman, C.E. (Capt) Anderson,

Frank Whitson, Thomas E. Jackson, Samuel T. Godfrey, William R. Arnold, Perry Izins, Walter McGrail, Russ Powell, Wong Chung, Lon Loy, LeRoy Mason, Frank Moran, Herman Bing, Wade Boteler, Arthur Aylesworth, John Ince, Jesse DeZorska, Syd Saylor, George MacQuarrie, Joan Woodbury, Frank Campeau, Pat Flaherty, Larry McGrath, Jack Stoney, Leon Beaumont, The Beef Trust Girls, and Buck

in *The Gangbuster*

in *Dude Ranch*

in *Tomahawk*

a personal appearance

with Dorothy MacKaill in
Hard To Get

with Buster Keaton — on the Paramount Baseball Team

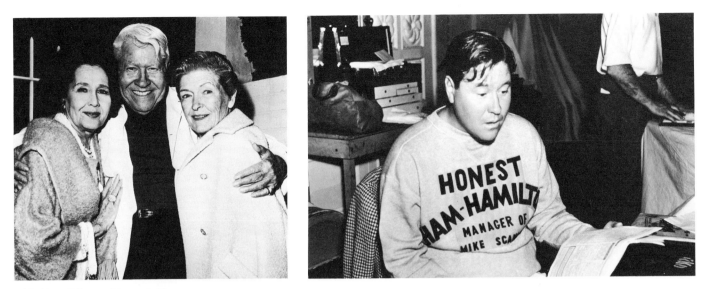

with Mary Brian and Laura LaPlante

with portrait, in Mexico

with Joan Blondell in *Colleen*

with Ann Sothern in *Super Sleuth*

with Bob Cobb at the Hollywood Brown Derby

with a couple of dummies

The Big Broadcast Of 1936, 1935, Paramount, Norman Taurog, director. Cast: Bing Crosby, Lyda Roberti, George Burns and Gracie Allen, Ethel Merman, Mary Boland, Charlie Ruggles, Wendy Barrie, Benny Baker, Bill Robinson, Henry Wadsworth, Ray Noble and his band, Gail Patrick, The Nicholas Brothers, (Freeman Gosden and Charles Correll) Amos 'n Andy, Sir Guy Standing, Jessica Dragonette, Samuel S. Hinds, Akim Tamiroff, Ina Ray Hutton and her band, Willie West and McGinty, David Holt, Virginia Weidler, The Vienna Boys Choir

Collegiate, 1935, Paramount, Ralph Murphy, director. Cast: Joe Penner, Frances Langford, Ned Sparks, Lynne Overman, Betty Grable, Betty Jane Cooper, Mack Gordon, Harry Revel, Henry Kolker, Julius Tannen, Georgia Coleman, Adrian Rosley, Nora Cecil, Kathryn Bates, Helen Brown, Ethel Wales

King Of Burlesque, 1935, Twentieth Century-Fox, Sidney Lanfield, director. Cast: Warner Baxter, Alice Faye, Mona Barrie, Arline Judge, Gregory Ratoff, Dixie Dunbar, Fats Waller, Nick Long Jr., Herbert Mundin, Kenny Baker, Charles Quigley, Paxton Sisters, Shaw and Lee, Andrew Tombes, Shirley Deane, Harry (Zoop) Welch, Claudia Coleman, Ellen E. Lowe, Herbert Ashley, Jerry Mandy, Keye Luke, Gareth Joplin, and Jane Wyman (one of the girls on the swings, and a loving lifetime friend)

Colleen, 1935, Warner's First National, Alfred Green, director. Cast: Ruby Keeler, Dick Powell, Joan Blondell, Luis Alberni, Paul Draper, Hugh Herbert, Louise Fazenda, Marie Wilson, Berton Churchill, J.M. Kerrigan, Spencer Charters, Charles Coleman, Addison Richards, Mary Treen, Hobart Cavanaugh

Florida Special, 1936, Paramount, Ralph Murphy, director. Cast: Sally Eilers, Frances Drake, Kent Taylor, Sam Hearn, Claude Gillingwater, J. Farrell MacDonald, Gail Sheridan, Irene Bennett, Wilma Francis, Jill Deen, Louise Small, Ann Evers, Jeanne Perkins, Dewey Robinson, Clyde Dilson, Dwight Frye, Sidney Blackmer, Matthew Betz

The Texas Rangers, 1936, Paramount, King Vidor, director. Cast: Fred MacMurray, Jean Parker, Lloyd Nolan, Edward Ellis, Bennie Bartlett, Frank Shannon, Frank Cordell, Richard Carle, Jed Prouty, Fred Kohler Sr., George Hayes, Elena Martinez

Champagne Waltz, 1936, Paramount, A. Edward Sutherland, director. Cast: Gladys Swarthout, Fred MacMurray, Veloz and Yolanda, Herman Bing, Vivienne Osborne, Frank Forest, Benny Baker, James Burke, Ernest Cossart, Fritz Leiber, Maude Eburne, Michael Visaroff, Guy Bates Post, Maurice Cass

That Girl From Paris, 1936, RKO, Leigh Jason, director. Cast: Lily Pons, Gene Raymond, Herman Bing, Mischa Auer, Frank Jenks, Lucille Ball, Patricia Wilder, Vinton Haworth, Gregory Gaye, Willard Robertson, Rafaela Ottiano, Ferdinand Gottschalk, Harry Jans, Landers Stevens, Edward Price, Alec Craig

Fight For Your Lady, 1937, RKO, Ben Stoloff, director. Cast: John Boles, Ida Lupino, Margot Grahame, Gordon Jones, Erik Rhodes, Billy Gilbert, Paul Guilfoyle, Georges Renavent, Charles Judels, Maude Eburne, Charles Coleman

Hitting A New High, 1937, RKO, Raoul Walsh, director. Cast: Lily Pons, Edward Everett Horton, John Howard, Eduardo Ciannelli, Vinton Haworth, Eric Blore, Luis Alberni, Jack Arnold, Leonard Carey

Radio City Revels, 1937, RKO, Ben Stoloff, director. Cast: Bob Burns, Helen Broderick, Kenny Baker, Jane Froman, Milton Berle, Ann Miller, Victor Moore, Buster West, Melissa Mason, Richard Lane, Marilyn Vernon

Super Sleuth, 1937, RKO, Ben Stoloff, director. Cast: Ann Sothern, Eduardo Ciannelli, Edgar Kennedy, Joan Woodbury, Alan Bruce, Paul Hurst, Bradley Page, Paul Guilfoyle, Willie Best, William Corson, Alec Craig, Richard Lane, George Rosener, Fred Kelsey, Robert E. O'Connor, Philip Morris, Dick Rush

Toast Of New York, 1937, RKO, Rowland V. Lee, director. Cast: Edward Arnold, Frances Farmer, Cary Grant, Donald Meek, Thelma Leeds, Clarence Kolb, Billy Gilbert, George Irving, Frank M. Thomas, Russell Hicks, Oscar Apfel, Dudley Clements, Lionel Belmore, Robert McClung, Robert Dudley, Dewey Robinson, Stanley Fields, Gavin Gordon, Joyce Compton, Virginia Carroll

Affairs Of Annabel, 1938, RKO, Ben Stoloff, director. Cast: Lucille Ball, Ruth Donnelly, Bradley Page, Fritz Feld, Thurston Hall, Elizabeth Risdon, Granville Bates, James Burke, Lee Van Atta, Anthony Warde, Leona Roberts, Edward Marr

Annabel Takes A Tour, 1938, RKO, Lew Landers, director. Cast: Lucille Ball, Ruth Donnelly, Ralph Forbes, Alice White, Bradley Page, Frances Mercer, Donald MacBride, Pepito, Chester Clute, Jean Rouverol, Clare Verdera, Edward Gargan

Thanks For Everything, 1938, Twentieth Century-Fox, William A. Seiter, director. Cast: Adolph Menjou, Binnie Barnes, Jack Haley, Tony Martin, Arleen Whelan, George Barbier, Warren Hymer, Gregory Gaye, Andrew Tombes, Renie Riano, Jan Duggan, Charles Lane, Charles Trowbridge, Frank Sully, Gary Breckner, Paul Hurst, James Flavin, Ed Dearing

The Great Dictator, 1939, Chaplin, Charlie Chaplin, director. Cast: Charlie Chaplin, Paulette Goddard, Reginald Gardiner, Henry Daniell, Billy Gilbert, Grace Hayle, Carter DeHaven, Maurice Moscovich, Emma Dunn, Bernard Gorcey, Paul Weigel, Chester Conklin, Esther Michelson, Hank Mann, Florence Wright, Eddie Gribbon, Robert O. Davis, Eddie Dunn, Nita Pike, Peter Lynn

Young People, 1940, Twentieth Century-Fox, Allan Dwan, director. Cast: Shirley Temple, Charlotte Greenwood, Arleen Whelan, George Montgomery, Kathleen Howard, Minor Watson, Frank Swann, Frank Sully, Mae Marsh, Sarah Edwards, Irving Bacon, Charles Halton, Olin Howland, Billy Wayne, Harry Tyler, Diane Fisher, Shirley Mills, Darryl Hickman, Bobby Anderson, Arthur Aylesworth, Billy Benedict, Robert Shaw, Syd Saylor, Dell Henderson, Ted North, Evelyn Beresford

Little Men, 1940, RKO, Norman Z. McLeod, director. Cast: Kay Francis, George Bancroft, Jimmy Lydon, Ann Gillis, Charles Esmond, Jimmy Zaner, Richard Nichols, Johnny Burke, Lillian Randolph, Casey Johnson, Isabel

with Maria Montez in *Bowery To Broadway*

with Irene Ryan and Arthur Treacher in *That's The Spirit*

with June Havoc, John Payne, and Alice Faye in *Hello Frisco Hello*

with Doris Day in *Lover Come Back*

with Joan Davis in *She Wrote The Book*

with Ida Lupino and Maude Eburne in *Fight For Your Lady*

with Thelma Todd in *Sitting Pretty*

with Peggy Ryan and Donald O'Connor in *The Merry Monahans*

Jewell, William Demarest, Sterling Holloway, Francesca Santore, Sammy McKim, Edward Rice, Anne Howard, Bobbie Cooper, Schuyler Standish, Paul Matthews, Tony Neil, Fred Estes, Douglas Rucker, Donald Rackerby, Sarah Edwards, Bud Jaimison, Hal K. Dawson, Russ Powell, Lew Kelly, Nella Walker, George Irving, Nora Cecil, Charles Arnt, Stan Blystone, Jack Henderson, George Green, Bill Irving, Duke York, Clarence H. Wilson, Howard Hickman

Tin Pan Alley, 1940, Twentieth Century-Fox, Walter Lang, director. Cast: Alice Faye, Betty Grable, John Payne, Allen Jenkins, Esther Ralston, Nicholas Brothers, Ben Carter, Elisha Cook Jr., Billy Gilbert, John Loder, George Watts, Fred Keating, Lillian Porter, Tyler Brooke, Princess Vanessa Ammon, Brian Sisters, Roberts Brothers, Hal K. Dawson, William B. Davidson, Lionel Pape, Billy Bevan, Jack Roper, Dewey Robinson, Robert Emmett Keane, John Sheehan, James Flavin, Franklyn Farnum, Harry Strang

The Great American Broadcast, 1941, Twentieth Century-Fox, Archie Mayo, director. Cast: Alice Faye, John Payne, Cesar Romero, Nicholas Brothers, Wiere Brothers, The Four Inkspots, Mary Beth Hughes, James Newill, Eula Morgan, William Pawley, Lucien Littlefield, Edward Conrad, Gary Breckner, Mike Frankovich, John Hiestand, Eddie Acuff, Mildred Gover, Syd Saylor, Eddie Kane, William Halligan, Frank Orth, Herbert Heywood, Charles Tannen, Dorothy Dearing, Sam McDaniel, Snowflake, John Sinclair, Arno Frey

Navy Blues, 1941, Warner Brothers, Lloyd Bacon, director. Cast: Ann Sheridan, Martha Raye, Jack Haley, Jack Carson, Herbert Anderson, Jackie C. Gleason, William T. Orr, Marguerite Chapman, DeWolfe Hopper, Hardie Albright, Ray Cooke, William Justice, Frank Wilcox, Howard Da Silva, John Ridgely, Richard Lane, Claire James, Lorraine Gettman, Peggy Diggins, Georgia Carroll, Katharine Aldridge, Nick Lukats, Renny McEvoy, Ralph Bird, Elliott Sullivan, William Newell, Jean Ames, Maris Wrixon, Lucia Carroll, Don Rowan, Fred Graham, Tom Dugan, Ed Gargan, Frank Orth, Gaylord Pendleton, George O'Hanlon, Arthur Gardner, Will Morgan, Garland Smith, G. Pat Collins, Emmett Vogan, Byron Barr, Murray Alper, Dick Wessel, Victor Zimmerman, Harry Strang, Selmer Jackson, Lane Allan, William Forrest, Ed Stanley, Pat McVeigh, Walter Sands

Rise And Shine, 1941, Twentieth Century-Fox, Allan Dwan, director. Cast: George Murphy, Linda Darnell, Ruth Donnelly, Donald Meek, Walter Brennan, Milton Berle, Emma Dunn, Sheldon Leonard, Raymond Walburn, Donald MacBride, Charles Waldron, William Haade, Dick Rich, John Hiestand, Mildred Gover, Claire DuBrey, Francis Pierlot, Paul Harvey, Matt Willis, Pat Flaherty, Billy Wayne, Edward Arnold Jr., Jimmy Butler, Robert Shaw, Mike Pecarovich, Robert Homans, Tim Ryan, Nestor Paiva, William Reade, Claire James, Edna Mae Jones, Mary Scott

Song Of The Islands, 1941, Twentieth Century-Fox, Walter Lang, director. Cast: Betty Grable, Victor Mature, Hilo Hattie, Lillian Porter, Thomas Mitchell, George Barbier, Billy Gilbert, Harry Owens and his Royal Hawaiians, Hal K. Dawson, Amy Cordone, Bruce Wong, Alex Pollard, Harold Lishman

Something To Shout About, 1942, Columbia, Gregory Ratoff, director. Cast: Don Amechi, Janet Blair, William Gaxton, Cobina Wright Jr., Veda Ann Borg, Hazel Scott, Jaye Martin, Kay Aldridge, Lily Norwood (Cyd Charisse), James (Chuckles) Walker, The Bricklayers (dog act), Harry Green, Jiggs (the ape), Shirley Patterson, Beatrice Blinn, Ludmila Toretzka

Iceland, 1942, Twentieth Century-Fox, Bruce Humberstone, director. Cast: Sonja Henie, John Payne, Felix Bressart, Osa Massen, Joan Merrill, Fritz Feld, Sterling Holloway, Duke Adlon, Adeline DeWitt Reynolds, Ludwig Stossel, Jody Gilbert, Ilka Gruning, Eugene Turner, James Flavin, William Haade, James Bush, Carol Curtis Brown, Sammy Kaye and his orchestra

Wintertime, 1943, Twentieth Century-Fox, John Brahm, director. Cast: Sonja Henie, Cornel Wilde, Cesar Romero, Carole Landis, S.Z. Sakall, Helene Reynolds, Matt Briggs, Don Douglas, Woody Herman and his orchestra, Geary Steffen, Jean De Briac, Jean Del Val, Charles Irwin, Dick Elliott, Charles Trowbridge, Nella Walker, Arthur Loft

Hello Frisco Hello, 1943, Twentieth Century-Fox, Bruce Humberstone, director. Cast: Alice Faye, John Payne, June Havoc, Lynn Bari, Laird Cregar, Ward Bond, Aubrey Mather, John Archer, Frank Orth, George Lloyd, Frank Darien, Harry Hayden, Eddie Dunn, Charles Cane, James Flavin, Edward Earle, Frank Thomas, Kirby Grant, Mary Field, George Barbier, Esther Dale, Gino Corrado, Fortunio Bonanova, Adia Kuznetzoff, James Sills, Ed Mundy, Marie Brown, Jackie Averill, Jimmie Clemans Jr., John Sinclair, Jack Stoney

It Happened Tomorrow, 1943, United Artists, Rene Clair, director. Cast: Linda Darnell, Dick Powell, Edgar Kennedy, John Philliber, Edward Brophy, George Cleveland, Sig Ruman, Paul Guilfoyle, George Chandler, Eddie Acuff, Marion Martin, Jack Gardner, Eddie Coke, Robert Homans, Robert Dudley, Emma Dunn

The Merry Monahans, 1943, Universal, Charles Lamont, director. Cast: Donald O'Connor, Peggy Ryan, Ann Blyth, Rosemary DeCamp, Isabel Jewell, John Miljan, Gavin Muir, Ian Wolfe, Robert Homans, Lloyd Ingraham, Marion Martin, Billy Benedict, Duke Johnson, Ronnie Rondell, Al Thompson, Bobby Barber, Herbert Heywood, Jimmy Bates, Arthur Loft, Lew Woods, Ray Turner, Cyril Ring, Jack Gardner, Harry Harvey, Harry Tyler, Al Bridge, Pearl Early, Lew Kelly, Robert Barron, Eddie Bruce, Emmett Vogan, Polly Bailey, Earle Hodgens, Herbert Weber, Albert Smith, Frank Kenny, Jack Rice, Andrew Toombes, Patsy O'Byrne, Phil Dunham, Edgar Dearing, Syd Saylor, Ernie Adams, Kernan Cripps, Ella Ethridge, Matt McHugh, Patsy Moran, Nolan Leary, Bobbie Hale, Art Miles, Pat Gleason, Murray Parker, Robert Emmett Keane, Doodles Weaver, Bill Cartledge

Sweet and Low Down, 1944, Twentieth Century-Fox, Archie Mayo, director. Cast: Linda Darnell, Benny Goodman and his band, Lynn Bari, James Cardwell, Allyn Joslyn, John Campbell, Roy Benson, Dickie Moore, Buddy Swan, Beverly Hudson, Dorothy Vaughan

Bowery To Broadway, 1944, Universal, Charles Lamont, director. Cast: Maria Montez, Leo Carillo, Turhan Bey, Susanna Foster, Ann Blyth, Donald Cook, Louise Albritton, Frank McHugh, Rosemary DeCamp, Andy Devine, Evelyn Ankers, Thomas Gomez, Donald O'Connor, Peggy Ryan, Mantan Moreland, Ben Carter, Maude Eburne, Robert Warwick, Richard Lane, George Dolenz

That's The Spirit, 1945, Universal, Charles Lamont, director. Cast: Peggy Ryan, Johnny Coy, June Vincent, Gene Lockhart, Edith Barrett, Andy Devine, Irene Ryan, Arthur Treacher, Buster Keaton, Victoria Horne, Rex Story, Karen Randle, Harry Tyler, Billy Newell, Jack Roper, Virginia Brissac, Charles Sullivan, Sid Troy, Monte Collins, Jack Shutta, Fred Kelsey, Dorothy Christy, Eddie Dunn, Mary Forbes, Ed Gargan, Mabel Forrest, Genevieve Bell, Herbert Evans, Lloyd Ingraham, Nelson McDowell, Wheaton Chambers, Herbert Heywood, Bobby Barber, Lou Wood, Brooks Benedict, Gloria Marlen, Mary McLeod, Teddy Infur, Eddie Cutler, Charles Teske, Jerry Maren, Billy Curtis

On Stage Everybody, 1945, Universal, Jean Yarborough, director. Cast: Peggy Ryan, Johnny Coy, Julie London, Otto Kruger, Esther Dale, Wallace Ford, The King Sisters, June Brady, Georgiana Bannister, Billy Usher, Eddie Russell, Jean Hamilton, Bob Hopkins, Beatrice Fung Oye, Ilene Woods, Ronnie Gibson, Cyril Smith, Milburn Stone, Stephen Wayne, Jimmy Clark, Jean Richey

She Wrote The Book, 1946, Universal, Charles Lamont, director. Cast: Joan Davis, Kirby Grant, Jacqueline de Witt, Gloria Stuart, Mischa Auer, John Litel, Thurston Hall, Lewis L. Russel, Raymond Largay, Verna Felton, Jack J. Ford, Phil Garris, Victoria Horne

Northwest Stampede, 1947, Eagle-Lion, Al Rogel, director. Cast: Joan Leslie, James Craig, Chill Wills, Victor Kilian, Polly Burson, Harry Shannon, Stanley Anders, Ray Bennett, Lane Chandler, Lane Bradford, Harry Cheshire, Eddie Acuff, Lee Roberts, Flame, (the dog)

When My Baby Smiles At Me, 1948, Twentieth Century-Fox, Walter Lang, director. Cast: Betty Grable, Dan Dailey, June Havoc, Richard Arlen, Jean Wallace, James Gleason, Vanita Wade, Robert Emmett Keane, Pati Behrs, Jerry Maren, George Lewis, Tom Stevenson, Sam Bernard, Kenny Williams, Maurtiz Hugo, Frank Scannell, Lee MacGregor, Charles Tannen, Noel Neill, Lu Anne Jones, Joanne Dale, Dorothy Babb, Hank Mann, Edward Clark, Charles La Torre, Lela Bliss

Thieves Highway, 1948, Twentieth Century-Fox, Jules Dassin, director. Cast: Richard Conte, Valentina Cortesa, Lee J. Cobb, Barbara Lawrence, Millard Mitchell, Joseph Pevney, David Clark, Morris Carnovsky, Tamara Shayne, Kasia Orzazewski, Norbert Schiller, Walter Baldwin, Hope Emerson, George Tyne, Edwin Max, Percy Helton, Ann Morrison, David Opatoshu, Maurice Samuls, Saul Martell, Al Eben, Holland Chamberlain, Irene Tedrow, Joe Haworth, Dick Wessel, Frank Kreig, Mario Siletti

Tomahawk, 1950, Universal, George Sherman, director. Cast: Van Heflin, Yvonne DeCarlo, Alex Nicol, Preston Foster, Tom Tully, Susan Cabot, Rock Hudson, John War Eagle, Arthur Space, Russell Conway, Ann Doran, Stuart Randall

Last Of The Buccaneers, 1950, Columbia, Lew Landers, director. Cast: Paul Henreid, Mary Anderson, Karin Booth, John Dehner, Eugene Borden, Harry Cording, Edgar Barrier, Jean Del Val, Pierre Watkin, Sumner Getchell, Paul Marion, Rusty Wescoatt

Around The World In 80 Days, 1955, Todd A-O, Michael Anderson, director. Cast: David Niven, Cantinflas, Robert Newton, Shirley MacLaine, Charles Boyer, Joe E. Brown, Martine Carol, John Carradine, Charles Coburn, Ronald Colman, Melville Cooper, Noel Coward, Finlay Currie, Reginald Denny, Andy Devine, Marlene Dietrich, Luis Miguel Dominguin, Fernandel, Sir John Gielgud, Hermoine Gingold, Jose Greco, Sir Cedric Hardwicke, Trevor Howard, Glynis Johns, Buster Keaton, Evelyn Keyes, Beatrice Lillie, Peter Lorre, Edmund Lowe, Victor McLaglen, Col. Tim McCoy, A.E. Matthews, Mike Mazurki, John Mills, Alan Mowbray, Robert Morley, Edward R. Murrow, George Raft, Gilbert Roland, Cesar Romero, Frank Sinatra, Red Skelton, Ronald Squires, Basil Sydney, Harcourt Williams

The Wonderful Country, 1958, United Artists, Robert Parrish, director. Cast: Robert Mitchum, Julie London, Gary Merrill, Charles McGraw, Albert Dekker, Pedro Armendariz, Victor Mendoza, Jay Novello, John Banner, Mike Kellin, Max Slaten, Chuck Roberson, Joe Haworth, LeRoy (Satchel) Page, Tom Lea, Chester Hayes, Mike Luna, Anthony Caruso, Claudio Brook, Judy Marsh

The Rat Race, 1960, Paramount, Robert Mulligan, director. Cast: Debbie Reynolds, Tony Curtis, Kay Medford, Don Rickels, Joe Bushkin, Gerry Mulligan, Sam Butera, Marjorie Bennett, Lisa Drake, Norman Fell, Hal K. Dawson, Jack (Tipp) McClure, Dick Winslow, Wally Cassell, David Joseph Landfield, Jacques Gallo, Stanley Adams, Joseph G. Sullivan, Louis M. Lettieri, Johnny Lee, Richard Keene, Barbara Mansell, Nancy Root, Helen Jay, Theona Bryant, Ruth Rickaby, Richard Adams, Joe Terry, Donald Lamont, Bob Kenaston, Mark Russell, Frank Mitchell

Lover Come Back, 1961, Universal-International, Delbert Mann, director. Cast: Doris Day, Rock Hudson, Tony Randall, Edie Adams, Jack Kruschen, Ann B. Davis, Howard St. John, Joe Flynn, Jack Albertson, Charles Watts, Ward Ramsey, Karen Norris, Donna Douglas, Willard Sage, Chet Stratton, Mina Vaughn, Joan Kelly, Barbara Fredrick, Nelson Olmstead, John B. Litel, Nelson Leigh, Emerson Treacy, Ed. Prentiss, Richard Deacon, Jo Anne Smith, Israel Kaufman, Hilda Plowright, Kathleen Mulqueen, Frank London, Penny Santon, Nolan Leary, Joan Patrick, Fletcher Allen, Russ Bender, Michael Ross, Al Hodge, Robert Cass, William Benedict, Micky Blair, John Morley, Pauline Drake, Ray Daley, Ted Bessell, Jimmie B. Smith, Henry Bernard, Dorothy Abbott, George Lymburn, Marla Ryan, Chris Seitz, John R. McKee, Don MacLeod, June Wilkinson, Bob Duggan, Rita D'Amico, Darlene Daye, Barbra Dorothy Clarke

with birthday cake and Gene Raymond at Chasen's

with Wynne Gibson and friend

with Debbie Reynolds in *The Rat Race*

with Mary Brian and Laura LaPlante

under portrait of Cantinflas at his home in Mexico

William O'Dwyer, Vickie, and Jack

with Helen Hayes

Rosemary DeCamp, Jack Oakie, Ann Blyth, Peggy Ryan, and Donald O'Connor in *The Merry Monahans*

The DeLaSalle Basketball Team — Jack is second from right, front row

JACK OAKIE'S MUSIC

"K-K-K-Katy" by Powell, Henderson, & O'Hara from *Tin Pan Alley.*

"Goodbye Broadway Hello France" by Reisner, Davis, & Backette from *Tin Pan Alley.*

"You Say The Sweetest Things Baby" by Warren & Gordon from *Tin Pan Alley.*

"Give My Regards To Broadway" by George M. Cohan from *Great American Broadcast.*

"I Take To You" by Warren & Gordon from *Great American Broadcast.*

"Boulevardier From The Bronx" by Warren & Dubin from *Colleen.*

"When Are We Going To Land Abroad" by Mercer & Schwartz from *Navy Blues.*

"In Waikiki" by Mercer & Schwartz from *Navy Blues.*

"Fifth Avenue" by Warren & Gordon from *Young People.*

"I Wouldn't Take A Million" by Warren & Gordon from *Young People.*

"Tra-La-La-La" by Warren & Gordon from *Young People.*

"Thanks For Everything" by Gordon & Revel from *Thanks For Everything.*

"Stay As Sweet As You Are" by Gordon & Revel from *College Rhythm.*

"I'm Shooting High" by Koehler & McHugh from *King Of Burlesque.*

"This Must Be Illegal It's So Nice" by Marion Jr., Rainger, & Harling from *Sea Legs.*

"You'd Be So Nice To Come Home To" by Cole Porter from *Something To Shout About.*

"Through Thick And Thin" by Cole Porter from *Something To Shout About.*

"Something To Shout About" by Cole Porter from *Something To Shout About.*

"Gee But It's Great To Meet A Friend From Your Home Town" by Tracy & Gavisk from *Hello, Frisco, Hello.*

"Miss Brown To You" by Whiting, Robin, & Rainger from *The Big Broadcast.*

"Why Dream" by Whiting, Robin, & Rainger from *The Big Broadcast.*

"Down The Old Ox Road" by Johnston & Coslow from *College Humor.*

"Rhythm-atic" by Gordon & Revel from *Collegiate.*

"I Feel Like A Feather In The Breeze" by Gordon & Revel from *Collegiate.*

"My Grandfather's Clock In The Hallway" by Gordon & Revel from *Collegiate.*

BING CROSBY

Dear Jack:

Congratulations on achieving this significant milestone — seven decades. That is really a point of reference. I achieve the same thing next year.

You should write a book now, Jack, and I know it would be entertaining — filled with your life and times in Hollywood.

I could contribute an episode or two — like the occasion when you pinched the shootin' iron from Nick Stuart's guard, and held the whole Paramount Studio at bay. What laughs we had in those days, eh?

And you were the ringleader in most of the shenanigans.

Have a happy and festive day, Jack —

Always your pal,

Bing

"You Hit The Spot" by Gordon & Revel from *Collegiate.*

"I'm In Love With A Tune" by Rainger from *Dancers In The Dark.*

"I've Got A Yen For You" by Whiting, & Marion Jr. from *Let's Go Native.*

"Let's Go Native" by Whiting, & Marion Jr. from *Let's Go Native.*

"Sometimes I'm Happy" by Youmans & Caesar from *Hit The Deck.*

"Hallelujah" by Youmans & Ceasar from *Hit The Deck.*

"Harbor Of My Heart" by Youmans & Caesar from *Hit The Deck.*

"Keepin' Myself For You" by Youmans & Caesar from *Hit The Deck.*

"Nothing Could Be Sweeter" by Youmans & Caesar from *Hit The Deck.*

"An Armful Of You" by Youmans & Caesar from *Hit The Deck.*

"Join The Navy" by Youmans & Caesar from *Hit The Deck.*

"Buckin' The Wind" by Johnston & Coslow from *Too Much Harmony.*

"Has Anybody Here Seen Kelly?" by Moore, Murphy, & McKenna from *Hello, Frisco, Hello.*

"Grizzly Bear" by Botsford & Berlin from *Hello, Frisco, Hello.*

"He's Got A Gal In Every Port" by Unknown from *Hello, Frisco, Hello.*

ASCAP "Dreadnaughts": George Greeley, Harry Ruby, L. Wolfe Gilbert, Harold Adamson, Sammy Fain, Jack Oakie and Jimmy McHugh (at the piano).

"Did You Ever See A Dream Walking" by Gordon & Revel from *Sitting Pretty*.

"You're Such A Comfort To Me" by Gordon & Revel from *Sitting Pretty*.

"Good Morning Glory" by Gordon & Revel from *Sitting Pretty*.

"June Moon" by Lardner & Kaufman from *June Moon*.

"It's You I'm Talking About" by Gordon & Revel from *Florida Special*.

"Sweet Sue" by Young & Harris from *The Fleet's In* (the sheet music was sent out to the theatres to accompany this silent picture).

"I Can't Play My Banjo With Susannah On My Knee" by Scholl & Boutelje (Stephen Foster) from *The Texas Rangers*.

"Woof Bloogle Jig" ("One Hour With You") by Robin & Whiting from *Million Dollar Legs*.

"Sing Me A Song Of The Islands" by Gordon & Owens from *Song Of The Islands*.

"What's Buzzin' Cousin" by Gordon & Owens from *Song Of The Islands*.

"Home On The Range" by Unknown from *Song Of The Islands*.

"No Matter Where You Are" by Brooks & Salter from *That's The Spirit*.

"Feller With The Flute" by Miller & James from *That's The Spirit*.

"I'm In Training For You" by Gilbert & Baer from *Paramount On Parade*.

"How I Wish I Could Sing A Love Song" by Harburg & Green from *Sap From Syracuse*.

"With My Eyes Wide Open I'm Dreaming" by Gordon & Revel from *Shoot The Works*.

"Alma Mammy" by Whiting & Marion Jr. from *Sweetie*.

"Bear Down Pelham" by Whiting & Marion Jr. from *Sweetie*.

"Prep Step" by Whiting & Marion Jr. from *Sweetie*.

"Lovely" by George & Bibo from *Merry Monahans*.

Joe Penner, Jack Oakie and Bing Crosby.

"Beautiful To Look At" by George & Bibo from *Merry Monahans*.

"We're Havin' A Wonderful Time" by George & Bibo from *Merry Monahans*.

"In My Merry Oldsmobile" by Bryan, Edwards, & Schoebel from *Merry Monahans*.

"I'm Always Chasing Rainbows" by Carroll & McCarthy from *Merry Monahans*.

"Lovable And Sweet" by Levant & Clare from *Street Girl*.

"Let's Call The Whole Thing Off" by Ira & George Gershwin from *Oakie College*.

"Little Old Lady" by Adams & Carmichael from *Oakie College*.

"Please" by Rainger & Robin from *The Big Broadcast*.

"Moonface" by Schwartz & Heyman from *That Girl From Paris*.

"Doin' The Racoon" by Coots & Klages from *Close Harmony*.

"The Dark Town Strutter's Ball" by Shelton Brooks from *Close Harmony*.

"Hail To Bolewciecwcz" by Rainger from *Rise and Shine*.

"I Want To Be The Guy" by Rainger from *Rise And Shine*.

"Get Thee Behind Me, Clayton" by Rainger from *Rise And Shine*.

THE OAKIE COLLEGE

"The Oakie College," my radio show for the Camel Caravan, was on the air for three years. I was the president of the comedy college, and it always added to the fun to be recognized socially as an educator. The radio show was considered a very good one. We had Benny Goodman's orchestra, Jo Stafford (one of the Stafford Sisters), Martha Tilton (who was a regular), and such guests as John Barrymore, Alice Faye, Ethel Waters, and little Judy Garland, who was only twelve at the time and showing us that she was one of the biggest talents in our business.

Because I was making movies at the studios all day, we rehearsed the radio show at night, and also made the weekly broadcast at night. For our rehearsals and the broadcast we took over the Music Box Theatre on Hollywood Boulevard. The little theatre was just one street away and around the corner from that restaurant on Vine Street where we all ate, drank, and held our meetings, so that it had become practically a theatrical club, known the world over as the Hollywood Brown Derby.

Wilson Mizner, a great writer and one of the most caustic wits of our day, held court nightly at his corner table. This private area was the gathering place of the greatest writing talent brought to Hollywood.

One night after one of the early broadcasts of my radio show, perhaps the third or fourth time I was on the air, I came into the Derby feeling pretty good. The big brass had just told me that although I was new to radio our show was a big hit. Mizner was exchanging witticisms with some of his peers. At his table that night was playwright Arthur Caesar, famous for his "Hollywood greetings" at the Derby.

As Arthur passed your table, if you were working, he would bend forward and reach for your hand and shake it warmly, as he said, "Hellooooo." But if, as he passed your table, he knew you were unemployed, he would paddle the atmosphere from his path with open palm as he hurried by, and let the breeze carry a curt "Hello." At the Brown Derby, his act was to extend a hand only to the guy with a job.

There was also Solly Violinski, the songwriter, whom my good friend Harold Adamson, the great lyricist, likes to quote. It seems one time Solly had an accident, and when asked if he was insured, ex-

"Hellzapoppin" Olson and Johnson guest on Jack Oakie's radio program.

claimed, "Certainly, but only for fire and theft!" Mark Kelly, the Hearst papers great sportswriter, was also at that table, along with Ralph Spence, the famous title writer for silent pictures, one of the "titular bishops" of Hollywood.

"Hey, Oakie," Mizner called to me, "come on over here, kid." I was glad to join the gathering of good friends after my busy day and night, and expected them to offer me a drink for a job well done. "Listen, young man," he threatened in his driest tone, as I sat down. "We've just taken a vote at this table and decided unanimously that if you don't get off the air, we're all going to stop breathing!"

"The Jack Oakie College," for Camel cigarettes, ran on the CBS network from 1936 to 1938. Below is a partial list of Jack's shows during the first part of 1937. His orchestras were Benny Goodman (from New York and Georgie Stoll (from Los Angeles); Judy Garland was under contract to him as a singer.

1/19/37
JUDY GARLAND
SHAW & LEE
GLEE CLUB OF UCLA
ORCHESTRAS OF GEORGIE STOLL and BENNY GOODMAN

198

April 1934, on the international broadcast celebrating the first anniversary of the new studio, 20th Century. From the left: Tulio Carminati, Fredric March, Jack Oakie, Ronald Colman, Rupert Hughes and Alfred Newman, music director.

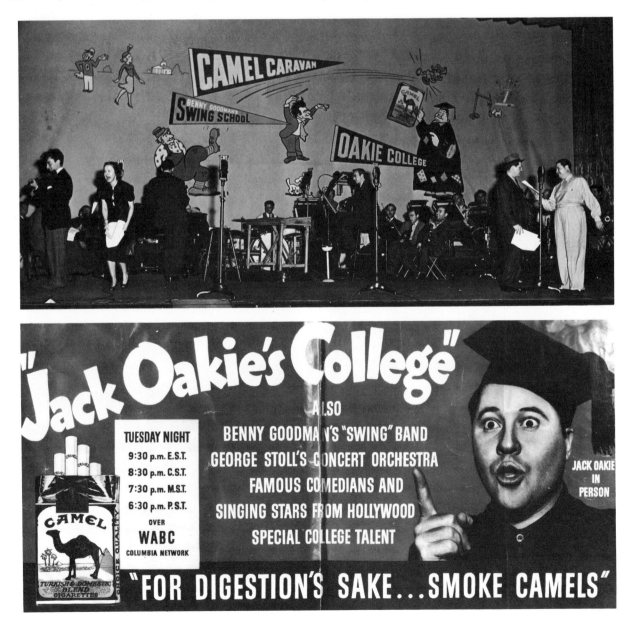

1/26/37
ORCHESTRAS OF GEORGIE STOLL and BENNY
GOODMAN
SHAW & LEE
BLOCK & SULLY
ROBERT WILDHACK
DOROTHY LAMOUR

2/2/37
EDDIE CANTOR
GERTRUDE NIESEN
SHAW & LEE
ORCHESTRAS OF BENNY GOODMAN and GEORGIE
STOLL
ALEXANDER'S SWING TIME CHORUS

2/9/37
BLOCK & SULLY
DONALD NOVIS
SHAW & LEE
ORCHESTRAS OF BENNY GOODMAN and GEORGIE
STOLL

2/16/37
GEORGE GIVIT
CLIFF EDWARDS
SHAW & LEE
ORCHESTRAS OF BENNY GOODMAN and GEORGIE
STOLL
ALEXANDER'S SWING TIME CHORUS

2/23/37
JUDY GARLAND
CORNELL UNIVERSITY GLEE CLUB
ORCHESTRAS OF BENNY GOODMAN and GEORGIE
STOLL
ALEXANDER'S SWING TIME CHORUS
SHAW & LEE

JACK OAKIE

3/2/37
HUGH HERBERT
JUDY GARLAND
MARY CARR
SHAW & LEE
ORCHESTRAS OF BENNY GOODMAN and GEORGIE
STOLL
ALEXANDER'S SWING TIME CHORUS

3/9/37
ALICE FAYE
ROY ATWELL
SHAW & LEE
ORCHESTRAS OF BENNY GOODMAN and GEORGIE
STOLL

3/16/37
ALICE FAYE
ROY ATWELL
SHAW & LEE
ORCHESTRAS OF BENNY GOODMAN and GEORGIE
STOLL
ALEXANDER'S SWING TIME CHORUS

3/23/37
FRANK FAYE and JOHN BOLES
ORCHESTRAS OF BENNY GOODMAN and GEORGIE
STOLL
SHAW & LEE

3/30/37
PAT O'BRIEN
JUDY GARLAND
SHAW & LEE
ORCHESTRAS OF BENNY GOODMAN and GEORGIE
STOLL
ALEXANDER'S SWING TIME CHORUS

George Jessel and Eddie Cantor guest on Oakie College
program.

Judy Garland, at age 13, solos for Oakie College.

4/6/37
JOE PENNER
SHAW & LEE
JUDY GARLAND
ORCHESTRAS OF BENNY GOODMAN and GEORGIE STOLL

4/13/37
EDWARD EVERETT HORTON and DEWEY ROBINSON
JUDY GARLAND
SHAW & LEE
ORCHESTRAS OF BENNY GOODMAN and GEORGIE STOLL
ALEXANDER'S SWING TIME CHORUS

4/20/37
STUART ERWIN
SHAW & LEE
ORCHESTRAS OF BENNY GOODMAN and GEORGIE STOLL
ALEXANDER'S SWING TIME CHORUS
JUDY GARLAND
RUFE DAVIS

4/27/37
BENNY GOODMAN AND HIS SWING TIME BAND
GEORGIE STOLL AND HIS ORCHESTRA
ROBERT WILDHACK
JUDY GARLAND
RUFE DAVIS
SHAW & LEE

5/4/37
BENNY GOODMAN AND HIS SWING TIME BAND
GEORGIE STOLL AND HIS ORCHESTRA
JUDY GARLAND
SHAW & LEE
JACK OAKIE GLEE CLUB

ST. LOUIS STAR-TIMES   SATURDAY EVENING, MAY 1, 1937.   ST. LOUIS STAR-TIMES

Jack Oakie Ridin' High on the Air Waves

STAR TELLS BRUNDIDGE HE'S 'LUCKIEST GUY THAT EVER ESCAPED FROM SEDALIA'

5/11/37
ROBERT BENCHLEY
JUDY GARLAND
SHAW & LEE
OAKIE COLLEGE GLEE CLUB
BENNY GOODMAN AND HIS SWING TIME BAND
GEORGIE STOLL AND HIS ORCHESTRA

5/18/37
JUDY GARLAND
SHAW & LEE
OAKIE COLLEGE GLEE CLUB
BENNY GOODMAN AND HIS SWING TIME BAND
GEORGIE STOLL AND HIS ORCHESTRA
SID SILVERS

5/25/37
BENNY GOODMAN AND HIS SWING TIME BAND
GEORGIE STOLL AND HIS ORCHESTRA
OLSEN & JOHNSON
JUDY GARLAND
SHAW & LEE
OAKIE COLLEGE GLEE CLUB

6/1/37
BENNY GOODMAN AND HIS SWING TIME BAND
GEORGIE STOLL AND HIS ORCHESTRA
JUDY GARLAND
SHAW & LEE
OAKIE COLLEGE GLEE CLUB
ERIC BLORE
HERBERT MUNDON

6/8/37
BENNY GOODMAN AND HIS SWING TIME BAND
GEORGIE STOLL AND HIS ORCHESTRA
HUGH HERBERT
JUDY GARLAND
SHAW & LEE
OAKIE COLLEGE GLEE CLUB

6/15/37
JOE PENNER
ORCHESTRAS OF BENNY GOODMAN and GEORGIE STOLL
JUDY GARLAND
SHAW & LEE
OAKIE COLLEGE GLEE CLUB

THE CANDID PICTURE MAGAZINE OF RADIO!

Radio Stars

MARCH
10 CENTS

THE LARGEST CIRCULATION OF ANY RADIO MAGAZINE

JACK OAKIE

COMPLETE COAST-TO-COAST PROGRAM LISTINGS

RADIO — STAGE — NIGHT SPOTS — PICTURES — OUTDOOR

NOVEMBER 20, 1937

The Billboard

15 Cents

The World's Foremost Amusement Weekly

JACK OAKIE

Jack Oakie and Major General J.O. Mauborgne

Damon Runyon's
The Brighter Side

Reg. U. S. Pat. Off.

(Copyright, 1940, King Features Syndicate, Inc. Distributed by International News Service)

IN "TIN PAN ALLEY," one of those nostalgic stories with music that Mr. Darryl Zanuck so dearly loves and does so well, we find the blubbery Jack Oakie turning in a performance that stamps him as one of the great comedians of the screen.

He has been something of an in-and-outer in our book, but his current display, following close on his depiction of Mussolini in Chaplin's "The Great Dictator," indicates that he may have settled down to being consistently good. There are not many great screen comedians. Perhaps ten. We put Oakie in the first five.

He has been on the screen for some years now, though he is still comparatively young. As a rule comedians do not mature early in their art. They require seasoning. Few of the great comedians of the day, stage or screen, are youthful. Most of them are of middle age, or even beyond. Perhaps this is because they are inclined to be more erratic than other actors and take life as more of a laugh and therefore do not settle down as soon. Then again maybe comedy just naturally takes more experience than straight acting.

Oakie's strength is that he can play character roles—human beings—and make them funny without too much burlesque or exaggeration. However, the broader the comedy the better he is, as in "The Great Dictator." He actually out-plays the mighty Chaplin in spots in that picture, and he walks away with "Tin Pan Alley" in an entirely different type of role. He has a sense o timing that you usually see only in the graduates of that finest o all prep schools for comedy—which is burlesque. We do not thir Oakie ever worked in burlesque. As we understand it, his stag experience was limited to minor assignments in musical shows.

HE IS WHAT you might call screen-trained, and few scree trained actors, especially comedians, have ever acquired his ease and proficiency. You put a screen-trained actor in with a bunch of other screen-traineds and he may seem pretty good, but spot him alongside a couple of slick stage actors and nine times out of ten they will make him look sick. It is even tougher on a screen-trained comedian when he runs up against a cunning veteran of the theatre laughs.

Oakie is amazingly versatile, and it is lack of versatility that keeps the number of great screen comedians limited. There are many comedians who simply kill audiences in theatres but who do not last long on the screen because they will not get away from tricks and mannerisms that are sure-fire laugh producers on the stage. And why screen audiences soon get tired of these tricks and mannerisms while the more sophisticated stage audiences go on laughing at them for years and years is something for you to answer yourself. We give it up.

Jack Oakie, Kate Smith and Betty Grable.

Twentieth Century-Fox Film Corporation

STUDIOS
BEVERLY HILLS, CALIFORNIA

OFFICE OF
DARRYL F. ZANUCK
VICE-PRESIDENT
IN CHARGE OF PRODUCTION

November 23, 1940

Dear Jack:

I can't thank you too much for your great help in
making the Kate Smith broadcast of TIN PAN ALLEY
last night such a brilliant success. I enjoyed your
work immensely and have already received reports
from listeners-in around the country, in which you
shared in the praise for the program.

It was a pleasure to have had you both in the picture
and the broadcast.

Sincerely,

Darryl Zanuck
m. d.

Mr. Jack Oakie
7243 Haskell Avenue
Van Nuys, Calif.

Jack and Bing.

Al Jolson, Parkyakarkas and Jack Oakie at foundation laying ceremonies, 1937, for the new CBS building on
Sunset Boulevard and Gower Street.

JACK OAKIE'S PRESS STORIES

Variety

Radio Review: August 26, 1936
WABC, New York
Lux Soap (Every Monday
night from Hollywood)
One Sunday Afternoon
August 24, 1936

Jack Oakie
Helen Twelvetrees
Alan Hale
Agnes Ayers
Cecil B. De Mille
Mrs. Evelyn Offield
(Jack Oakie's mother)

"Mrs. Offield was a wow. Her presence represented showmanship on the part of the auspices. Her performance also represented showmanship. She handled one of the longest of the Lux commercials. She'd be a cinch to peddle a lot of kickapoo Indian elixir off the back end of a wagon under a gasoline flare."

The Chicago Daily News, August 17, 1935

AN INTIMATE CHARACTER PORTRAIT OF JACK OAKIE THE JOKER

By Dave Keene

A great new star was arriving from Europe. In her honor, a banquet had been arranged. Newspaper men by the score were there to meet the gorgeous, glamorous person. The speaker introduced her. "And I want her," he said, "to tell us in her own words what she was doing last night. What she thought, what she felt, as that great ship was nearing New York and she could see the first outlines of this great country that is to be her home. I want her to tell us what she was doing last night!"

Amid thunderous applause, Europe's most beautiful star rose to her feet.

"Hey, baby," shrilled a male voice as silence fell. "Never mind last night! What are you doing tonight?"

That was when the press from all over the country met Jack Oakie. With one line he had stolen the show from Marlene Dietrich, and was an instant pal of every newspaper man in the place.

The Gang Buster

This Story Is Exclusive . . . .
(*Herald Express,* 1930)

OAKIE BECOMES HILARIOUS AT A DOLLAR — A — WORD

By Jack Oakie

Somewhere I read about a fellow named Calvin Coolidge getting $1 a word for writing for the papers. So I said to myself, "What one comedian, does another can do; after all, we both write English." The only thing Coolidge has on me is being president and I'm still young and willing. So when asked to write something funny, which happened on the set of *The Gang Buster* the other day, I quickly asked for that one buck per.

This, therefore is a sample, and I wish all readers would write me whether they think I should get a $1 or more. If anyone, however, is going to go below the dollar mark in suggestions, I'd just as soon they wouldn't write. Now that I've made an introduction (at $1 a word), "I'll hasten into my story," as I've noted other great authors say; and no doubt you have too if you read, and of course you do read (just look at the dollars pile up).

You see it was this way. I had just come onto the set to start work on *The Gang Buster,* having come from my dressing room which is at the studio, and to which I went when arriving from what I laughingly call my apartment. By the way, I drive my own car to work and how I drive it. Why let me tell you, that car . . . . but let's get to the story. Edward Sutherland (since initials should count as much as a word, I'll say A. Edward Sutherland), who is my director, and a "boy's best friend is his director," was there.

He was waiting for me, as directors have a habit of doing. You know Eddie is a swell guy. He's the sort of fellow who appreciates a good joke. (At a dollar a word, I can certainly afford to tell what sort of a person he is, can't I?)

Then he asks sharply: "Jack, where have you been?"

"To the doctor's office," I reply, thinking quickly. Oh yes comedians often think, quickly.

"What?" he interjected. (That word ought to be worth $2.) "I thought the doctor said he didn't have to see you again."

"I didn't go to see him," I retorted ($1.25 word). "I'm reading a continued story in one of his waiting room magazines." Well I thought I'd die

laughing and I guess Eddie wished I had. Now here is where I get going on that dollar a word thing. Everyone on the set laughed. Percy Heath, who wrote the story, laughed. Joseph L. Mankiewicz, who was writing the dialogue, laughed. Jean Arthur, who was playing the part of Sylvia, laughed. William Boyd, who was playing the part of Mike, laughed. Wynne Gibson, who was playing the part of Zella, laughed. The assistant director laughed. The first cameraman laughed, the second cameraman laughed. The third cameraman laughed. The script girl laughed. The film editor laughed. In fact, he laughed twice, because his assistant wasn't there. The property boy laughed the loudest. I had just loaned him $10. Well, they all laughed and laughed, and laughed, and laughed, and laughed, and laughed. Well I hate to take any more dollars, so I'll just finish with a laugh.

Los Angeles Herald Express
May 14, 1932

JACK OAKIE WRITES HIS OWN LAFF STORY AHEAD OF TIME
Paramount comic goes
literary for a day.

JACK OAKIE

I always said the best time to write an autobiography is while you are alive; then you'll know it's done right — and I'd rather be right than president. Unless, of course, the country really wants me, and then I'd stretch a few points.

Well sir, I'm just a country boy who made goodness knows how many errors, but I keep up on the old farm tricks, and can still tell a Jersey cow as long as I'm in that state. I was the cause of Missouri's admission day. For years New York claimed I was born in Oklahoma and Oklahoma insisted I was a native of New York. Finally Missouri had to admit I was from Sedalia. And that's some admission — one that congress can't tax.

When I started out learning things, my mother always told me not to ask for a second piece of cake at a party, so I always took two pieces the first time.

I then became an actor in spite of advice. The first one to oppose my career was the high school principal in Kansas City. On graduation day, he caught me ringing the fire bell. When he stopped my performance he asked: "Jack, why do you act so badly?" To make amends I told him I was willing to put myself out for him, and he said that was fine because it relieved him of the responsibility.

So I went to New York and started on Wall Street. But I don't take any stock in bonds. One morning when I finally got to work at 11:30, the boss wanted to know why.

"Honestly," I explained, "I just couldn't sleep any longer." But honesty wasn't the best policy; he sent me uptown to appear in a benefit stage show. I knocked the audience so cold, they had to sit on their hands to warm them. But then, I never was one to crave applause.

Then Lulu McConnell took me into vaudeville with her, and everyone shook their heads and said that Lulu was acting strange. But she really wasn't so dumb, she knew that no one could look awfully bad alongside me.

At last I woke up one day and decided that all the walking I was doing ought to be getting me somewhere besides from one agent's office to another, so I came to Hollywood. I could see right off that Hollywood was right up my alley, and everyone kept in touch with me until all my dough was gone and when there weren't any more touches, I went to work. Right then and there it was apparent that something was wrong with either the motion picture industry or me. Because as soon as folks saw me in some silent pictures they began saying: "Too bad you can't hear Oakie." Being an optimist I decided to take it the right way.

Finally some technicians got together and decided to give me the breaks, they invented talking pictures so that people could hear me. Of course they let Al Jolson try it out first and then they turned me loose.

Well I'm still at large and I'm still at Paramount.

Frank Sinatra, Jack Oakie, and Gene Kelly.

JACK OAKIE'S TELEVISION

1950, *The Ken Murray Show* (CBS, live). Cast: Basil Rathbone, Jack Mulhall, Darla Hood, Tony Labriola, Joe Wong, Elizabeth Walters

1950, *The Jack Carter Show* (KNBH, live). Cast: Wendy Barrier, Marion Hutton, Vincent Price, June Christy

1955, *The Shower Of Stars* (CBS, live). Cast: Dan Dailey, Marilyn Maxwell, Joan Blondell, James Gleason, Dick Foran, Helene Stanley, Leon Devoh, Sam Flint, Laurie Mitchell

1955, *The Shower Of Stars* (CBS, live). Cast: Edgar Bergen & Charlie McCarthy, Dan Dailey, Betty Grable & Harry James, Tony Martin, Ethel Merman, Red Skelton, Dick Foran, Shirley MacLaine, Marilyn Maxwell, Gene Nelson, Bill Lundigan, David Rose (Musical Director)

1958, *The Battle For Wednesday Night*, **Kraft Theatre** (NBC, live). Cast: Earl Holliman, Virginia Gibson, Rudy Vallee, Richard O'Neill, Lee Krieger, J. Pat O'Malley, David Doyle, Bernard Kates, Bob Van Scoyk

1958, *The Award Winner*, **Studio One** (CBS, live). Cast: Eddie Bracken, Joanna Moore, Gale Gordon, Ross Ford, Sheila Bromley, Joe Conley, Leon Tyler, Sally Todd, Arthur Gould-Porter, Marilyn Maxwell

1961, *I Remember Murder*, **The New Breed** (KABC) Goldwyn Studios. Cast: Ilka Chase, Tina Louise, John Beradino, Robert Middleton, David Lewis, Virginia Field, Sandra Joselyn, Leslie Nielsen, Byron Morrow, John Clark, Greg Roman

1961, *Viva Vegas*, **Target The Corrupters** Republic-Four Star. Cast: Steve McNally, Suzanne Pleshette, Joey Foreman, Robert Harland, Allyson Ames, Troy Melton, James F. Stone, Charles Couch, George Neise, Kenneth Toby, Mitchell Rhein, Ken P. Strong, Lorraine Wilson, Jerry Catron

1962, *Musical Milker, Up To Ears In Corn, Uncle Rightly*, **The Real McCoys** Pathe-Desilu Studios. Cast: Richard Crenna, Kathleen Nolan, Andy Clyde, Madge Blake, Lydia Reed, Tony Martinez, Michael Winkleman, Percy Helton

1963, *Child Of The Center Ring*, **The Breaking Point** RKO. Cast: Paul Richards, Eduard Franz, Susan Strasberg

1964, *Kilroy* Walt Disney Studios. Cast: Warren Berlinger, Joan Blondell, Celeste Holm, Allyn Joslyn, Philip Abbott, Robert Emhardt, Arthur Hunnicutt, Cheryl Miller, Vaughn Taylor, Tom Lowell, Don Beddoe, Alvy Moore, Philip Coolidge, Chick Chandler, Elisabeth Fraser, Bryan Russell, Marcus James, Mike Barton, Dennis Rush, Joie Russo, Herb Vigran, Renie Riano, Jon Lormer, William Fawcett, Richard Collier, Pitt Herbert, Gary Goetzman, Jeff Kirkpatrick, Maudie Prickett, Patrick Campbell, Michael Flatley, Keith Green, Terry Murphy, Donald Losby, George Cisar, Howard Wendell, Randy Hanson, Shug Fisher, Myron Healy, "Dwight Moore's Mongrel Revue" (the dog act), Will J. White, Ray Walker, Dick Winslow, Sam Flint, Gail Bonney, Belle Montrose, Alice Backes, Aline Towne, Olan Soule, Rodney Bell, Charles Wagenheim, Johnny Jensen, Claire Carleton, Herbert C. Lytton, Baron Powers, Nino Candido, Alvin Roberts

1966, *Goliath*, **Daniel Boone** Fox Western Avenue Studio. Cast: Fess Parker, Darby Hinton, Woody Strode, Jerome Cowan, Ed Ames, Albert Salmi, Patricia Blair, Veronica Cartwright, Cal Bolder, Roosevelt Grier

1966, *A Christmas Story*, **Bonanza** Paramount Studios. Cast: Wayne Newton, Mary Wickes, Dabbs Greer, Lorne Greene, Dan Blocker, Michael Landon, Victor Sen Yung, Ray Teal, Bing Russell

1972, *Sun City Scandals*, **Johnny Carson Special** (NBC). Cast: Johnny Carson, Bette Davis, Eddie Foy Jr., Ethel Waters, Sammy Fain, Harry Ruby, Jerry Colonna, Beatrice Kay, Gene Sheldon

with Johnny Carson

with Henry Winkler ("The Fonz") Receiving the "Joakie" Award

with Fess Parker

with Ethel Waters

with Bette Davis

with Wayne Newton

James Gleason, Dan Dailey, Marilyn Maxwell, Jack Oakie, and Helene Stanley

with Marilyn Maxwell and Eddie Bracken

with Eddie Bracken

with Sally Todd

with Joey Foreman

with Johnny Carson

with Richard Crenna

with Warren Berlinger

with Ilka Chase

with Tina Louise

with Joanna Moore

with Virginia Gibson

as a clown in *The Breaking Point*

JACK OAKIE'S VAUDEVILLE

LULU

I was still in *Artists And Models* at the Winter Garden when the company was asked to take a cut in salary. Lulu McConnell and her husband, Grant Simpson, were in the show and objected.

"Not I!" said Lulu. "We'll go back into vaudeville before I'll cut my salary!" So she and Grant booked their act again. Their son, Bunk, had just married and didn't want to go out on the road, so they asked me to take his place in the act. The sketch was called "At Home" and was billed "Lulu McConnell and Company." I was "the Company."

We opened at the Fordham Theatre in the Bronx. Just as I came up out of the subway, it started to pour down rain. I took it on "the Arthur Duffy" for the stage door, and got in out of the downpour chilled and dampened. But not for long! My whole body quickly warmed up with excitement as I read the call board.

There we were, "Lulu McConnell and Company," listed with names like Ted Lewis and Bill Robinson! That stormy night was November 12, 1925, my twenty-second birthday. What a birthday present! Rain and all, the proverbial cup was sure running over! I was now in vaudeville!

That night, as always, Bill Robinson tore the place to pieces. The audiences loved him and I was his best audience. We became good friends and he worked with me on dance numbers. Ever after, as we played theatres throughout the country, I would read *Variety* to see who was going to be on the bill with us. Whenever I saw old "Bo Jangles" listed, I always looked forward to a session in dance improvement.

He taught me to dance on stairs. "The military buck" he called it. "Copesetic, Oakie!" he'd say, if I was doing all right.

It also became my job to get to each new theatre before show time and ask for "center door fancy." That described the kind of set we worked in. Every stage manager knew what "center door fancy" meant. Three flats were set up to look like three walls of a room. The two side flats were angled to converge on the rear flat without touching it or meeting each other. The space left between the flats, upstage center, was the area through which we made our entrances and exits.

Those three flats made up the "center door," and the "fancy" was a table and chairs. Sometimes a piano would make it "very fancy," that is, if the following act was a singer who worked in "one." The stagehands would put the piano in our set first, so that it could easily be pushed forward in front of the curtain to become "one." Our act was just what the title implied, some byplay, "at home."

Grant and I would come on first. I'd throw my hat on the piano. If there was no piano I'd compromise, I'd throw my hat on a chair. When Lulu made her entrance, there was no funnier woman on the stage ever. She got her laughs and applause immediately and kept those laughs coming all through the sketch. She kept up her incessant chatter as she did some tricks with a carpet sweeper. I lifted my legs so that she could work it under my feet. She broke it on Grant's leg and used the stick handle for a crutch in a very funny routine. During the sketch she set the table, covered it with a large tablecloth and dishes, prepared some food, and we finally sat down to dinner. The laughs never stopped while she served and we ate. At the end of the sketch, she grasped one corner of the tablecloth and with a magic yank, pulled it out from under the dishes. The dishes resisted the motion, and just sat there serenely, on the uncovered table in their original positions. To this day I don't know how she did it! She never missed! Then with a single brushing stroke of her arm she quickly swept the dishes into the tablecloth and holding onto all four corners, she threw it over her shoulder like a knapsack for her exit, never letting up on her chatter.

Lulu always envied what she called "a dumb act." She often pointed out a dog act called "the house builders." "See?" she said. "There's nothing to stop them from playing any place in the world. Because they don't talk!"

The truth of her observations was proven just a few years later when I was making the movie *Something To Shout About*. The dog act was in the picture. The little dogs started their "house building" when the cameraman called "Cut!" He was having some trouble with the roll of film in the camera. "We'll have to take that over," he called to our director, Gregory Ratoff.

"All right, that's enough," Ratoff called to the little animals in his Russian accent. "We're going to take it over from the top again. So you can stop now." The dogs kept right on doing their act.

"All right, dogs, that's enough!" Ratoff shouted. "We've got to start over from the top!" The dogs kept right on doing their well-learned routine. Ratoff got up from his director's chair and started toward them.

"Come on, stop it! What's a matter with you dogs? Don't you understand English?" As he neared the little stage where the action was taking place, the trainer stepped in front of him and pushed at his chest hard, Ratoff stumbled backward to his chair and sat right down into it again.

"Don't you dare talk to those dogs!" the trainer ground through his teeth at him. "Don't you dare interrupt those dogs!"

The poor man was white with anger and shook as he tried to explain. It takes years to train dogs and work them into a routine. Any confusion could destroy those years and years of very hard work. Once the dogs start their act they must go straight through the routine without any disturbance.

So that morning at Columbia Studios, we all sat down and watched Lulu's favorite "dumb act." As she said, nothing could stop them from playing any place in the world, because they don't talk!

Lulu not only played my mother on the stage, she also played "interference" more than a couple of times off the stage. Once the "understander" of the acrobatic act asked me to meet him after the show. The understander of the hand-to-hand, hand-balancing act is the biggest and strongest of the group. He is the one who at the climax of the act holds all the others on his shoulders. Six build a pyramid by climbing over him as he holds first three on his shoulders, then two above them, and then the topper.

When Lulu heard the high thin falsetto of this mammoth specimen of masculinity ask, "Oh Jack, would you like to join me for a cup of coffee?" she stepped right in, playing the part of a raucous Irish washerwoman and put a damper on the invitation.

"Too bad," she often said regretfully. "I bet he made a darn good cup of coffee."

Another time Lulu played "interference" was in Louisville, the week of the Kentucky Derby. We were in the lobby of the Seelbach Hotel. Everyone was looking up at the mezzanine, I more hopefully than most. That balcony was bulging with girls! I never saw so many beautiful girls. They were so crowded up there they hung over the railing. Even draped themselves over the ironwork. But they were ensconced up there, as if told they must not leave the meeting place. My neck

Jack Oakie and Lulu McConnell.

hurt for holding my head back so long.

"Must be a girls' school around here," I said to Lulu, still looking up. My mother had had a school for girls when I was a boy, and I guess I was conditioned to think of a school whenever I saw a large gathering of girls.

"A girls' school!" Lulu snapped at me. "This is Derby week! Bangtail week! These girls come from all over the country for just this one week! They are ladies of the evening, not schoolgirls. But they sure have class when it comes to knowing where the pickins are good." I relaxed my neck and dropped my sights.

In vaudeville you became a member of a family, and those family ties were knotted in arteries called "the circuit." Among the many treasured arteries in which we became thicker than water, were the B.F. Keith circuit, the Pantages circuit, and the Interstate Time circuit that year.

We were booked on "the Interstate," as a unit, a group of acts that played the circuit together. Practical jokes gamboled through that family of acts constantly. I was initiated at the Majestic Theatre, Wichita Falls, Texas. The Klein Brothers,

Lulu McConnell.

grooves into my face that hurt, and I couldn't breathe, but I was fighting for something much more important than breathing! I kept hearing my cues and was trying to answer them!

When the Klein Brothers' act was over and those cards were flipped to read the name of the next feature, I was released. I swung around to meet the foe and faced two merry, hysterically laughing Arnaut Brothers. Their act was called "The Two Loving Birds," and I could have plucked their feathers!

However, we did six a day, so the Klein Brothers got their stooge the next show. This time I had one eye on the stage, one eye on my lap, and one in the back of my head. I was the best stooge anyone ever had! My reward was a suit of clothes. I still have the snapshot of me standing in the theatre alley, proudly wearing it.

Lulu's humor was a world of warmth and love and fun in a wonderous pixieland. Millions were introduced to her when she played on the panel of the radio and T.V. show "It Pays To Be Ignorant." That humor was just as much a part of her life off the stage as it was on.

She and Grant had a beautiful home in Floral Park, Long Island. It was a big house with spacious grounds near the Merrick Road. One day I was out on the back lawn with Grant, keeping him and his bottle company, while Lulu was in town. Alan Dinehart and Donald Meek and their wives came through the house on the run and joined us.

"Help! Hide us! Quick! The police are after us!" all four were breathless and asking for refuge. They were carrying a tripod and phony large box camera.

"Sure, sure," said Grant, "have a drink." They did.

"We were making believe we were movie moguls," Dinehart explained, and demonstrated by putting his cap on backwards. They were pretending to shoot a movie right out in the middle of the Merrick Road and held up the traffic. When

Al and Harry, asked me to stooge for them. "Here are all the cues, see? And then this is what you say," Al handed me an old piece of white oilcloth with his printing on it in large black letters.

"Remember now, yell real loud. You're supposed to heckle us," Harry instructed.

It was a matinee, and a blinding snowstorm kept people at home. The Klein Brothers, not wanting to louse up their act before a full house, thought it a good time to try me out. I went up to the balcony, as they suggested, spread the oilcloth out on my lap, and read and reread the cues and my lines. I was intent on being the best stooge anybody ever had!

At last the cards at each end of the stage changed to read the billing of The Klein Brothers. Readying myself with one eye on the stage, one eye on my lap, and deep breaths for yelling, I finally heard my first cue! I took the deep breath that was going to project to the stage and reverberate throughout the theatre, but before I could utter a sound, hands were firmly clasped over my mouth. The more I grappled to free myself the harder the hands gagged me, and there weren't just two hands, they seemed octopus-like. Rings squeezed

Al and Harry Klein.

they heard the police sirens they picked up their props and dashed for Lulu's.

When Lulu got home we were all well into more than one of Grant's bottles. "Saw Mike Bentham," Lulu said as she joined the party. (Mike Bentham was her agent.)

"Good, good, good," Grant remarked. He was too relaxed, so I poured Lulu's drink.

"I also went by the Palace and saw Eddie Darling." (Eddie Darling was one of the most important booking agents in vaudeville.) "Oh, screw Eddie Darling," Grant mumbled. "I did!" Lulu shot at him, quick as a wink! "We open in Weehawken, Thursday!"

C. WILLIAM DEMAREST

March 14, 1974

Dear Jack,

I hear you just passed the seventy mark and I want to be among those congratulating you and wishing you many more. And, by the way, thanks for your telegram on my 82nd. It brings back memories — like when we were on the bill together in vaudeville. You were in Lulu McConnell's act at the time, hadn't been in the business very long, but one could see you had that genius for comedy right from the start — not alone on the stage — but off as well. After that I went into a show and you came to Hollywood, where you were successful in pictures.

When I came to the Coast later, Edward Small was my agent, but the best he could get me was a headwaiter part in "Diamond Jim Brady", which lasted three days. I went to Eddie and said, "To hell with this — I want to be an agent with you." He agreed. In going over the client list of stars, my big thrill was when I saw the name of Jack Oakie there. It gave me great satisfaction to represent you during the year I remained an agent. I never had to worry about when you got the script, because you had a photographic memory . . . . . . you could read the part once and go right in and do it. And in all my visits on the set while you were performing, you always got it on the first take. There were never retakes unless some other actor blew his lines or there were mechanical problems.

You may not have known it, but every agent was looking for another "Jack Oakie" type. After I had left the agency business and I was under contract to Paramount, I had an outside interest in a medicine company. Working in the factory was a young man who had such a natural flair and told gags in such a funny way that he had everybody laughing and slowed up production. Every time I heard him I thought of Jack Oakie. So, I called Bill Meiklejohn, head of casting at Paramount Studios and arranged a test for him. I personally took him to Paramount and when he passed through the studio gates, he left all his charm and comedy outside. He had it in person, but he couldn't project it on the screen. He made the test in Hollywood and you could smell it all the way to New York!

There always was and still is only one JACK OAKIE — many happy returns!

Love and Kisses,
Bill Demarest

"BANANA OIL" IS RIGHT—Milt Gross

The Arnaut Brothers.

Ol' Bojangles.

Peggy Hopkins Joyce and W. C. Fields.

ACKNOWLEDGMENTS TO OTHER PUBLISHERS

Holiday
"Benchley" (Published as "Saved by a Zipper," September/October 1975)
"Call of the Wild" (Shortened version, January/February, 1975)
"Chaplin" (Shortened version entitled, "Sound and Der Führer," June/August, 1975)

Hollywood Studio
"Car Barns" (August 1977)

Kansas City Star
"Counting" (April 6, 1977)

Modern Maturity
"Fame at Last" (Shortened version, February/March, 1975)
"Garbo" (August/September, 1974)
"It's a Fascinating Business"
"My Mother Had a Feeling" (December/January, 1975/76)
"My Biggest Bow" (August/September, 1975)

"Sweatshirt"
"Titular Bishops (or "Words We Never Said")
"Unsuitable"
"Wall Street"
"When We Learned to Talk" (October/November, 1976)

Performing Arts
"Shoes" (September, 1977)

Photoplay
"Jackie O" (January, 1977)
"Pundits" (Published as "Laughter is My Lifestyle," November, 1975)

Saturday Evening Post
"Chaplin" (April, 1978)

Valley News
"Fame At Last" (April 2, 5, 1978)

Variety
"Right Place At the Right Time" (June 10, 1977)
"Sin Town" (November, 1975)

All photographs which appear in this book are from the Jack Oakie Personal Collection.
Grateful acknowledgement is made to the following:
CBS, Inc.
Columbia Pictures, A Division of Columbia Pictures Industries, Inc.
Walt Disney Productions (© 1965 Walt Disney Productions)
Metro-Goldwyn-Mayer, Inc.

RKO General Pictures
The Tonight Show
Twentieth Century-Fox
United Artists Corporation ("Navy Blues," Copyright © 1941, Warner Bros. Pictures, Inc.; Renewal © 1969, United Artists Television, Inc. "Colleen," Copyright © 1936; Renewal United Artists Television, Inc. All rights reserved.)
Universal Pictures

INDEX

Abbott and Costello — 179
Abbott, Bud — 179
Adams, Stanley — 8
Adamson, Harold — 178, 198
Adler, Paul — 12
Adrian — 107, 183-184
Adrian, Robin — 183-184
Alba, Maria — 82
Allen, Gracie — 45
Allen, Hugh — 29
Allen, Judith — 129
Anthony, Joseph — 25
Archer, Everett A. — 113
Arlen, Jobyna (Mrs. Richard Arlen) — 123
Arlen, Richard — 51, 57, 63, 73, 119, 123-124, 180

Arlen, Richard Jr. — 118-119, 123
Arliss, George — 160
Arms, Frances ("Frankie") (Mrs. Abe Lastfogel) — 165
Arnaut Brothers — 213
Arnaz, Desi — 25
d'Arrat, H. d'Abbadie (Harry) — 99
Arthur, Jean — 204
Asta — 121-122
Astaire, Fred — 23
Ayers, Agnes — 204

Bacon, Lloyd — 28
Badrutt, Hans — 109
Ball, Lucille — 25, 120, 135

Bambi — 8
Bancroft, George — 51
Bankhead, Tallulah — 95-96
Banky, Vilma — 107
Banton, Travis — 94
Baravalle, Victor — 103
Barrett, Gene — 37-38
Barrie, Wendy — 45
Barrymore, Ethel — 41
Barrymore, John — 8, 121-122, 198
Barrymore, Lionel — 31, 82, 121-122, 179
Basquette, Lina — 30
Basserman, Albert — 71
Bassetti, *Chef* Henri — 169
Baxter, Warner — 160

Bayes, Nora — 132
Beery, Wallace (Wally) — 8, 57, 81, 162
Bell, Rex — 87
Bell, Rex Jr. — 87
Benchley, Peter — 170
Benchley, Robert — 170-172
Bentham, Mike — 214
Bergen, Edgar — 9
Berman, Bobby Burns (B.B.B.) — 119-120
Binyon, Claude — 107, 118, 120, 180
Binyon, Claude Jr. — 118
Black, Shirley Temple — 169, 180
Blondell, Joan — 74
Blumenthal, A.C. — 72

Boardman, Eleanor — 99
Bojangles (Bill Robinson) — 211
Borge, Victor — 9
Bow, Bob (Clara Bow's father) — 87
Bow, Clara — 38, 51, 81-87, 94, 101, 107, 125
Boyd, William (Bill) (Hopalong Cassidy) — 29, 204
Boylan, Malcolm Stuart — 25, 81
Breese, Edmund — 27-28
Brendel, El — 8
Brennan, Walter — 71, 80
Brent, Evelyn — 41, 51, 176
Brent, George — 107
Brian, Mary — 37, 51, 107
Bricker, Sammy — 54
Brook, Clive — 51
Brown, Senator (Hawaii) Francis I.I. — 169
Brown, Joe E. — 81, 99
Brown, Johnny Mack — 119
Bruce, Virginia — 123
Brynner, Yul — 72
Buck — 45, 48, 50, 122
Bulova, P.R. — 155
Burdee, Bill — 150
Burke, Warren — 82
Burns, Bob ("Bazooka") — 9, 11
Burns, George — 45
Butler, David — 180
Byfield, Ernie — 170
Byington, Spring — 168

Caesar, Arthur — 198
Caesar, Irving — 103
Calhern, Louis — 9
Cameron, Fay — 108
Campbell, Mrs. Patrick — 116
Cantor, Eddie — 9
Carol, Sue — 118
Caron, Pat — 18-19
Carrol, Nancy — 51, 89
Carter, Jimmy — 161-163
Cartier, Jack ("Animal Jack") — 179
Caruso, Enrico — 131, 135
Castle, Nick — 169
Chaplin, Betty — 78
Chaplin, Charlie — 58, 67-68, 71-80, 101, 157-158
Chaplin, Syd — 71-72, 76
Chatterton, Ruth — 40, 51, 161
Chevalier, Maurice — 51, 56
Clair, René — 72
Clemens, Clara — 9
Clemens, Samuel (Mark Twain) — 9
Cline, E. Francis ("Eddie") — 95-96
Cody, Lew — 180
Cohan, George M. — 41
Cohen, Manny — 89
Cohen, Sammy — 81-82
Cohn, Alex — 155
Colbert, Claudette — 159
Cole, Lester — 39-40
Coleman, Johnny — 12
Colima, Bert — 28
Collier, William Jr. — 108
Colvin, Zeke — 23-24, 150, 152
Conley, Lige — 25, 82
Converse, George — 56-57
Coogan, Bobby — 123-125
Coogan, Jackie — 123
Coolidge, Calvin — 204

Cooper, Gary — 38, 51-52, 57, 94
Cooper, Gordon — 29-30
Cort, John — 165
Costello, Lou — 179
Cousteau, Jacques — 57
Cracker, The (Jack's stand-in) — 65, 131-132
Crawford, Joan — 107, 153
Cromwell, John — 40, 161
Cronjager, Eddie — 43-44
Crosby, Bing — 9, 11, 55, 63-64, 118, 129, 163, 169
Crosby, Gary — 118

Damita, Lily — 18
Dandy, Dr. Walter — 1
Darling, Eddie — 213
Darnell, Linda — 58, 152
Davey, Bill — 4
Day, Juliette — 165
Dell, Claudia — 38-39
Dell, Dorothy — 180
Delmar, Gene — 118-119
Delmar, Vina — 118
Demarest, C. William — 213
DeMille, Cecil B. — 30, 204
Dempsey, Jack — 182
Deverich, Nat — 54
Devine, Andy — 27
Dietrich, Marlene — 204
Dinehart, Alan — 212
Disney, Walt — 121
Dix, Richard — 52
Donlin, Mike — 152
Dorsey, Jimmy — 136
Dover, Bill — 50
Dressler, Marie — 119
Dummy, The (Joe Hermano) — 100
Dundee, Jimmy — 83, 86
Durante, Jimmy — 179
Dwan, Allan — 152

Eddy, Nelson — 56, 165
Eglevsky, André — 80
Eisenhower, Dwight D. and Mamie — 177
Elsie, The Cow — 61
Ellis, Robert — 141
Errol, Leon — 51, 54
Erwin, Stuart — 119
Erwin, Stuart Jr. — 118-119

Fairbanks, Douglas — 157
Faire, Eleanor — 29
Faye, Alice — 62, 71, 198
Fehr, Rudy — 75
Felix, Seymour — 152
Fields, Carol (Mrs. Walter Lang) — 94
Fields, W. C. — 41, 94-96, 113, 116, 118
Fineman, Bernie — 102
Finis Fox — 25
Finston, Nathaniel — 89
Fleck, Freddy — 29-30
Fleming, Susan — 169
Flynn, Errol — 18
Ford, Gerald — 161-162
Ford, Helen — 39
Francis, Kay — 91
Freund, Karl — 25
Frisco, Joe — 17-19, 170

Gable, Clark — 45-50, 55
Gable, Ria — 46
Gabrilowitsch, Ossip — 9, 11
Gallagher, Richard J. — 118
Gallagher, Richard "Skeets" — 41-42, 44, 51, 54, 91, 129, 171-172, 176
Garbo, Greta — 107-108
Gargan, William — 71
Garland, Judy — 198
Gaudio, Tony — 61
Gaynor, Janet (Mrs. Adrian) — 183-184
Gershwin, George — 1
Gibson, Wynne — 204
Gilbert, John — 38, 56, 62
Goddard, Paulette — 77
Goetz, Bill — 50
Goldstein, Leonard — 51-54
Goldwyn, Samuel — 160
Goodman, Benny — 198
Goodwin, Bill — 58
Gordon, Arthur (Arturo Gordoni) — 132
Gordon, Mack — 141, 169
Grable, Betty — 62, 96, 109
Grant, Cary — 7, 113, 117
Grant (Jack's chauffeur) — 118-119
Grant, Sidney — 165
Grauman, Sid — 54, 155-158
Green, Alfred E. — 74
Green, Hettie — 42
Green, Mitzi — 51
Greenwood, Charlotte — 169, 181
Grey, Virginia — 73
Gulliver, Dorothy — 27

Hale, Alan — 204
Haley, Flo MacFadden — 119
Haley, Jack — 119
Haley, Jack Jr. — iii, 118
Hall, Jimmy — 82-83
Hanaford, Puddles — 81
Hardy, Sam — 41, 99
Harlow, Jean — 169
Harrison, Mace — 152-153
Harron, Johnny — 27
Hart, Moss — 17
Hart, Rodgers and — 17
Harvey, Forrester — 115
Hayakawa, Sessue — 83
Head, Edith — 94
Heath, Percy — 204
Hecht, Ben — 96
Heermann, Victor — t1
Heifetz, Jascha — 57
Hellinger, Mark — 58, 152
Henie, Sonja — 141-143
Herbert, Hugh — 38, 74
Hermano, Joe ("The Dummy") — 100
Hernandez, Joe — 181
Hillman, Hill Billy — 136
Hoctor, Harriet — 163
Holman, Libby — 172
Hopkins, Miriam — 108
Hopkins, Sherbourne C. — 113
Horton, Edward Everett — 122
Houdini — 30
Hughes, Howard — 125, 169
Humberstone, Bruce "Lucky" — 141
Hunt, J. Roy — 161-162
Hurok, Sol — 23
Huston, Walter — 41, 44

Ihnen, Bill — 141, 143
Ince, Ada — 8
Ince, Bill — 8
Ivey, Tom — 17

Jacobson, Artie — 99-101
Jaffee, Sam — 91
Janss (Mr.) — 30
Jenkins, Florence Foster — 136
Jenner (George Arliss' valet) — 160
Jiggs (the movie Chimpanzee) — 146
Jolson, Al — 9, 89-90, 205
Johnson, Jack — 35
Jones, Grover — 96, 123
Jones, Pardner — 38
Joyce, Peggy Hopkins — 113-116
Joyce, Stanley — 113
Jump, Rev. Albert (Jack Oakie's grandfather) — 176
Jump, Mrs. Harriet Murray (Jack Oakie's grandmother) — 173, 175-176

Kane, Elmer — 44
Kane, Helen — 51, 89-90
Karns, Roscoe — 64-65
Katzman, Sam — 81
Kaufman, Al — 125
Kaye, Sammy — 141
Keeler, Ruby — 61, 74
Kellerman, Annette — 86
Kelly, Mark — 198
Kennedy, Edward T. (Teddy) — 109, 111
Kennedy, Joseph P. Jr. — 109, 111
Kenyon, Ethel — 170-171
Kiepura, Jan — 132
King, Dennis — 51
Klein, Al — 211-212
Klein, Harry — 211-212
Klein, The Brothers (Al and Harry) — 211-212
Kober, Arthur — 103, 105
Kohler, Fred — 161
Kostelanetz, Andre — 5, 136
Kress, Sam — 6
Kuhl, Cal — 9, 11

Laemmle, Carl — 27
Lang, Walter — 94
Langdon, Harry — 8, 122
LaPlante, Laura — ii, 19, 25, 27, 161
Lardner, Ring — 41, 152, 176
Lasky, Jesse — 52, 54
Lastfogel, Abe — 165
Laughton, Charles — 109
Leahy, Agnes Brand — 123
Le Baron, William — 141
Lee, Dixie (Mrs. Bing Crosby) — 118, 163
Lee, Gwen — 27
Leisen, Mitch — 35-36
Leontovich, Eugenie (Mrs. Gregory Ratoff) — 145-146
Lerner, Murray — 12, 15, 16
Levenson, Sam — 8
Levy, Mike — 52-54
Lewis, George — 27
Lewis, Jerry — 157
Lewis, Ted — 210

Lindbergh, Charles (Lucky Lindy) — 17
Lloyd, Harold — 94
Logan, Helen — 141
Lombard, Carole — 55, 94-96
London, Jack — 45
Love, Winona — 169
Lowe, Edmund ("Eddie") — 81
Luce, Clare Booth — 1
Luden, Jack — 52
Lugosi, Bela — 86-87
Lund, Ed — 125
Lunt, Alfred — 80
Lupino, Stanley — 166
Lyman, Abe — 54, 155, 170

MacArthur, Charles — 96
MacDonald, Jeanette — 56, 91
MacMahon, Aline — 162
MacMurray, Fred — 32, 35, 132
MacNamara, Ted — 81-82
McCarey, Leo — 91
McConnell, Lulu — iii, 7, 17, 81, 153, 170, 205, 210-213
McInnes, Dick — 150-151
McLaglen, Margaret — 35
McLaglen, Victor — 35-36, 81
McLeod, Norman — 62-65
McNutt, Bill — 96
Mack, Russell — 159
Main, Marjorie — 23
Mankiewicz, Joseph L. — 42, 123, 204
Manly, Nellie Marie — 68
March, Fredric — 40, 51, 54, 113, 115, 161
Marion, George — 25
Marion, George Jr. — 89
Martin, Dean — 157
Martin, "Doc" (Louella Parson's husband) — 56
Mason, Jack — 166
Meek, Donald — 72, 212
Meiklejohn, Bill — 213
Menjou, Adolphe — 107
Merlin, Harry — 42-43
Mickey (a wardrobe man) — 123-124
Miller, Virgil — 61, 67, 161
Milton, Robert — 39-40, 161-162
Mistinguett — 23, 150, 152, 166
Mix, Ruth — 101
Mix, Tom — 38-39, 101
Mizner, Wilson — 198
Mook, Dick — 57
Moore, Grace — 169
Moore, Victor — 122
Moran, Polly — 119
Morner, Count Gosta — 113
Morros, Boris — 73
Mountbatten, Lord Louis — 80
Muller, Frank — 101
Murphy, George — 58
Murray, Rev. James and Mary Long Atkinson (Jack Oakie's great grandparents) — 176

Nechtow, Dr. — 50
Nelson, Eddie — 165

Nichols, Dudley — 72
Nijinsky, Vaslar — 158

Oakie, Victoria Horne (Mrs. Jack) — ii, 4, 23, 68-69, 87, 116, 158, 180, 183-185
Offield, Lewis Delaney (Jack Oakie) — ii, 1
Offield, Mary Evelyn, "Ev" — 1, 4, 5, 7, 8, 23, 42, 44, 68, 115-116, 119-120, 125, 129, 135, 175-177, 180, 204
Olsen, Otto — 158
O'Neal, Zelma — 51, 54
Owen, Reginald — 50

Pallette, Eugene — 50, 91, 101, 108
Palmer, Ernie — 62
Pan, Hermes — 58, 152
Parker, Jean — 32
Parrish, Imboden — 52
Parsons, Louella — 56
Pasternak, Joe — 25
Patrick, Gail — 98
Patterson, Louise — 152
Pavlova, Anna — 23-24
Payne, John — 71, 141
Percy (a sound technician) — 78
Perry, Bob — 30
Phillips, Eddie — 27
Phillips, Gordon — 179
Pickford, Mary — 80
Pitts, ZaSu — 38, 40, 72, 101-102, 161-162
Pomeroy, Roy — 37, 161-162
Pons, Lily — 65-66, 132-136
Porter, Cole — 182
Powell, William (Bill) — 51, 95
Powell, Dick — 74
Pressburger, Arnold — 72
Pringle, Harry — 62-63
Pugh, Harvey — 37

Rachmaninoff, Sergei — 145-146
Raft, George — 94, 96, 108
Rainger, Ralph — 58, 152
Ralston, Bud — 180
Ralston, Vera Hruba — 141
Ralston, Jobyna (Mrs. Richard Arlen) — 57
Rapf, Harry — 153
Ratoff, Gregory — 78, 145-146, 210-211
Reader, Ralph — 165-166
Reed, Luther — 103-105
Reed, Thomas (Tom) — 25, 27-28
Reynolds, Smith — 172
Richman, Harry — 153
Rinehart, Mary Roberts — 27
Rin Tin Tin — 122
Roberti, Lyda — 45, 122
Roberts, Stephen — 123
Robin, Leo — 58, 103, 152
Robinson, Bill ("Bojangles") — 210
Rocker, Louis P. — 12, 15, 16
Rockne, Knute — 1

Rodgers and Hart — 17
Rodgers, Richard — 17
Rogers, Charles "Buddy" — 37, 51, 55, 80
Rogers, Ginger — 51, 56, 118, 169
Rogers, Margaret — 37
Rogers, Will — 41, 120, 178
Romberg, Sigmund — 152
Rooney, Mickey — 35
Roosevelt, Franklin Delano — 58
Rosson, Richard — 82
Roth, Lillian — 51
Ruggles, Wesley — ii, 7, 19, 25, 35, 39, 61, 82-83, 119
Ruggles, Wesley Jr. — 118-119, 161
Ryans, J. H. — 179

St. Clair, Malcolm — 82-83
Sandrich, Mark — 158
Saunders, John Monk — 113
Savalas, Telly — 72
Savo, Jimmy — 155-156
Sawyer, Geneva — 169
Schroeder, Frieda — 87
Schubert(s) — 153
Schulberg, Ad — 89
Schulberg, Budd — 89
Schwartz, Arthur — 136
Schwartz, Jean — 152
Scott, Randolph — 123, 129
Selznick, David O. — 102
Sennett, Mack — 50
Shakespeare, William — 31, 37-39
Shamroy, Leon — 68
Shearer, Norma — 27, 107
Sheldon, Lloyd — 38
Siegel, David W. — 155
Siegel, Mo — 155
Silvey, "Big" Ben — 50, 142-143
Simpson, Bunk — 210
Simpson, Grant — 17, 210
Skolsky, Sidney — 74
Small, Eddie — 54, 213
Small, Morris — 4, 5, 8, 72-73, 96-98, 178
Smid, Dr. Rufus von Klein — 58
Smith, Stuff — 57
Smith, Whispering Jack — 120
Sparks, Ned — 35
Spence, Ralph — 25, 27, 198
Spitz, Carl — 48
Stafford, Jo — 198
Starr, Jimmy — 55
Stephenson, James — 71
Stevens, Ruby (Barbara Stanwyck) — 17
Stewart, Anita (Mrs. George Converse) — 56-57
Stoll, Georgie — 198
Stoloff, Benny — 38, 81
Stone, Lewis — 35
Struss, Karl — 67, 75
Stuart, Nick — 118
Sullivan, Charlie — 27-28
Sutherland, A. Edward (Eddie) — 7, 42, 125, 129, 170-172, 204
Swanson, Gloria — 4, 107
Swarthout, Gladys — 131-132
Sydney, Sylvia — 94

Symington, Senator Stuart — 58-59

Taurog, Norman — 56, 122
Temple, Shirley — 169, 180
Tetrick, Teddy — 77-78
Thalberg, Irving — 27
Thomas, John Charles — 135-136
Thompson, Alexis — 172
Thorpe, Jim — 62-63
Tilton, Martha — 198
Tippett, Mrs. Cloyce (Liz Whitney) — 183
Todd, Mike — 155
Topping, Dan — 141
Totheroh, Roland — 77
Tracy, Spencer — 160
Truman, Harry S. — 178
Tucker, Sophie — 157
Twain, Mark — 9
Tuttle, Frank — 89
Twelvetrees, Helen — 204

Valentino, Rudolph — 46
Velez, Lupe — 28, 157, 178
Veloz (Frank) and Yolanda — 180-181
Vidor, Florence (Mrs. Jascha Heifetz) — 57
Vidor, King — 35
Violinski, Solly — 198

Wadsworth, Henry — 45
Walker, Polly — 103
Walker, Stuart — 113
Wall, Berry — 120
Walsh, Raoul — 55
Warren, Harry — 141, 169
Washington, Ned — 178
Waters, Ethel — 198
Wellman, "Wild Bill" — 46-50, 57, 162
Wesson, Al — 60
Wheeler, Neely — 44
White, Harry — 150
Whiting, Richard — 89, 91
Whitney, Liz (Mrs. Cloyce Tippett) — 183
Wilkerson, Billy — 19, 81
Williams, Guinn ("Big Boy") — 119-120
Wilson, Woodrow — 175
Windsor, Duke of — 120
Wrigley, Phil — 45
Wurtzel, I. Sol — 82

Yates, Herbert — 141
York, Duke — 99
Youmans, Vincent — 103
Young, Loretta — 45-50

Zanuck, Darryl — 50, 58, 72, 74, 143, 160